802.11 Wireless LAN Fundamentals

Pejman Roshan
Jonathan Leary

Cisco Press

800 East 96th Street
Indianapolis, IN 46240 USA

802.11 Wireless LAN Fundamentals

Pejman Roshan

Jonathan Leary

Copyright© 2004 Cisco Systems, Inc.

Published by:
Cisco Press
800 East 96th Street
Indianapolis, Indiana 46240 USA

Printed in the United States of America 1 2 3 4 5 6 7 8 9 0

First Printing December 2003

Library of Congress Cataloging-in-Publication Number: 2001097378

ISBN: 1-58705-077-3

Trademark Acknowledgments

All terms mentioned in this book that are known to be trademarks or service marks have been appropriately capitalized. Cisco Press or Cisco Systems, Inc., cannot attest to the accuracy of this information. Use of a term in this book should not be regarded as affecting the validity of any trademark or service mark.

Warning and Disclaimer

This book is designed to provide information about wireless LAN (WLAN) technologies. Every effort has been made to make this book as complete and as accurate as possible, but no warranty or fitness is implied.

The information is provided on an "as is" basis. The authors, Cisco Press, and Cisco Systems, Inc., shall have neither liability nor responsibility to any person or entity with respect to any loss or damages arising from the information contained in this book or from the use of the discs or programs that may accompany it.

The opinions expressed in this book belong to the author and are not necessarily those of Cisco Systems, Inc.

Feedback Information

At Cisco Press, our goal is to create in-depth technical books of the highest quality and value. Each book is crafted with care and precision, undergoing rigorous development that involves the unique expertise of members from the professional technical community.

Readers' feedback is a natural continuation of this process. If you have any comments regarding how we could improve the quality of this book or otherwise alter it to better suit your needs, you can contact us through e-mail at feedback@ciscopress.com. Please make sure to include the book title and ISBN in your message.

We greatly appreciate your assistance.

Corporate and Government Sales

Cisco Press offers excellent discounts on this book when ordered in quantity for bulk purchases or special sales. For more information, please contact:

U.S. Corporate and Government Sales 1-800-382-3419 corpsales@pearsontechgroup.com

For sales outside of the U.S. please contact:

International Sales 1-317-581-3793 international@pearsontechgroup.com

Publisher	John Wait
Editor-in-Chief	John Kane
Executive Editor	Brett Bartow
Cisco Representative	Anthony Wolfenden
Cisco Press Program Manager	Sonia Torres Chavez
Cisco Marketing Communications Manager	Scott Miller
Cisco Marketing Program Manager	Edie Quiroz
Production Manager	Patrick Kanouse
Development Editor	Grant Munroe
Senior Project Editor	Sheri Cain
Copy Editor	Kris Simmons
Technical Editors	Bruce Alexander, Daryl Kaiser, Bruce McMurdo
Team Coordinator	Tammi Barnett
Cover Designer	Louisa Adair
Composition	Mark Shirar
Indexer	Brad Herriman

Corporate Headquarters
Cisco Systems, Inc.
170 West Tasman Drive
San Jose, CA 95134-1706
USA
www.cisco.com
Tel: 408 526-4000
    800 553-NETS (6387)
Fax: 408 526-4100

European Headquarters
Cisco Systems International BV
Haarlerbergpark
Haarlerbergweg 13-19
1101 CH Amsterdam
The Netherlands
www-europe.cisco.com
Tel: 31 0 20 357 1000
Fax: 31 0 20 357 1100

Americas Headquarters
Cisco Systems, Inc.
170 West Tasman Drive
San Jose, CA 95134-1706
USA
www.cisco.com
Tel: 408 526-7660
Fax: 408 527-0883

Asia Pacific Headquarters
Cisco Systems, Inc.
Capital Tower
168 Robinson Road
#22-01 to #29-01
Singapore 068912
www.cisco.com
Tel: +65 6317 7777
Fax: +65 6317 7799

Cisco Systems has more than 200 offices in the following countries and regions. Addresses, phone numbers, and fax numbers are listed on the **Cisco.com Web site at www.cisco.com/go/offices.**

Argentina • Australia • Austria • Belgium • Brazil • Bulgaria • Canada • Chile • China PRC • Colombia • Costa Rica • Croatia • Czech Republic
Denmark • Dubai, UAE • Finland • France • Germany • Greece • Hong Kong SAR • Hungary • India • Indonesia • Ireland • Israel • Italy
Japan • Korea • Luxembourg • Malaysia • Mexico • The Netherlands • New Zealand • Norway • Peru • Philippines • Poland • Portugal
Puerto Rico • Romania • Russia • Saudi Arabia • Scotland • Singapore • Slovakia • Slovenia • South Africa • Spain • Sweden
Switzerland • Taiwan • Thailand • Turkey • Ukraine • United Kingdom • United States • Venezuela • Vietnam • Zimbabwe

About the Authors

Pejman Roshan is a product line manager with the Wireless Networking Business Unit at Cisco Systems. He manages the Cisco wireless LAN software products, including security and network management. Prior to joining the Wireless Networking Business Unit, Pej spent six years working as a network engineer, most recently as a technical leader in the Cisco IT networking group where he helped design and deploy the Cisco campus network in San Jose, CA.

Jonathan Leary is a product line manager with the Wireless Networking Business Unit at Cisco Systems. His primary focus is the usage of WLAN technology in outdoor applications. His responsibilities include defining products and roadmaps for wireless bridging as well as providing assistance and guidance in the area of outdoor WLAN deployments to systems engineers. Jon holds a B.S. degree in engineering science from Harvard University and an M.S. in electrical engineering from Stanford University. He has authored several technical papers on the subject of signal processing for wireless systems and is a U.S. patent holder on channel estimation for orthogonal frequency-division multiplexing (OFDM) signals.

About the Technical Reviewers

Bruce Alexander is the technical marketing manager for the Cisco Systems Wireless Networking Business Unit. Bruce joined Cisco as a result of the Cisco acquisition of Aironet Wireless Communication, where Bruce was the director of technical support. Bruce has been in the radio frequency (RF) technology area for more than 25 years and in RF WLAN technology for the past 16 years. His previous duties include working in both software and hardware areas of the RF engineering group at Telxon, serving as senior instructor for National Education centers, and co-founding the Ameritron Amateur Radio Company. Bruce attended Akron University, where he majored in computer programming and business administration.

Daryl Kaiser joined the Cisco Systems Wireless Networking group in 2001 with the goal of enhancing WLAN performance by making the network aware of its radio environment. As an active participant in the IEEE 802.11 standards development process, he helped draft the IEEE 802.11k Radio Measurement supplement. In previous work, he was responsible for the management and technical performance of wireless signal processing for GSM base stations—from pico-cell to macro-cell with macro-diversity combining. Prior to these commercial applications, Daryl worked with Silicon Valley defense contractors, developing custom algorithms for signal detection, automatic recognition, and content enhancement.

Bruce McMurdo, CCIE No. 1537, has been with Cisco for seven years as a network consulting engineer and a technical marketing engineer. For the last three years, Bruce has focused on WLANs and mobility.

Dedications

Pejman Roshan:

To my wife, Shelby, for selflessly supporting me in all my pursuits. I don't know what I did to deserve such a patient, loving, and understanding partner. Now that this book is done, the weekends are ours again!

To my parents, Bijan and Jaleh. You two have always believed in me, encouraged me, and given me the support I need, directly or indirectly. And as lucky as you two are to have a son like me (ha ha!), I am even more fortunate to have you as parents.

Jonathan Leary:

To my parents, Norita and Edward, for providing me with the will to succeed and the strength to dream. Without your love and support, this book and many other accomplishments never would have been realized.

Acknowledgments

Pejman Roshan:

I started my career as a network administrator, managing and designing networks of all sizes. When WLANs became mainstream for enterprises back in 2000, I did what I always do when it is time to learn a new technology: I looked for the Cisco Press book. I found nothing and had to resort to reading IEEE specs (yuck!) to figure out this wireless stuff. That was not a task I had to endure alone. Many people around me thought it possible for me to write a book about WLANs. It is them whom I would like to acknowledge.

I was fortunate enough to work with Raul Romero, my close friend. Raul has always been a positive force in my life and career and a voice of reality when I am going nuts. This book would not be a reality if it were not for him and his always-sound advice.

It was my management team, Christine Falsetti, Eric Blaufarb, and Bruce Alexander, who gave me the opportunity to write this book. Christine is the eternal "networker" with a million and one contacts. Her encouragement and support throughout my career in the Cisco wireless team has been without end.

To Eric Blaufarb, my friend and co-worker, a thank you just doesn't seem like enough. Eric gave me the push I needed to start work on this book and the skills to upgrade to business class on international flights for free.

Bruce Alexander is a technical editor for this book; my manager at one time; and, most importantly, my friend. Bruce is the man to go to for RF and deployment questions. He is a living, breathing encyclopedia of RF, and it is an honor to have him be a part of this book.

Bruce McMurdo is another technical editor for this book. Bruce is the WLAN technical guru I can only aspire to be. I have never met anyone so dedicated to doing the right thing both for this book and his work. His attention to detail and his focus on the end result is what helped Jon and me through the grinding process of writing a technical book.

Daryl Kaiser is the master of the MAC and, lucky for us, a technical editor for this book. You can ask Daryl a question about anything related to 802.11—quality of service (QoS), RF, or mobility—and he will have a simple and easy-to-understand answer for you. He also works cheap. All I have to do is buy lunch at Le Boulanger. (A Classico and a cup of soup is all it takes.) Thanks for being a technical editor, a great co-worker, and a friend.

Tim Olson wisely refused to work on this book, either as a co-author or a technical editor. Lucky for me, I get to ask him tons of questions and he stills answer them, ever the undying technologist. A big thanks to Tim for the technical help, both on this book and my golf swing. Now that I am finished with this book, we can go to where the beer flows like wine and play a little Golden Tee.

I thank Brett Bartow and Chris Cleveland, the editors and task masters of this book. How these two professionals deal with the likes of me and Jon, I don't know! A big thanks to them for e-mailing, pushing, nagging, and motivating us.

Last but not least, a hearty thank-you to my co-author, Jon Leary, who made the diving catch when I was crumbling under the pressure of this book. If he had not signed on to co-write this book, I would be a guy with a bunch of unpublished chapters, far too many wasted weekends, and nothing to show for it.

Jonathan Leary:

First and foremost, I must thank Pej Roshan for giving me the opportunity to make the "diving catch." From the moment he mentioned that he was writing a book for Cisco Press and that he needed a co-author, I was inspired to be a part of it.

Co-authoring this book pushed me to new heights of understanding the writing process, where it is necessary to not only understand a technical solution but also describe it in everyday terms. Explaining in words what can succinctly be described with a single equation was my greatest challenge in this book, as I am sure the technical reviewers can attest to. I must truly thank Bruce Alexander, Daryl Kaiser, and Bruce McMurdo for putting up with the first drafts and the figures that were out of alignment with the text.

Finally, Pej and I owe a lot to Brett Bartow, Grant Munroe, and Christopher Cleveland for keeping us focused and more or less on schedule and guiding us through the process.

Contents at a Glance

Table of Contents

Icons Used in This Book

 Router

 Bridge

 Hub

 DSU/CSU

 Catalyst Switch

 Multilayer Switch

 ATM Switch

 ISDN/Frame Relay Switch

 Communication Server

 Gateway

Access Server

PC

 PC with Software

Sun Workstation

Macintosh

 Terminal

 File Server

 Web Server

 Cisco Works Workstation

 Modem

 Printer

Laptop

IBM Mainframe

 Front End Processor

 Cluster Controller

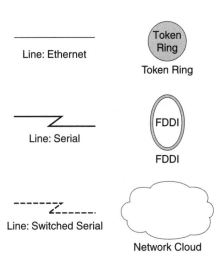

Command Syntax Conventions

The conventions used to present command syntax in this book are the same conventions used in the Cisco IOS Command Reference. The Command Reference describes these conventions as follows:

- Vertical bars (|) separate alternative, mutually exclusive elements.

- Square brackets [ ] indicate optional elements.

- Braces { } indicate a required choice.

- Braces within brackets [{ }] indicate a required choice within an optional element.

- **Boldface** indicates commands and keywords that are entered literally as shown. In actual configuration examples and output (not general command syntax), boldface indicates commands that are manually entered by the user (such as a **show** command).

- *Italics* indicate arguments for which you supply actual values.

Foreword

Wi-Fi is changing the world around us. It's changing the way we work, play, and interact with each other. The economics of Wi-Fi are rapidly changing the landscape for the delivery of high-speed wireless data services. It allows you to stay connected, compressing time by allowing you to be productive no matter where you are. In fact, as I write this, I'm sitting in the Tokyo airport waiting for a flight to Beijing connected to the local Wi-Fi network syncing up e-mail from the long flight from the United States.

With humble beginnings in 1997 as a 1 Mbps and 2 Mbps wireless standard in the unlicensed 2.4 GHz band, data rates jumped to 11 Mbps in 1999 and, most recently, to 54 Mbps in both the 2.4 GHz and 5 GHz frequency bands. It quickly became popular as a way for businesses to make their employees more productive by allowing them to remain connected to the network when they were away from the office. With multiple vendors building to a common standard and an interoperability certification program provided by the Wi-Fi Alliance, the performance of Wi-Fi equipment increased while the cost rapidly declined. Wi-Fi soon became popular as a consumer technology and is now a standard feature on many laptop computers and handheld devices. Today, readily available single PC cards can operate from 1 Mbps to 54 Mbps in both the 2.4 GHz and 5 GHz bands at a cost that's less than what most people might pay for a cellular phone. Compare this speed, mobility, and cost to the $700 that one might have paid for a 9600 Kbps modem about ten years ago, and you can see that Wi-Fi technology is accelerating at a pace comparable to few technologies before it.

IEEE 802.11, or Wi-Fi, has expanded from its vertical application roots of warehousing, inventory management, and linking cash registers together to a horizontal application used by many of us at home and at work. Today, Wi-Fi is primarily used as a high-speed wireless extension of the Ethernet network that is all around us, connecting us effortlessly and conveniently to the Internet and our office applications, wherever we might be—in the office, at an airport, at home, at our favorite coffee shop, or at the park down the street.

Wi-Fi will continue to mushroom into applications that its inventors surely never envisioned. New extensions to the standard are being developed that will improve security, provide quality of service (QoS) support, improve manageability, and take data rates well beyond 100 Mbps. These new extensions will not only improve the performance of Wi-Fi in today's applications, but will allow new applications like toll quality calls using Voice over Wi-Fi to streaming video from consumer electronics devices to a display panel on your wall. Many of these applications are already here and more are still to come as Wi-Fi becomes a part of our everyday lives. And with the continued convergence between computers and consumer electronics comes a desire to connect these devices effortlessly. You might one day be able to go to your favorite electronics store and buy a new AV receiver that will wirelessly hook to your home network stream video content to a flat panel display located in another part of your home.

New standards extensions, client mobility, and rapid evolving equipment all create the potential for confusion. What do the alphabet soup of 802.11 standards mean and which ones should you be interested in? How many access points will you need, and where should you deploy them? What about user mobility and its impact on legacy applications? Should any special considerations be given for your particular business? We are still early in the adoption and growth of Wi-Fi technology, and many exciting things lie ahead. This book helps you grasp the fundamentals of Wi-Fi networking and prepares you for the best that's yet to come.

Dennis Eaton
Chairman, Wi-Fi Alliance
www.wi-fi.org

Introduction

How many times have you needed network or Internet access at home and wished you could work in a different room, or even outside, without having to run a long Ethernet cable? How many times have you been in a public spot, such as an airport or hotel, and realized you needed to send a quick e-mail? How many hours have you wasted sitting in conference rooms between meetings while your e-mails pile up?

If you are like thousands of other corporate network users, telecommuters, business travelers, and home users, the answer is more than once. Network users take heed: 802.11-based WLANs hold the answer for you. 802.11-based networks provide the much sought-after mobility and bandwidth that network users have been asking for.

WLANs are not a new concept. They have been around for decades. The 802.11 standard was ratified in 1997, so why is it that WLANs are really starting to take off now? The answers are bandwidth and cost. Early wireless networks, such as Aloha, ARDIS, and Ricochet, offered data rates of less than 1 Mbps. The 802.11 standard offers vendor interoperable rates as high as 2 Mbps. The ratification of 802.11b in 1999 raised the bar to 11 Mbps, competing against wired 10 Mbps Ethernet rates. The 802.11a and 802.11g standards offer data rates as high as 54 Mbps, giving wired Fast Ethernet a run for its money.

As early implementers of WLANs, vertical industries such as retail stores, healthcare providers, and manufacturers see the value that WLANs and wireless applications bring. Many of these industries rely on WLANs as core components of their business. As a result, vendors are rising to meet the challenge of delivering cost-effective WLAN solutions for these customers. Vendors can increase their manufacturing volumes and lower their costs and as a result their prices, making WLAN hardware available to consumer and enterprise customers at reasonable prices.

Although 802.11 networks are a LAN topology, they present new challenges to network administrators who are accustomed to a world of wires and wired-based network technologies such as 802.3 Ethernet networks. Issues like site surveys, security, QoS, and network-device mobility require attention that a network administrator might not have the experience to give.

The premise to this book is to discuss the aspects of 802.11 in terms that IT and network engineers can relate to. This book is a reference guide to operating and troubleshooting 802.11 networks and also serves as the first stepping stone to bridge the gap between wired and wireless networks.

How This Book Is Organized

Beginning in Chapter 1, "Ethernet Technologies," we cover the different flavors of Ethernet networks, from 10 Mbps Ethernet to Gigabit Ethernet. This chapter provides a review of Ethernet as a point of contrast for you as you continue with this book. Examining a simple yet mature technology should give you some perspective on the challenges of deploying and planning 802.11 WLANs.

Chapter 2, "802.11 Wireless LANs," provides an overview of the technology in the frame of reference of Ethernet. It provides an overview of the 802.11 wireless Media Access Control (MAC) layer while detailing the basic functions that it performs.

Chapter 3, "802.11 Physical Layer Technologies," overviews the physical layer (PHY) technologies used to create the 802.11, 802.11b, 802.11a, and 802.11g physical layers. They are reviewed in the context of the basic building blocks of radios. We also present the specific interface between the MAC and the PHY that has allowed the easy expansion of newer PHYs.

Chapter 4, "802.11 Wireless LAN Security," provides a primer on security, including authentication and encryption. This information is a prelude to examining security as defined in the 1997 802.11 standard and its associated vulnerabilities. This chapter also provides details on the 802.11i draft standard for wireless security and a look at WiFi Protected Access (WPA) and interim vendor-interoperable WLAN security specifications.

Chapter 5, "Mobility," describes the mobility of 802.11 client devices, with specific focus on how wireless applications directly impact access point (AP) deployment. Client mobility impacts the 802.11 MAC protocol but also has an impact on IP-based networks, so a brief discussion of mobile IP is also included.

Chapter 6, "QoS for 802.11 Wireless LANs—802.11e," discusses the challenges of deploying wireless applications that require low-latency network connectivity, such as Voice over IP (VoIP). This chapter provides an overview by examining the 802.11 protocol and taking a sneak peak at the forthcoming 802.11e 802.11 QoS standard.

Chapter 7, "Radio Frequency Essentials," overviews the essentials of radio technology as it applies to WLANs. Topics include antennas, receivers, and radio system performance. We discuss different unlicensed frequencies used throughout the world. The intent of this chapter is to provide you with the knowledge to evaluate the physical layer performance of different vendors radios.

Chapter 8, "Deploying Wireless LANs," considers the deployment aspects of a wireless network from the physical layer through the application layer. First considering the applications to be used, it derives the requirements for the lower layers while providing specific network-setting suggestions. We discuss coverage- and capacity-oriented WLANs. This chapter outlines several different approaches to the site survey process while indicating the necessary tools for a successful survey. We detail the deployment aspects of your WLAN security policy and the tools for managing your network.

Chapter 9, "The Future of Wireless LANs," provides a glimpse at technology trends. The specific technologies considered are Bluetooth, Ultra Wide Band, Free Space Optics, and future higher-speed 802.11 technologies.

Chapter 10, "WLAN Design Considerations," steps through several WLAN application areas while providing insight into their unique requirements. The application areas are retail stores, healthcare organizations, branch offices, and education organizations. Also considered are scenarios that are likely to use client devices from multiple vendors. We detail the specific potential pitfalls of WLANs for remote locations. We delineate design considerations for public access networks and the unique requirements of WLANs for public-safety entities.

One thing to note: The WLAN industry is moving at an exponential pace. With each passing day, new innovations from vendors are making WLANs more secure; easier to deploy and manage; and, most importantly, more cost-effective. This book is not designed to be a finite description of WLANs. Its goal is to provide the fundamental foundations necessary for you, the network administrator, to understand how to plan, deploy, and operate a WLAN. We chose the topics and examples from real-world problems we have encountered in internal product development at Cisco Systems and from the many companies that are evaluating or actively deploying WLANs.

This chapter covers

- 10 Mbps Ethernet
- 100 Mbps Fast Ethernet
- 1000 Mbps Gigabit Ethernet and topology variants

CHAPTER 1

Ethernet Technologies

Wireless LANs (WLANs) are the latest access technology to take the industry by storm. WLANs, sometimes referred to as wireless Ethernet or Wireless Fidelity (Wi-Fi), are popular because they parallel wired Ethernet so well. As such, it makes sense to review wired Ethernet before diving into wireless Ethernet. You have to know where you have been to understand where you are going!

In general, networks have hierarchies consisting of three logical units:

- **Access layer**—Provides end stations with connectivity to the network.

- **Distribution layer**—Segments the networks into distinct Layer 2 broadcast domains by using routers or Layer 3 switches. Network services, such as access control lists (ACLs), route filtering, and Network Address Translation (NAT), are applied at the distribution layer.

- **Core layer**—Designed to simply forward frames between distribution layers as fast as possible. You should not find any network services applied at this layer because most network services require processing frames or packets, which impacts the throughput of the layer. The core layer can be either Layer 2, a flat core, or Layer 3.

Although Ethernet technologies can operate at any other these layers, the focus of this chapter is Ethernet as an access layer technology and, more to the point, the specifics of how the 802.3 Ethernet family functions.

802.3 Ethernet

Any networking standard works well in isolated, homogenous environments. As is the case in most networks, many differing topologies are interconnected to best facilitate the user experience. 802.3 Ethernet networks are bridged or routed into 802.5 Token Ring networks; ASNI X3T9.5 FDDI networks are bridged or routed into 802.3 Fast Ethernet networks; and so on. To place some perspective on how 802.11-based WLANs operate and interoperate with wired networks, the next few sections cover the following topics:

- 802.3 and the Open System Interconnection (OSI) reference model

- 802.3 frame format

- Ethernet addressing

- Carrier sense multiple access with collision detection (CSMA/CD) architecture

• Common media

802.3 Ethernet and the OSI Model

Diving deep in the OSI model is not the goal of this chapter, but you do need to focus on Layer 2, the data link layer, to put Ethernet technologies into perspective. The data link layer has two sublayers, as illustrated in Figure 1-1:

• **Data link sublayer**—Also known as the MAC layer, this sublayer focuses on topology-specific implementations. For example, 802.5 Token Ring networks have a different MAC than 802.3 Ethernet networks.

• **Logical link (LLC) sublayer**—Standard across all 802-based networks, this sublayer provides a simple frame protocol that provides connectionless frame delivery. There is no mechanism to notify the sender that the frame was or was not delivered.

Figure 1-1   *The OSI Reference Model*

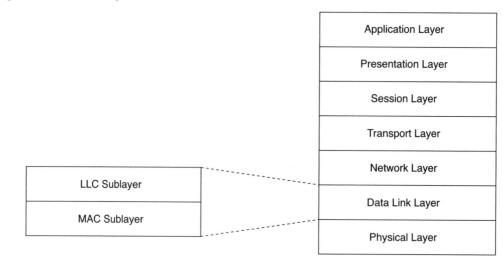

The focus of the subsequent sections surrounds the MAC layer. This layer is unique to 802.3 networks and as such provides a reference point as you progress through the chapters on the wireless MAC.

The 802.3 Frame Format

Figure 1-2 depicts an Ethernet frame.

Figure 1-2   *The Ethernet Frame*

Preamble	SFD	Destination Address	Source Address	Type	Data or Payload	FCS
56 Bits	8 Bits	48 Bits	48 Bits	16 Bits	Up to 1500 Bytes	32 Bits

As Figure 1-2 illustrates, the Ethernet frame consists of the following fields:

- **Preamble**—The preamble is a set of 7 octets (an octet is a set of 8 bits) totaling 56 bits of alternating 1s and 0s. Each octet has the following bit pattern: 10101010. The preamble indicates to the receiving station that a frame is being transmitted on the medium. It is important to note that Ethernet topologies subsequent to 10 Mbps Ethernet still include the preamble but do not require one.

- **Start of frame delimiter (SFD)**—The SFD is an 8-bit field that has a bit pattern similar to the preamble, but the last 2 bits are both 1s (10101011). This pattern indicates to the receiving station that the frame's contents follow this field.

- **Destination MAC address**—The destination address field is a 48-bit value that indicates the destination station address of the frame.

- **Source address**—The source address field is a 48-bit value that indicates the station address of the sending station.

- **Type/length value (TLV)**—The TLV field uses 16 bits to indicate what type of higher-layer protocol is encapsulated in the data or payload field. The value contained in this field is also referred to as the *Ethertype value*. Table 1-1 lists some common Ethertype values.

Table 1-1   *Some Common Ethernet Ethertypes*

Ethertype Value	What It Stands For
0800	Internet Protocol (IP)
0806	Address Resolution Protocol (ARP)
0BAD	Banyan Systems
6004	DEC Local Area Transport (LAT)
8037	Internetwork Packet Exchange (IPX) (Novell NetWare)
809B	EtherTalk (AppleTalk over Ethernet)
80D5	IBM Systems Network Architecture (SNA) Services over Ethernet
80F3	AppleTalk Address Resolution Protocol (AARP)
86DD	IP Version 6

- **Payload or data**—The data or payload field carries upper-layer packets and must be a minimum of 46 bytes and a maximum of 1500 bytes in length. The minimum data or payload size is required to allow all stations a chance to receive the frame. This topic is discussed further in the section, "Ethernet Network Diameter and Ethernet Slot Time." If the data or payload is less than 46 bytes, the sending station pads the payload so it meets the minimum 46 bytes.

- **Frame check sequence (FCS)**—The FCS field contains a cyclic redundancy check (CRC) value calculated against the bit pattern of the frame. When the receiving station receives the frame, it calculates a CRC and compares it to what is in the FCS field. If the values match, the frame is considered error free (see Figure 1-3).

Figure 1-3 *Calculating the FCS*

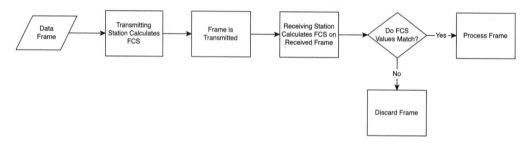

Ethernet Addressing

Ethernet addresses are 48-bit values that uniquely identify Ethernet stations on a LAN. Ethernet addresses are in part issued by a global authority, the IEEE, and in part by device vendors. The IEEE assigns unique 24-bit organizational unique identifiers (OUIs) to vendors. The OUI is the first 24 bits of the Ethernet address. The vendors themselves assign the remaining 24 bits. This process ensures that every Ethernet address is unique, and any station can connect to any network in world and be uniquely identified. Because this addressing describes a physical interface, it is also referred to as *MAC addressing*. For the most part, MAC addresses are expressed in hexadecimal form, with each byte separated by a dash or colon, or with every 2 bytes delimited with a period. For example, the following is an Ethernet address from a Cisco router:

00-03-6b-48-e9-20

You can also represent this value as

00:03:6b:48:e9:20 or 0003.6b48.e920

The IEEE has assigned the first 24 bits, 00-03-6b, to Cisco. The remaining 24 bits, 48-e9-20, have been assigned by Cisco to the device. The OUI of 00-03-6b allows the vendor to assign a range of addresses starting from 00-03-6b-00-00-00 to 00-03-6b-ff-ff-ff. This provides the vendor a total of 2^{24} or 16,777,216 possible addresses.

CSMA/CD Architecture

The Ethernet networking standard is based on the CSMA/CD architecture. CSMA/CD is a half-duplex architecture, meaning only one station can transmit at a time. You can compare the CSMA/CD architecture to people communicating in a conference-call meeting:

- Each participant doesn't know when the other person is going to speak.

- A participant wanting to say something has to wait for the phone line to become quiet before she can start speaking.

- When the phone line becomes quiet, it is possible for two or more participants to start speaking at the same time.

- If two people speak at the same time, it is difficult for listeners to understand, so the speakers must stop talking and again wait for the line to become quiet before trying to speak again.

Ethernet functions in the same way as the conference call. The carrier-sense portion of CSMA/CD refers to the capability of stations to determine whether the Ethernet medium is currently in use. There is no actual carrier signal, so the stations are actually sensing a lack of signal, indicating the medium is not is use. The multiple-access portion of CSMA/CD refers to the capability of the medium to support many users at the same time. Like the conference-call participants, all stations have equal access to the medium, but they must wait until the medium is available for transmitting. As the number of stations on the Ethernet medium increases, so does the possibility of frame *collision*. A collision occurs when two stations transmit at the same time on the medium. Neither station's transmitted data is usable, so the stations must retransmit. Finally, collision detection refers to the capability of the stations to detect that a collision has occurred. The Ethernet specification provides a fair mechanism for the stations whose frames have collided to retransmit.

Ethernet Network Diameter and Ethernet Slot Time

The *network diameter* consists of the distance between Ethernet stations at the extreme ends of a broadcast domain. You can interconnect the devices with hubs, repeaters, switches, or bridges. The rules for 802.3 Ethernet networks state that a collision needs to be detectable within the time it takes to transmit the smallest legal Ethernet frame. The smallest legal frame is 64 bytes or 512 bits. Given the speed of electricity across the wire and the data rate of the medium (10 Mbps), the maximum wire length for Ethernet networks is 2800 meters (m). The time it takes for an Ethernet frame to traverse the network diameter is known as the *Ethernet slot time*.

Consider Figure 1-4 where two stations are at extreme ends of the broadcast domain:

- Station A transmits a frame and that is smaller than 512 bits.
- At the same moment, Station B begins transmitting a frame.
- Station A transmits the last bit of its frame.
- Station A does not detect a collision during transmission and discards the frame from its transmit buffer.
- Station A assumes that the destination station of its frame received the frame.
- Station A's frame collides with Station B's frame.
- Station A has already discarded the frame from its transmit buffer, so Station A has no frame to retransmit.

Figure 1-4   *Collision Within a Broadcast Domain*

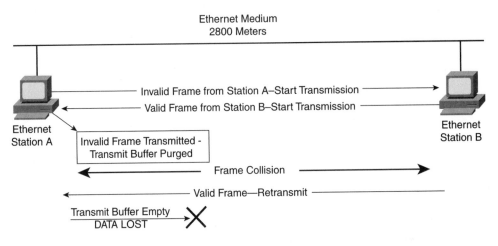

This scenario also holds true if the media length extends beyond the 2800 m limit.

Unicast, Multicast, and Broadcast Frames

A station can address its frames for transmission using one of three methods:

- **Broadcast addressing**—The station sends the frame to all stations in the broadcast domain.

- **Group or multicast addressing**—The station addresses its frames to a subset of all stations in the broadcast domain that belong a predefined group.

- **Unicast addressing**—The station addresses its frames to a specific station.

Figure 1-5 depicts these addressing types. Ethernet networks use all three methods. No one method is a panacea. Each method has pros and cons for its use.

Figure 1-5 *Addressing Types*

An Ethernet broadcast address has a special 48-bit destination address. It is called the "all 1s" address because every bit is a 1 (or every byte is the ff value in hex). A broadcast address can look like ff-ff-ff-ff-ff-ff or ffff.ffff.ffff. A station wanting to transmit a frame to all stations on the medium sends the frame with a destination address of the broadcast address.

Broadcast frames are received and processed by every station on the medium. Every station runs through the logic in Figure 1-6 to determine whether the frame contains data that is destined for it. You don't want the station to process a large number of frames that are not destined for it. A station receiving the unwanted broadcast frames uses its CPU to process the frames that could be and should be used by other station resources. This process might seem trivial, but broadcast storm have been known to cripple networks and the stations that the networks interconnect.

Figure 1-6 *Station Determining Whether to Process a Frame*

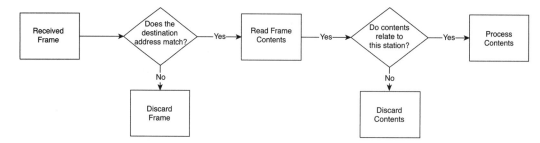

Multicast frames are similar to broadcast frames in that they allow the sender to address a group of receivers as opposed to a single receiver. This process reduces overall network utilization in some cases by eliminating the need for a station to retransmit the same frame several times to reach all the intended receivers. Multicast frames must be "subscribed to," meaning that the receiver must desire to receive them. If the receiver does not subscribe to receive multicasts from a particular group address, it discards the frames.

As an example, take streaming video to a station. Video generally has a high packet rate, and if the source broadcasts the video stream to all the stations in the broadcast domain, a station that is not actively using the video stream expends a large number of CPU cycles to process and discard the frame contents. A common mechanism for streaming video content is *IP multicast*. IP multicast frames are sent to a special destination IP address and with a special destination MAC OUI of 01-00-5E. For example, Enhanced Interior Gateway Routing Protocol (EIGRP), an IP routing protocol, sends routing updates to the IP multicast group of 224.0.0.10. This group corresponds to an Ethernet address of 01-00-5E-00-00-0A. All devices that care to receive EIGRP routing updates accept frames destined to that address. Devices that do not subscribe to EIGRP routing updates discard the frame.

In theory, multicast and broadcast frames can reduce network utilization by allowing a station to send a single frame to many destinations simultaneously. But if the sending station targets a small number of destination stations, or even a single destination station, broadcast and multicast traffic can create additional processing for unintended stations.

Unicast addressing is the simplest and most straightforward manner of sending data to a destination station. The transmitting station sends the frame with the specific Ethernet address of the receiving station as the destination address. Only the receiving station accepts and processes the frame and its contents.

Ethernet provides these three modes of addressing so applications can use the most appropriate mode that has the least impact to the network.

Common Media

Ethernet comes in a number of forms, including 10BASE2, 10BASE5 10BASE-T, and 10BASE-FL. Each of the Ethernet variants has advantages and drawbacks over the other types. In addition, similar media types are not mentioned because of a lack of installed base and customer acceptance.

10BASE-T is the most common twisted-pair Ethernet media. It allows for network connectivity over voice grade Category 3 unshielded twisted-pair (UTP) cabling using only two pairs of wire. Although 10BASE-T requires only Category 3 cabling, a large number of deployments are on Category 5 cabling for upgradeability to enhanced topologies such as 100BASE-TX or 1000BASE-T. Also, Category 5 cabling provides a higher grade of cable that allows for enhanced signal quality. The term *10BASE-T* refers to the capability of the medium to operate at 10 Mbps using a baseband signal over twisted-pair cabling. 10BASE-T allows for cable runs of roughly 100 m, although Ethernet itself supports distances up to 2800 m. This difference is because of signal degradation across the UTP cabling.

10BASE-T stations are physically connected to an aggregation device of some kind (a repeater, hub, or switch) to form a physical star topology. Although the network is a physical star, it operates as a logical bus architecture, as shown in Figure 1-7. The benefit of the physical-star topology is that a break in any one station's cable does not impact the network connectivity of any other station.

Figure 1-7   *10BASE-T Topology*

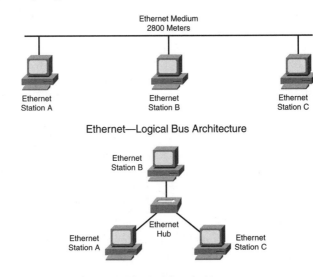

Ethernet—Logical Bus Architecture

Ethernet—Physical Star Architecture

Before 10BASE-T was popular, 10BASE2 was the topology that ruled the smaller networks of the Ethernet world. The naming of 10BASE2 refers to the 10 Mbps baseband signaling that can run roughly 200 m over RG-58 coaxial cable (see Figure 1-9 in the next section). Although the "2" in 10BASE2 refers to 200 m, 10BASE2 networks can only span 185 m. Evidently, the IEEE likes to be optimistic and round up. 10BASE2 was popular because cabling was relatively inexpensive and networks could be rapidly deployed. 10BASE2 runs over RG-59 or RG-59 coaxial cabling, and the entire network is physically connected to a contiguous length of wire. Stations are connected directly to the media using T connectors. A break anywhere in the cabling brings the entire network down.

Another common media type is 10BASE5, which runs over a much thicker coaxial cable (about the girth of a garden hose). The cable is far more expensive and unwieldy to manage. Adding stations to 10BASE5 requires costly transceivers as well. Each station is connected to a transceiver, which in turn taps into the media. As with 10BASE2, a break in the media causes all stations to lose network connectivity.

10BASE-FL is the most common implementation of Ethernet over multimode fiber. 10BASE-FL supports distances of up to 2 kilometers (km), and it would not be uncommon to see 10BASE-FL links connect distant Ethernet networks together. 10BASE-FL requires two strands of multimode fiber, one strand for transmit and the other for receive.

802.3u Fast Ethernet

As Ethernet became more accepted as a standard for data networking, users began demanding more bandwidth. To calm the screaming masses, the IEEE announced 802.3u, the standard for 100 Mbps Ethernet in 1995. Although there were a number of 100 Mbps solutions for Ethernet, two have become the most common options: 100BASE-TX and 100BASE-FX (both are collectively referred to as 100BASE-X). 100BASE-X technology is based on the non-IEEE standard FDDI (ANSI X3T9.5). FDDI was the de facto 100 Mbps standard before Fast Ethernet and had a number of advantages to shared Ethernet.

100BASE-TX applies the 100BASE-X specification to Category 5 twisted-pair cabling. 100BASE-TX is similar to 10BASE-T in many ways, but unlike 10BASE-T, 100BASE-TX requires Category 5 cabling. 100BASE-TX performs a great deal of high-frequency signaling that requires a higher grade of cable than the Category 3 required for 10BASE-T. 100BASE-TX also has the same distance limitation of roughly 100 m that 10BASE-T has, meaning the same cabling infrastructure can be leveraged (assuming it is Category 5 or better).

The network diameter and Ethernet slot time for Fast Ethernet networks change from Ethernet to 100BASE-X networks. The Ethernet slot time defines the maximum network diameter by stipulating that the diameter should not exceed the distance a 512-bit frame can travel before the transmitting station is done sending that frame. Fast Ethernet systems maintain the use of the 512-bit frame size to maintain backward compatibility with legacy Ethernet systems.

For Ethernet networks, the maximum diameter is 2800 m. With 100BASE-TX, the transmit operations occur 10 times faster than the transmit operations of Ethernet stations. Accordingly, for a sending station to detect a collision after sending the 512-bit frame, the frame can only travel one-tenth the distance. This limit reduces the maximum network diameter from 2800 m to roughly 200 m. The loss of distance does not pose a real issue because most Fast Ethernet deployments use 100BASE-TX, which has a maximum distance of 100 m anyway.

100BASE-FX is a variant of 100BASE-X that uses multimode fiber as the medium to transmit data. The network interface card (NIC) converts electric signals into pulses of light that are sent over the fiber medium to the receiving NIC. The receiving NIC then translates the light pulses back into electrical signals that the receiving station can process.

100BASE-FX uses the same encoding mechanism as 100BASE-TX, but that is where the similarities end between 100BASE-TX and 100BASE-FX. Because 100BASE-FX uses light to carry data through the medium, there is no electromagnetic interference to be concerned with. This setup allows for a more efficient signaling scheme. The maximum network diameter for 100BASE-FX is roughly 400 m in half-duplex mode. 100BASE-FX can also operate in full-duplex mode. (Duplex modes are discussed next.) Full-duplex operation essentially eliminates the issues surrounding collisions, so 100BASE-FX can safely extend to distances beyond 400 m. In fact, using standard 62.5/125 micron multimode fiber, 100BASE-FX can extend to 2 km while in full-duplex mode. If connectivity requirements dictate distances beyond 2 km, single-mode transceivers are available that allow 100BASE-FX to operate over single-mode fiber to distances up to 40 km. The cost of single-mode transceivers and single-mode fiber is an order of magnitude more expensive than its multimode brethren, but the solution exists if needed.

Full-Duplex Operation

CSMA/CD is the methodology that half-duplex Ethernet and Fast Ethernet is based on. As described earlier, CSMA/CD is like a telephone conference call. Each participant must wait until the medium is available before he can speak. In 1995, the IEEE ratified 802.3x, which specifies a new methodology for transmission in Ethernet networks known as *full-duplex* operation. Full-duplex operation allows a station to send and receive frames simultaneously, allowing greater use of the medium and higher overall throughput (see Figure 1-8). Full-duplex operation significantly changes the requirements placed on end stations, however.

Figure 1-8   *Full-Duplex Operation*

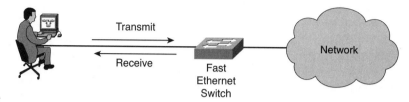

Full-duplex operation works only in a point-to-point environment. There can be only one other device in the collision domain. Stations connected to hubs, repeaters, and the like are unable to operate in full-duplex mode. Stations connected back-to-back or connected to Layer 2 switches (that support full-duplex mode) are able to use full-duplex mode.

The capability to transmit and receive at the same rate allows stations to better utilize the network medium. The bandwidth available to the station is theoretically doubled because the station has full access to the medium in the send direction and the receive direction. In the case of 100BASE-X, this access gives each station up to 200 Mbps of maximum bandwidth. For end stations, such as PCs, the truth is that few stations transmit and receive at the same time. Stations such as servers and networking infrastructure such as routers and switches can take advantage of full-duplex mode in a manner that end stations cannot. The devices aggregate sessions and connections from the edge of the network to the core and back. They send and receive traffic distributed in both the send and receive directions, so these links are able to really take advantage of the extra bandwidth that full-duplex operation provides.

Full-duplex operation allows Ethernet topologies to break free from the distance limitations that half-duplex operations impose on them. Ironically, only fiber-based interfaces can take advantage of additional distances (as 100BASE-FX does) because twisted-pair deployments are distance-limited by the physical medium itself and not the network diameter imposed by Ethernet or Fast Ethernet time slots.

NOTE   Full-duplex devices are not interoperable with half-duplex devices. A common issue in mixed media networks is duplex mismatch errors. These errors are caused by a full-duplex station connecting to a half-duplex station. The result from such a scenario is a large number of packet errors, such as late collision, and dropped frames. A full-duplex device transmits when it is ready to do so, without sensing carrier on the medium. If a half-duplex device is in the midst of transmitting, the resulting collision goes unnoticed by the full-duplex device. For this reason, it is important to verify device operation mode.

Gigabit Ethernet

The jump from Ethernet to Fast Ethernet gave users 10 times more available bandwidth. Gigabit Ethernet, with a data rate of 1000 Mbps, offers the same proportioned jump for Fast Ethernet users, but the difference is 900 Mbps more available bandwidth as opposed to 90 Mbps. This substantial increase in bandwidth places a strain on developers who must solve network diameter issues and cabling issues. Gigabit Ethernet has two main areas:

- **1000BASE-T**—Like its 10BASE-T and 100BASE-TX brethren, 1000BASE-T supports UTP cabling at a distance of up to 100 m.

- **1000BASE-X**—1000BASE-X has three subcategories:

  - **1000BASE-SX**—A fiber-optic–based medium designed for use over standard multimode fiber for short-haul runs up to 200 m.

  - **1000BASE-LX**—A fiber-optic–based medium designed for use over single-mode fiber for long runs of up to 10 km, although it is possible to use mode-conditioned multimode fiber in some cases.

  - **1000BASE-CX**—A shielded copper medium designed for short patches between devices. 1000BASE-CX is limited to distances of 25 m.

802.3ab 1000BASE-T

The development of the 1000BASE-T standard stemmed from the efforts of Fast Ethernet development. The search for the ideal Fast Ethernet copper solution drove the adoption of 100BASE-TX. Although not well known, there were two other standards: 100BASE-T4 and 100BASE-T2. 100BASE-T4 was not a popular solution because it required the use of all four pairs of Category 3 or 5 cabling. Some installations wired only two-pair Category 3 or 5 cabling in accordance with the requirements of 10BASE-T. 100BASE-T4 also missed the mark by not supporting full-duplex operation.

100BASE-T2 was a more far-reaching specification, enabling 100 Mbps operation over Category 3 cabling using only two pairs. The problem is that no vendor ever implemented the standard. When the time came to develop the gigabit solution for the Ethernet standard, developers took the best of all the 100 Mbps standards and incorporated them into the 1000BASE-T specification.

802.3z 1000BASE-X

802.3z was ratified in 1999 and included in the 802.3 standard. 1000BASE-X is the specification for Gigabit Ethernet over a fiber-optic medium. The underlying technology itself is not new because it is based on the ANSI Fibre Channel standard (ANSI X3T11). 1000BASE-X comes in three media types: 1000BASE-SX, 1000BASE-LX, and 1000BASE-CX. 1000BASE-SX is the most common and least expensive media, using standard multimode fiber. The low cost is not without shortcomings; 1000BASE-SX has a maximum distance of 220 m (compared with full-duplex 100BASE-FX at 2 km). 1000BASE-LX generally utilizes single-mode fiber and can span distances up to 5 km.

1000BASE-CX is the oddball of the three media types. It is a copper-based solution that requires precrimped shielded twisted-pair cabling. The connector is not the familiar RJ-45 of 10/100/1000BASE-T. Instead, you use either a DB-9 or HSSDC connector to terminate the two pairs of wire. 1000BASE-CX can span lengths of up to 25 m, relegating it to wiring closet patches. 1000BASE-CX is not all that common because 1000BASE-T provides the same function for a fraction of the price, and four times the cable length, using standard four-pair, Category 5 cabling.

Gigabit Ethernet Slot Time

The network diameter for Gigabit Ethernet presents a challenge. In half-duplex mode, the rules of Ethernet state that a 512-bit frame is the minimum frame size required for all stations to "hear" the frame and propagate a collision-detect message to all stations before the sending station discards the frame. Using the methodologies from previous sections, a 1000BASE-T or 1000BASE-X link would be limited to 20 m because the medium is able to transmit frames 10 times faster than its predecessor (roughly 200 m for 100BASE-TX divided by 10 equals 20 m).

The 20 m doesn't scale all that well in most situations, so to overcome this limitation, the IEEE required that the minimum frame size be increased 8-fold to 4096 bits (512 bytes) for Gigabit Ethernet. Instead of padding the payload portion of the frame, the standard instead opted to employ the use of a new feature known as *carrier extensions*.

For example, suppose a Gigabit Ethernet station detects a clear medium and wants to transmit a 512-bit frame. The NIC adds to the end of the frame 3,584 carrier-extension bits. These bits are known to other Gigabit Ethernet stations not to be data yet are considered part of the frame itself (see Figure 1-9). When the receiving station receives the frame, it discards the carrier extension. This process allows a small frame to be transmitted without concern for late collisions.

Although the use of carrier extensions solves the network-diameter problem, it creates a new one in its wake. For every small 512-bit frame transmitted, seven times that amount of carrier extension is also transmitted. It is a waste of bandwidth. To alleviate this overhead, the standard specifies a *burst mode* as an optional method to solve the slot-time issue and the carrier-extension overhead issue.

Figure 1-9   *Gigabit Ethernet Carrier Extensions*

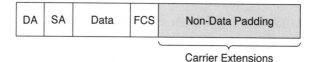

Burst mode allows small frames to chain together by sending carrier extensions in the interframe gap. Other stations wanting to transmit see the interframe gap but still detect carrier and avoid transmission. The standard allows for up to 64 kilobits (Kb) of burst-mode traffic to pass before sending a standard interframe gap.

The mechanism first sends a small frame with the full 4096-bit frame size (including carrier-extension bits). It does so to weed out any possible collisions with other stations. After the first frame is sent successfully, the subsequent interframe gap contains the extension bits to prevent other stations from accessing the medium (see Figure 1-10). Subsequent frames are transmitted without any carrier-extension padding. The station can burst up to 64 Kb of additional frames before relinquishing control of the medium. This mechanism, although not perfect, allows better utilization of the medium than carrier extensions alone.

Figure 1-10   *Gigabit Burst Mode*

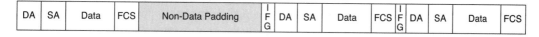

NOTE   Carrier extensions and burst mode are only necessary in half-duplex mode. In full-duplex mode, no contention exists, so there is no need to be concerned with slot time and, therefore, no need to be concerned with frame size.

Auto Negotiation

Given the numerous possible combinations of Ethernet data rates and duplex modes, auto negotiation takes the guesswork out of determining device compatibility. In general, auto negotiation of speed and duplex is designed for twisted-pair media because fiber-optic devices do not support auto negotiation, nor is it practical for fiber-optic media types.

The auto-negotiation process begins when the device detects link activity on its interface:

- The device sends out a fast link pulse (FLP) signal, advertising its desired speed and duplex. Table 1-2 lists the hierarchy of preferred modes of operation.

- If the remote station supports auto negotiation, it sends an FLP with its preference.

- The two stations negotiate the best possible matching speed and duplex mode.

Table 1-2   *Auto Negotiation Hierarchy*

Priority	Mode of Operation
1	100BASE-TX full duplex
2	100BASE-T4
3	100BASE-TX
4	10BASE-T full duplex
5	10BASE-T

If one station supports auto negotiation and the other does not, the auto negotiation uses medium auto sense. For example, an older 10BASE-T station can connect to a switch that supports auto negotiation. The switch sends a FLP to the 10BASE-T station requesting 100 Mbps full-duplex operation. The 10BASE-T station does not understand the FLP and ignores the auto-negotiation signaling. By the same token, the 10BASE-T station cannot send a FLP as it does not support them. The switch port senses the lack of FLP support and assumes the station is a 10BASE-T station. In this case, because the 10BASE-T station does not support auto negotiation, the switch reverts to the lowest common denominator, which is 10BASE-T.

Yet, what if the station is a 100BASE-TX station running in half-duplex mode and does not support auto negotiation either? Will these stations be doomed to run in 10BASE-T mode? The answer is no. FLPs are based on the network link pulse (NLP) specified in the Ethernet standard. NLPs are periodic pulses that are essentially the network heartbeat. FLPs provide a similar function for 100BASE-X networks, just 10 times as often. So although the 100BASE-TX station does not engage in auto negotiation, it does send FLPs, which indicate to the switch that the station does support 100 Mbps operation. This indication is what allows an auto-sense device to determine whether a station is 100BASE-TX or 10BASE-T.

Gigabit Ethernet Auto Negotiation

Auto negotiation is somewhat different in Gigabit Ethernet networks than in Fast Ethernet and Ethernet networks. Copper-based 1000BASE-T conforms to the same FLP mechanism that the other topologies use, as would be expected. But 1000BASE-X uses a different mechanism. Auto negotiation is medium dependant, and as a result, only like 1000BASE-X devices can auto negotiate with each other. Because access rate is predetermined (that is, speed negotiation is not supported), the only option is duplex mode. Unlike Ethernet and Fast Ethernet, FLPs are not used for negotiation and are instead abandoned in favor of signaling that is specific to each of the 1000BASE-X media types.

Summary

Ethernet has evolved to support new requirements that users and network administrators demand. It continues to evolve beyond Gigabit Ethernet with its next iteration, 10 Gigabit Ethernet, on the horizon. Table 1-3 gives a summary of the Ethernet family of topologies and their media types. Each topology has a place in networking today, determined by requirements such as cost, required data rate, distance, and existing cable plant. Wired Ethernet shows that backward compatibility is what allows new topologies to prosper, develop, and become accepted standards.

Table 1-3   *Summary of Ethernet Topologies*

Topology	Data Rate (Mbps)	Medium	Max Media Distance (m)
10BASE5	10	Thick coax	485
10BASE2	10	Thin RG-58 coax	185
10BASE-T	10	CAT 3/5 two-pair UTP	100
10BASE-FL	10	Two-strand multimode fiber	2000
100BASE-TX	100	CAT 5 two-pair UTP	100
100BASE-FX	100	Two-strand multimode fiber	2000
1000BASE-T	1000	CAT 5 four-pair UTP	100
1000BASE-CX	1000	Shielded twisted-pair	25
1000BASE-SX	1000	Two-strand multimode fiber	200
1000BASE-LX	1000	Two-strand single-mode fiber	10,000

This chapter covers the following topics:

- Overview of wireless LAN (WLAN) topologies
- 802.11 medium access mechanisms
- 802.11 MAC layer operations
- 802.11 frame formats

CHAPTER 2

802.11 Wireless LANs

802.11 WLANs are becoming pervasive in network deployments primarily because they are easy to implement and easy to use. From the perspective of the user, they function and perform exactly like a shared Ethernet LAN. Ironically, the 802.11 architecture is anything but simple. The challenges of an uncontrolled medium are more complex than those of the controlled wired Ethernet medium.

The 802.11 MAC must orchestrate an access mechanism that allows fair access to the medium. 802.11 stations do not possess the ability to sense collisions that the carrier sense multiple access/collision detect (CSMA/CD)–based wired Ethernet stations do. As a result, a more robust and scalable MAC is required for medium access with minimized overhead.

This chapter provides an overview of the 802.11 basic access mechanism.

Overview of WLAN Topologies

802.11 networks are flexible by design. You have the option of deploying three types of WLAN topologies:

- Independent basic service sets (IBSSs)
- Basic service sets (BSSs)
- Extended service sets (ESSs)

A *service set* is a logical grouping of devices. WLANs provide network access by broadcasting a signal across a wireless radio frequency (RF) carrier. A receiving station can be within range of a number of transmitters. The transmitter prefaces its transmissions with a service set identifier (SSID). The receiver uses the SSID to filter through the received signals and locate the one it wants to listen to.

IBSS

An *IBSS* consists of a group of 802.11 stations communicating directly with one another. An IBSS is also referred to as an ad-hoc network because it is essentially a simple peer-to-peer WLAN. Figure 2-1 illustrates how two stations equipped with 802.11 network interface cards (NICs) can form an IBSS and communicate directly with one another.

Figure 2-1 *An IBSS WLAN*

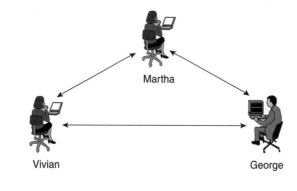

Martha

Vivian   George

Ad Hoc/IBSS

An ad hoc or independent basic service set (IBSS) network is created when individual client devices form a self-contained network without the use of an access point. These networks do not involve any pre-planning or site survey, so they are usually small and only last long enough for the communication of whatever information needs to be shared. Unlike the case of an ESS, the clients are directly connected to each other, which creates only a single BSS that has no interface to a wired LAN (i.e., no distribution system that is essential to tying BSSs to create an ESS). There is no standards-based limit as to the number of devices that can be in an IBSS. But because every device is a client, often, certain members of the IBSS cannot talk to each other because of the hidden node issue. In spite of this, there is no mechanism for a relay function in an IBSS.

Because no access point is in an IBSS, timing is controlled in a distributed manner. The client that starts the IBSS sets the beacon interval to create a set of target beacon transmission times (TBTT). When the TBTT is reached, each client in the IBSS takes the following steps:

- Suspend any pending backoff timers from the previous TBTT.
- Determine a new random delay.
- If a beacon arrives before the end of the random delay, resume the suspended backoff timers. If no beacon arrives prior to the end of the random delay, send a beacon and resume the suspended backoff timers.

You can see that the maintenance of the beacon timing is distributed in the ad hoc network rather than being owned by an AP or one of the clients. Because there is often an inherent hidden node problem, it is possible that multiple beacons from different clients will be sent in the beacon interval, and so some clients might receive multiple beacons. However, this is allowed in the standard and should not create any issues because the clients are only looking for the reception of the first beacon relative to their own random timer.

Embedded within the beacon is a timer synchronization function (TSF). Each client compares the TSF in the beacon to its own timer and, if the received value is greater, meaning the clock in the transmitting station is running faster, it updates its timer to the received value. This has the long-term effect of updating the timing throughout the ad hoc network to the client with the fastest timer. In a large distributed ad hoc network where many clients cannot directly communicate, it might take some time for the timing to distribute.

BSS

A *BSS* is a group of 802.11 stations communicating with one another. A BSS requires a specialized station known as an *access point (AP)*. The AP is the central point of communications for all stations in a BSS. The client stations do not communicate directly other client stations. Rather, they communicate with the AP, and the AP forwards the frames to the destination stations. The AP might be equipped with an uplink port that connects the BSS to a wired network (for example, an Ethernet uplink). Because of this requirement, a BSS is also referred to as an infrastructure BSS. Figure 2-2 illustrates a typical infrastructure BSS.

Figure 2-2   *An Infrastructure BSS WLAN*

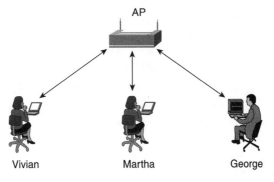

ESS

Multiple infrastructure BSSs can be connected via their uplink interfaces. In the world of 802.11, the uplink interface connects the BSS to the distribution system (DS). The collection of BSSs interconnected via the DS is known as the *ESS*. Figure 2-3 shows a practical implementation of an ESS. The uplink to the DS does not have to be via a wired connection. The 802.11 specification leaves the potential for this link to be wireless. For the most part, DS uplinks are wired Ethernet.

Figure 2-3 *An ESS WLAN*

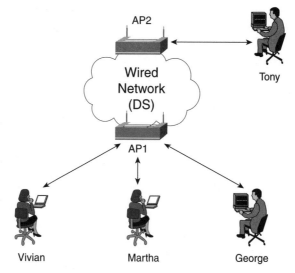

802.11 Medium Access Mechanisms

Chapter 1, "Ethernet Technologies," described CSMA/CD as the medium access mechanism for 802.3-based Ethernet networks. 802.11-based WLANs use a similar mechanism known as carrier sense multiple access with collision avoidance (CSMA/CA). CSMA/CA is a listen before talk (LBT) mechanism. The transmitting station senses the medium for a carrier signal and waits until the carrier channel is available before transmitting.

Wired Ethernet is able to sense a collision on the medium. Two stations transmitting at the same time increase the signal level on the wire, indicating to the transmitting stations that a collision has occurred. 802.11 wireless stations do not have this capability. The 802.11 access mechanism must make every effort to avoid collisions altogether.

Overview of CSMA/CA

Chapter 1 compares CSMA/CD to a telephone conference call. Each participant wanting to speak needs to wait for everyone else to stop speaking. Once the line is quiet, the participant can attempt to speak. If two participants begin speaking at the same time, they must stop and try again.

CSMA/CA is more ordered than CSMA/CD. To use the same telephone conference call analogy, you make some changes to the scenario:

- Before a participant speaks, she must indicate how long she plans to speak. This indication gives any potential speakers an idea of how long to wait before they have an opportunity to speak.

- Participants cannot speak until the announced duration of a previous speaker has elapsed.

- Participants are unaware whether their voices are heard while they are speaking, unless they receive confirmation of their speeches when they are done.

- If two participants happen to start speaking at the same time, they are unaware they are speaking over each other. The speakers determine they are speaking over each other because they do not receive confirmation that their voices were heard.

- The participants wait a random amount of time and attempt to speak again, should they not receive confirmation of their speeches.

As you can see, CSMA/CA has more stringent rules than CSMA/CD. These rules help prevent collisions. This prevention is key for wireless networks because there is no explicit collision-detection mechanism. CSMA/CA implicitly detects a collision when a transmitter does not receive an expected acknowledgment.

The 802.11 implementation of CSMA/CA is manifested in the distributed coordination function (DCF). To describe how CSMA/CD works, it is important to describe some key 802.11 CSMA/CA components first:

- Carrier sense
- DCF
- Acknowledgment frames
- Request to Send/Clear to Send (RTS/CTS) medium reservation

In addition, two other mechanisms pertain to 802.11 medium access but are not directly tied to CSMA/CA:

- Frame fragmentation
- Point coordination function (PCF)

Carrier Sense

A station that wants to transmit on the wireless medium must sense whether the medium is in use. If the medium is in use, the station must defer frame transmission until the medium is not in use. The station determines the state of the medium using two methods:

- Check the Layer 1 physical layer (PHY) to see whether a carrier is present.
- Use the virtual carrier-sense function, the network allocation vector (NAV).

The station can check the PHY and detect that the medium is available. But in some instances, the medium might still be reserved by another station via the NAV. The NAV is a timer that is updated by data frames transmitted on the medium. For example, in an infrastructure BSS, suppose Martha is sending a frame to George (see Figure 2-4). Because the wireless medium is a broadcast-based shared medium, Vivian also receives the frame. The 802.11 frames contain a duration field. This duration value is large enough to cover the transmission of the frame and the expected acknowledgment. Vivian updates her NAV with the duration value and does not attempt transmission until the NAV has decremented to 0.

Note that stations only update the NAV when the duration field value received is greater than what is currently stored in their NAV. Using the same example, if Vivian has a NAV of 10 milliseconds, she does not update her NAV if she receives a frame with a duration of 5 milliseconds. She updates her NAV if she receives a frame with a duration of 20 milliseconds.

Figure 2-4   *The NAV Update Process*

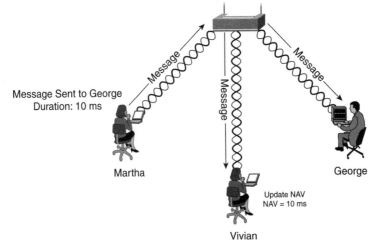

Message Sent to George
Duration: 10 ms

Martha

George

Update NAV
NAV = 10 ms

Vivian

DCF

The IEEE-mandated access mechanism for 802.11 networks is DCF, a medium access mechanism based on the CSMA/CA access method. To describe DCF operation, we first define some concepts. Figure 2-5 shows a time line for the scenario in Figure 2-4.

Figure 2-5   *Timeline for DCF Medium Access*

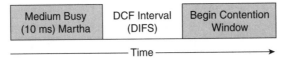

Medium Busy (10 ms) Martha	DCF Interval (DIFS)	Begin Contention Window

————————— Time —————————→

In DCF operation, a station wanting to transmit a frame must wait a specific amount of time after the medium becomes available. This time value is known as the DCF interframe space (DIFS). Once the DIFS interval elapses, the medium becomes available for station access contention.

In Figure 2-5, Vivian and George might want to transmit frames when Martha's transmission is complete. Both stations should have the same NAV values, and both will physically sense when the medium is idle. There is a high probability that both stations will attempt to transmit when the medium becomes idle, causing a collision. To avoid this situation, DCF uses a random backoff timer.

The random backoff algorithm randomly selects a value from 0 to the contention window (CW) value. The default CW values vary by vendor and are value-stored in the station NIC. The range of values for random backoff start at 0 slot times and increment up to the maximum value, which is a moving ceiling starting at CW_{min} and stopping at a maximum value known as CW_{max}. For the sake of this example, assume that the CW_{min} value begins at 7 and CW_{max} value is 255. Figure 2-6 illustrates the CW_{min} and CW_{max} values for binary random backoff.

A station randomly selects a value between 0 and the current value of the CW. The random value is the number of 802.11 slot times the station must wait during the medium idle CW before it may transmit. A *slot time* is a time value derived from the PHY based on RF characteristics of the BSS .

Getting back to the example, Vivian is ready to transmit. Her NAV timer has decremented to 0, and the PHY also indicates the medium is idle. Vivian selects a random backoff time between 0 and CW (in this case, CW is 7) and waits the selected number of slot times before transmitting. Figure 2-7 illustrates this process, with a random backoff value of four slot times.

Figure 2-6   *Random Backoff with DCF Medium Access*

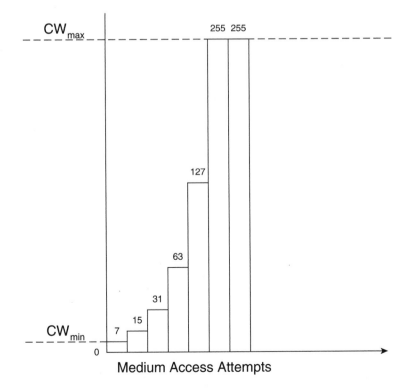

Figure 2-7   *Frame Transmission After Random Backoff*

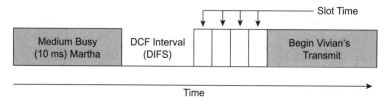

Once the four slot times pass, Vivian can transmit. But what if George's station has a random backoff time of two time slots? Vivian hears a new duration from George's frame when he begins his transmission, and Vivian updates her NAV with that new value. Vivian must wait for her NAV to decrement to 0 and her PHY to report that the medium is available again before she can resume her backoff. (In this example, Vivian must wait an additional two slot times before attempting to transmit.)

Assuming that Vivian is able to defer transmission for all four slot times, she transmits the frame. So how does Vivian know that the frame made it to its destination? The 802.11 specification requires that the receiving station send an acknowledgment frame to the frame sender. This acknowledgment frame allows the sending station to indirectly determine whether a collision took place on the medium. If the sending station does not receive an acknowledgment frame, it assumes that a collision occurred on the medium. The sending station updates its retry counters, doubles the CW value, and begins the medium access process again. Figure 2-8 summarizes the steps a DCF station must iterate through to transmit a frame.

Figure 2-8   *The DCF Medium Access Process*

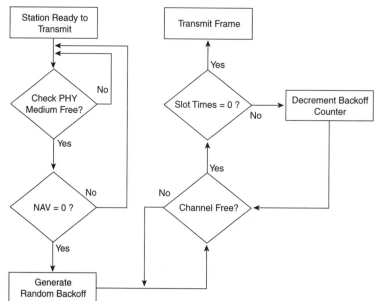

The Acknowledgment Frame

A station receiving a frame acknowledges error-free receipt of the frame by sending an acknowledgment frame back to the sending station. Knowing that the receiving station has to access the medium and transmit the acknowledgment frame, you would assume that it is possible for the acknowledgment frame to be delayed because of medium contention. The transmission of an acknowledgment frame is a special case. Acknowledgment frames are allowed to skip the random backoff process and wait a short interval after the frame has been received to transmit the acknowledgment. The short interval the receiving station waits is known as the *short interframe space (SIFS)*. The SIFS interval is shorter than a DIFS interval by two slot times. It guarantees the receiving station the best possible chance of transmitting on the medium before another station does.

Referring to Vivian's transmission to George, Vivian deferred her transmission attempt for four slot times. The medium was still available, so she transmitted her frame to George, as depicted in Figure 2-9. The AP receives the frame and waits a SIFS interval before sending an acknowledgment frame.

Figure 2-9   *Frame Transmission and Acknowledgment*

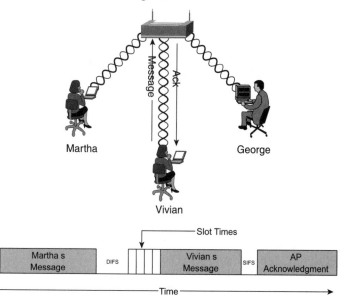

Supposing that Vivian never receives an acknowledgment frame, she doubles the CW value to 15 and repeats the backoff process. For every medium access attempt that fails, the 802.11 station increments a retry counter. CW continues to double until it is equal to CW_{max}. The MAC layer may continue to attempt to transmit the frame, but once the frame retry counters reach a administrator-defined retry threshold, Vivian's station attempts to reserve the medium.

The Hidden Node Problem and RTS/CTS

Vivian might be unable to access the medium because of another station that is within range of the AP yet out of range of her station. Figure 2-10 illustrates this situation. Vivian and George are in range of each other and in range of the AP. Yet neither of them is in range of Tony. Tony is in range of the AP and attempts to transmit on the medium as well. The situation is known as the *hidden node problem* because Tony is hidden to Vivian and George.

Figure 2-10 *The Hidden Node Problem*

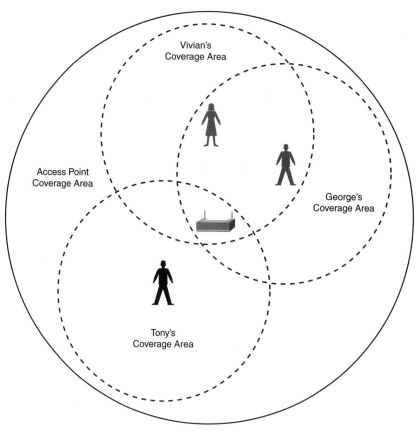

Vivian attempts to reserve the medium using a special control frame known as an RTS frame. The RTS frame is sent to the AP and indicates to the AP, and all stations that are within range of Vivian, the expect duration of Vivian's frame exchange. The frame exchange includes the frame she wants to initially transmit as well as the expected acknowledgment frame.

The AP receives Vivian's RTS frame and reply with a CTS control frame. The CTS frame contains a duration field value long enough to allow Vivian to complete her frame exchange. All stations within range of the AP, including Tony and George, receive the CTS frame and update their NAVs, as illustrated in Figure 2-11.

Figure 2-11 *Medium Reservation with RTS/CTS Frames*

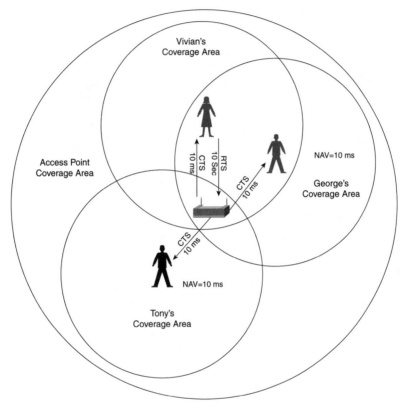

The initial RTS frame that Vivian transmits must go through the DCF process, as would any normal frame. But similar to the acknowledgment frame, the corresponding CTS frame from the AP skips the random backoff procedure and only needs to wait the SIFS interval before being transmitted. Figure 2-12 details Vivian's RTS frame transmission. Both George and Tony update their NAVs accordingly, but the acknowledgment frame the AP sends back to Vivian does not have to conform to the DCF rules. When George receives the frame, George immediately sends back an acknowledgment frame. Although George's NAV is nonzero, he still sends an acknowledgment frame back to the AP after a SIFS interval.

Figure 2-12 *Example of RTS/CTS*

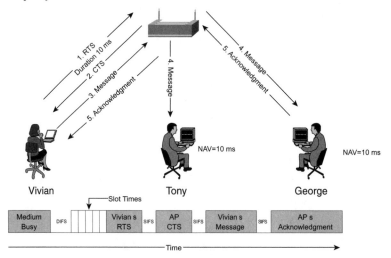

802.11 Frame Fragmentation

Frame fragmentation is a MAC layer function that is designed to increase the reliability of frame transmission across the wireless medium. The premise behind fragmentation is that a frame is broken up into smaller fragments, and each fragment is transmitted individually, as depicted in Figure 2-13. The assumption is that there is a higher probability of successfully transmitting a smaller frame fragment across the hostile wireless medium. Each frame fragment is individually acknowledged; therefore, if any fragment of the frame encounters any errors or a collision, only the fragment needs to be retransmitted, not the entire frame, increasing the effective throughput of the medium.

Figure 2-13 *Frame Fragmentation*

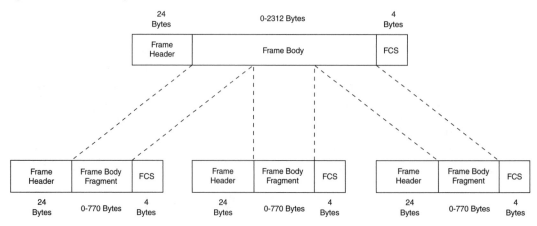

The network administrator can define the fragment size (see Figure 2-14). Fragmentation occurs only on unicast frames. Broadcast or multicast frames are transmitted as a whole. Also, the frame fragments are sent as a burst, using a single iteration of the DCF medium access mechanism.

Although fragmentation can increase the reliability of frame transmission in a WLAN, it does increase the 802.11 MAC protocol overhead. Every frame fragment includes the 802.11 MAC header information as well as require a corresponding acknowledgment frame. This increase in MAC overhead decreases the actual wireless station throughput. Fragmentation is a balance between medium reliability and medium overhead.

Figure 2-14 *Fragmentation Setup on Cisco Aironet Wireless Adapters*

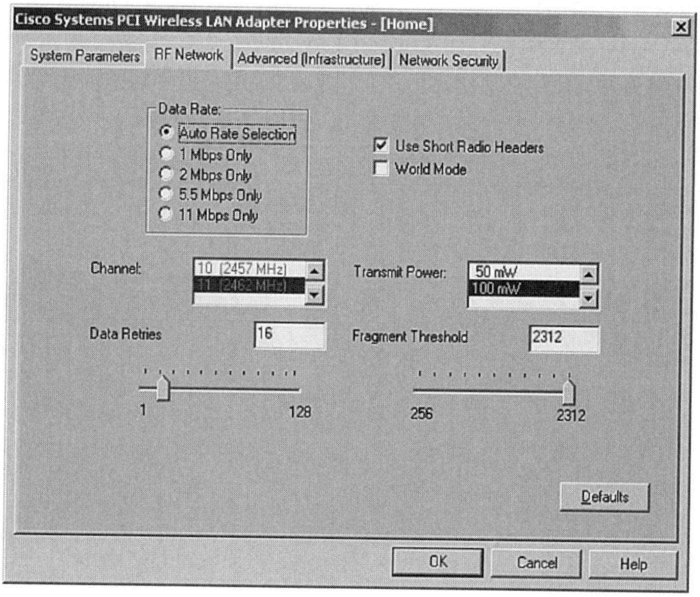

PCF

PCF is an 802.11 optional medium access mechanism that is used in addition to DCF. PCF is an access mechanism that provides contention-free frame delivery to and from the AP. Most vendors do not include PCF support because it increases the protocol overhead of the BSS. As a result, it is not widely deployed. Forthcoming quality-of-service (QoS) enhancements to the 802.11 specification build on PCF to create a more useful mechanism.

This section covers PCF operation, detailing the operation of the point coordinator (PC) and PCF-aware stations (referred to as CF-Pollable stations in the 802.11 specification).

The Contention Free Period

The *Contention Free Period (CFP)* is the window of time for PCF operation. The CFP begins at set intervals following a beacon frame containing a delivery traffic indication map (DTIM) information element (described later in the chapter). The frequency of CFPs is determined by the network administrator. Once the CFP begins, the AP assumes the role of the PC (and as such, PCF operation is only supported in infrastructure BSSs). Each 802.11 client sets its NAV to the CFPMaxDuration value. This value is included in the CF parameter set information element (detailed later in the chapter). The CFPMaxDuration defines the time value that is the maximum duration for the CFP. The PC can end the CFP before the CFPMaxDuration time elapses. The AP transmits beacon frames at regular intervals, and beacon frames sent during the CFP contain the CFPDurationRemaining field to update station NAVs of the remaining duration of the CFP. Figure 2-15 depicts the CFP and contention period (CP) as a function of time.

Figure 2-15 *The CFP and CP Timeline*

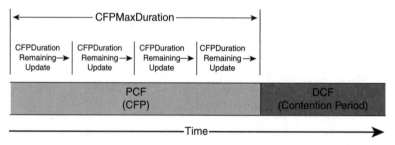

Unlike DCF operation, PCF does not allow stations to freely access the medium and transmit data. Stations can only send data (one frame at a time) when the PC polls them. The PC can send frames to stations, poll stations for frame transmission, acknowledge frames requiring MAC-level acknowledgments, or end the CFP.

PC Operation

When the CFP begins, the PC must access the medium in the same manner as a DCF station. Unlike DCF stations, the PC attempts to access the medium after waiting an interval of time known as the priority interframe space (PIFS). The PIFS interval is one slot time longer than the SIFS interval and one slot time shorter than the DIFS interval, allowing PCF stations to access the medium before DCF stations yet still allowing control frames, such as acknowledgment frames, to have the highest probability of gaining access to the medium. Figure 2-16 illustrate the SIFS, PIFS, DIFS, and slot time relationships.

Figure 2-16 *SIFS, PIFS, DIFS, and Slot Time Relationships*

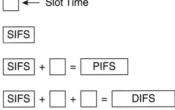

After waiting a PIFS interval, the PC sends the initial beacon frame containing the CF parameter information element. The PC waits for one SIFS interval subsequent to the beacon frame transmission and then sends one of the following to a CF-Pollable station:

- A data frame
- A poll frame (CF-Poll)
- A combination data and poll frame (Data+CF-Poll)
- A CFP end frame (CF-End)

If the PC has no frames to send and no CF-Pollable stations to poll, the CFP is considered null, and immediately following the beacon frame, the PC sends a CF-End frame terminating the CFP.

PCF Operation Example

Continuing the same example as before, Vivian, Martha, and George are communicating with AP1. Figure 2-17 depicts this example.

AP1 sends a beacon frame indicating the start of a CFP. The CFP is set for 20 seconds (sec). Vivian, Martha, and George all update their NAVs to reflect the 20-sec CFP. After waiting a SIFS interval, AP1 sends a frame buffered for Vivian's station and also sends a poll to Vivian's station to see whether she has any frames to send using the Data+CF-Poll frame. Vivian receives the Data+CF-Poll frame and sends one data frame and a contention-free acknowledgment (Data+CF-ACK) frame after waiting a SIFS interval. Note that Vivian's station ignores her NAV setting when transmitting frames in response to a CF-Poll frame.

AP1 iterates through its polling list to Martha's station. AP1 uses another combination frame to send a data frame to Martha, acknowledge Vivian's frame, and poll Martha's station for frame transmission (Data+CF-ACK+CF-Poll). Note that the frame is destined for Martha's station, yet it acknowledges Vivian's last frame. The multiple access nature of 802.11 allows for this arrangement. Martha waits a SIFS interval and sends a Data+CF-ACK frame.

Figure 2-17 *PCF Medium Access Operation*

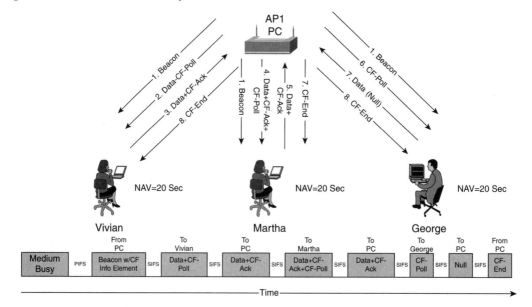

AP1 finally iterates to George's station. The AP has no data frames buffered for George's station, so it sends a CF-Poll frame to see whether George has any frames to send. George has no frames buffered either, so George sends a null data frame. Although the CFP has not exceeded the maximum duration allowed, AP1 sends a CF-End frame to end the CFP and proceed to the CP and normal DCF medium access. Vivian, Martha, and George receive the CF-End frame and reset their NAVs.

Nonstandard Devices

Although the previous section described how 802.11-standards–based devices access the wireless medium, this section discusses devices that fall outside of the 802.11 standard. These devices use the 802.11 technology in a way that violates or extends an area of the standard and that might prove useful in your network. The specific devices under consideration are

- Repeater APs
- Universal clients (workgroup bridges)
- Wireless bridges

Although each of these devices provides useful networking tools, you should remember that they are not currently defined in the 802.11 standard, and there are no interoperability guarantees because different vendors may define different mechanisms for implementing these tools. For the reliability of your network, should you choose to use these, you should ensure that they are only interfacing to devices from the same vendor or devices for which the vendor ensures interoperability.

Repeater APs

You might find yourself in situations where it is not easy or convenient to connect an AP to the wired infrastructure or where an obstruction makes it difficult for an AP on your wired network to directly associate clients in an area of your deployment. In such a scenario, you can employ a repeater AP. Figure 2-18 shows this scenario, where Elaine is not directly visible to AP2 but she can see AP3, which is not connected to the wired network but can see AP2.

Figure 2-18 *Repeater AP Application*

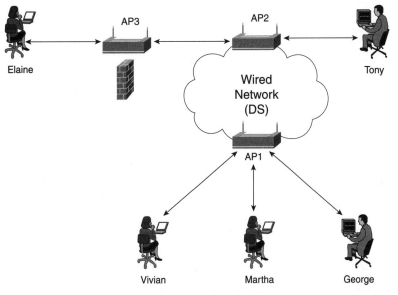

Much like a wired repeater, what a wireless repeater does is merely retransmit all the packets that it receives on its wireless interface. This retransmission happens on the same channel upon which the packet was received. The repeater AP has the effect of extending the BSS and also the collision domain. Although it can be an effective tool, you must take care when employing it; the overlapping of the broadcast domains can effectively cut your throughput in half because the originating AP also hears the retransmit. The problem can become even more exacerbated with a chain of repeater APs. In addition, the use of a repeater AP might limit you to utilizing clients with extensions that enable them to support associating to and running services over repeater APs. In spite of these limitations, it is highly likely that you will find applications for repeater APs in your network.

Universal Clients and Workgroup Bridges

As you migrate from a wired to a wireless network architecture, you might find that you have network devices that provide a wired Ethernet or serial interface but lack an interface slot for a wireless NIC. If it would be advantageous for you to have these devices on your wireless network, you can use a universal client or workgroup bridge. This scenario is illustrated in Figure 2-19.

Figure 2-19 *Universal Client and Workgroup Bridge Application*

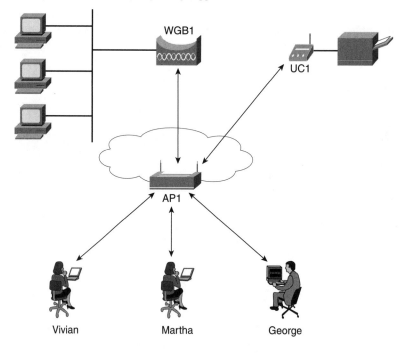

Examples of devices that might fall into this category include retail point-of-sale devices, printers, older PCs, copiers, and small mobile networks. The universal client or workgroup bridge encapsulates the wired packets it receives into wireless packets and thereby provides the 802.11 interface to the AP. The term *universal client* is most often used when a single wired device is being connected, whereas *workgroup bridges* are used for a small network of multiple devices. There is no standards-based approach for encapsulating or forwarding this wired interface data, so you often need to make sure that your universal client or workgroup bridge is certified to interoperate with your AP.

Wireless Bridges

If you extend the concept of a workgroup bridge even further to the point where you are connecting two or more wired networks, you arrive at the concept of wireless bridges. Similar to wired bridges, wireless bridges connect networks. You might bridge wirelessly because you need to connect networks that are inherently mobile. Alternatively, the networks to be connected might not be co-located, in which case wireless bridging provides a method for connecting these networks. The main distinction between bridges and workgroup bridges is that the latter are only wirelessly enabling a small network in an office environment, whereas the former can connect larger networks often separated by distances much greater than what is found in the WLAN environment. In fact, many vendors offer products that provide ranges which far exceed the definitions and limitations of 802.11. Figure 2-20 shows a wireless bridging example.

Figure 2-20 *Wireless Bridging Application*

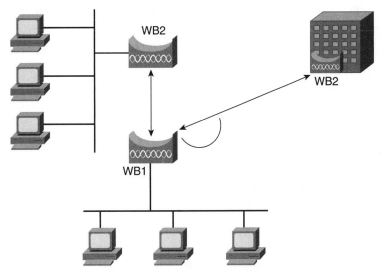

As shown in the figure, one of the bridges assumes the role of the AP in a WLAN network, and the other bridges act as clients. Although the basic 802.11 MAC and PHY sublayer technologies are utilized in wireless bridging, individual vendors have their own proprietary methods for the encapsulation of wired network traffic and for extending the range from a MAC and PHY sublayer perspective. For this reason, once again you should ensure that your wireless bridges are certified to interoperate.

802.11 MAC Layer Operations

The previous section described how a station accesses and contends for the wireless medium. This section focuses on the following:

- **Station connectivity**—Detailed explanation of how 802.11 stations select and communicate with APs

- **Power save operation**—Detailed explanation of frame delivery for power save stations

- **802.11 frame formats**—Detailed explanation of the frame formats described in previous sections

Station Connectivity

Earlier in the chapter, we discussed how George, Martha, Vivian, and Tony shared the medium in their BSS. This section takes a step back and details how an 802.11 wireless station joins a BSS. Three exchanges take place between the wireless station and the AP:

- The probe process
- The authentication process
- The association process

The Probe Process

In Figure 2-21, Vivian's station is in range to three APs. Two of the APs belong to the service set marketing, and the remaining AP belongs to the service set sales. Vivian's station is configured for the service set marketing.

The client station sends an 802.11 probe request frame. Generally, an 802.11 station sends the probe request frame on every channel it is allowed to use (channels 1 through 11 in North America). This process is not mandated by the 802.11 specification. The probe request frame contains information about an 802.11 wireless station, such as which data rates the station supports and what service set the station belongs to. Figure 2-22 is a protocol decode of a probe request frame.

The key fields in the probe request are

- **SSID element**—The SSID element contains the SSID that the client station is configured with.

- **Support rates element**—The support rates element describes all data rates the client supports.

Figure 2-21 *Vivian and the Surrounding APs*

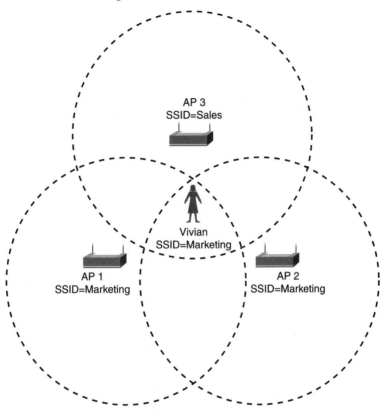

Client stations send probe requests frames blindly, meaning they don't know anything about the APs they are probing for. As such, most probes are sent at the lowest possible data rate of 1 Mbps. Figure 2-22 illustrates this process.

When an AP receives a probe request frame that successfully passed a frame check sequence (FCS), it replies with a probe response frame. Figure 2-23 is a protocol decode of a probe response frame.

Figure 2-22 *A Protocol Decode of a Probe Request Frame*

```
DLC: Signal level                    = 100%
DLC: Channel                         = 1
DLC: Data rate                       = 2 ( 1.0 Megabits per second)
DLC:
DLC: Frame Control Field #1 = 40
DLC:                .... ..00 = 0x0 Protocol Version
DLC:                .... 00.. = 0x0 Management Frame
DLC:                0100 .... = 0x4 Probe request (Subtype)
DLC: Frame Control Field #2 = 00
DLC:                .... ...0 = Not to Distribution System
DLC:                .... ..0. = Not from Distribution System
DLC:                .... .0.. = Last fragment
DLC:                .... 0... = Not retry
DLC:                ...0 .... = Active Mode
DLC:                ..0. .... = No more data
DLC:                .0.. .... = Wired Equivalent Privacy is off
DLC:                0... .... = Not ordered
DLC: Duration                        = 0 (in microseconds)
DLC: Destination Address             = BROADCAST FFFFFFFFFFFF, Broadcast
DLC: Source Address                  = Station Airont502F3F
DLC: Basic Service Set ID            = BROADCAST FFFFFFFFFFFF, Broadcast
DLC: Sequence Control                = 0x5690
DLC: ..Sequence Number               = 0x569 (1385)
DLC: ...Fragment Number              = 0x0   (0)
DLC: Element ID                      = 0 (Service Set Identifier)
DLC: ...Length                       = 9 octet(s)
DLC: ...Service Set Identity         = "marketing"
DLC:
DLC: Element ID                      = 1 (Supported Rates)
DLC: ...Length                       = 4 octet(s)
DLC: ...Supported Rates information field = 02
DLC:                0... .... = Not Basic Service Set Basic Rate
DLC:                .000 0010 = 1.0 Megabits per second
DLC: ...Supported Rates information field = 04
DLC:                0... .... = Not Basic Service Set Basic Rate
DLC:                .000 0100 = 2.0 Megabits per second
DLC: ...Supported Rates information field = 0B
DLC:                0... .... = Not Basic Service Set Basic Rate
DLC:                .000 1011 = 5.5 Megabits per second
DLC: ...Supported Rates information field = 16
DLC:                0... .... = Not Basic Service Set Basic Rate
DLC:                .001 0110 = 11.0 Megabits per second
```

The key fields in a probe response frame follow:

- **Timestamp field**—The value of the TSFTIMER of the frame sender. It is used to synchronize the clock of the client station to the clock of the AP.

- **Beacon interval field**—The number of time units (TUs) between beacons. A TU is 1024 microseconds.

- **Capability information field**—MAC and PHY layer capabilities. This field is described in detail in the section, "802.11 MAC Frame Formats," later in the chapter.

- **SSID element**—The SSID that the AP is configured with.

- **Support rates element**—All data rates that the AP supports.

- **PHY parameter set element**—Either frequency hopping or direct sequence. This element provides PHY-specific information to the client station. Both elements are described in detail in the section, "802.11 MAC Frame Formats," later in the chapter.

Figure 2-23 *A Probe Response Frame*

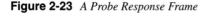

```
DLC: Frame Control Field #1 = 50
DLC:                .... ..00 = 0x0 Protocol Version
DLC:                .... 00.. = 0x0 Management Frame
DLC:                0101 .... = 0x5 Probe response (Subtype)
DLC: Frame Control Field #2 = 00
DLC:                .... ...0 = Not to Distribution System
DLC:                .... ..0. = Not from Distribution System
DLC:                .... .0.. = Last fragment
DLC:                .... 0... = Not retry
DLC:                ...0 .... = Active Mode
DLC:                ..0. .... = No more data
DLC:                .0.. .... = Wired Equivalent Privacy is off
DLC:                0... .... = Not ordered
DLC: Duration                  = 213 (in microseconds)
DLC: Destination Address       = Station Airont502F3F
DLC: Source Address            = Station 00097CAC4391
DLC: Basic Service Set ID      = 00097CAC4391
DLC: Sequence Control          = 0x2C30
DLC: ...Sequence Number        = 0x2C3 (707)
DLC: ...Fragment Number        = 0x0   (0)
DLC: Timestamp                 = 72298844
DLC: Beacon Interval           = 100
DLC: Capability information field #1 = 21
DLC:                .... ...1 = Extended Service Set is on
DLC:                .... ..0. = Independent Basic Service Set is off
DLC:                .... 00.. = No point coordinator at Access Point
DLC:                ...0 .... = No privacy
DLC:                ..1. .... = Short Preamble option is allowed
DLC:                .0.. .... = Packet Binary Convolutional Coding Modulation mode option is not allowed
DLC:                0... .... = Channel agility is not in use
DLC: Capability information field #2 = 00
DLC:                0000 0000 = Reserved
DLC:
DLC: Element ID               = 0 (Service Set Identifier)
DLC: ...Length                = 9 octet(s)
DLC: ...Service Set Identity  = "marketing"
DLC:
DLC: Element ID               = 1 (Supported Rates)
DLC: ...Length                = 4 octet(s)
DLC: ...Supported Rates information field = 82
DLC:                1... .... = Basic Service Set Basic Rate
DLC:                .000 0010 = 1.0 Megabits per second
DLC: ...Supported Rates information field = 84
DLC:                1... .... = Basic Service Set Basic Rate
DLC:                .000 0100 = 2.0 Megabits per second
DLC: ...Supported Rates information field = 8B
DLC:                1... .... = Basic Service Set Basic Rate
DLC:                .000 1011 = 5.5 Megabits per second
DLC: ...Supported Rates information field = 96
DLC:                1... .... = Basic Service Set Basic Rate
DLC:                .001 0110 = 11.0 Megabits per second
DLC:
DLC: Element ID               = 3 (Direct Sequence Parameter set)
DLC: ...Length                = 1 octet(s)
DLC: ...dot11CurrentChannelNumber = 1
```

When the client station receives the probe response frame, it is able to determine the signal strength of the received frame. The station compares the probe response frames and determines which AP to associate with. The mechanism for how a station chooses an AP to associate with is not specified by the 802.11 specification, so it is left to vendor implementation. In general, the AP selection criteria can include matching SSIDs, signal strength, and vendor proprietary extensions.

For the sake of this example, assume that matching SSIDs, supported data rates, and signal strength are the criteria (see Figure 2-24).

Figure 2-24 *The Probe Process*

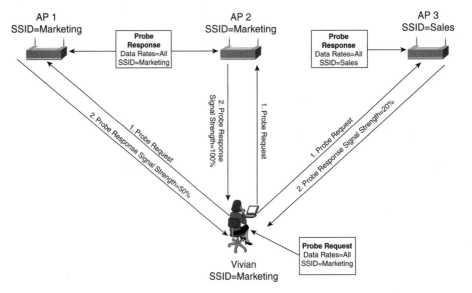

Table 2-1 summarizes the data from the probe response frames Vivian receives.

Table 2-1 *Probe Response Information*

Access Point Name	Support Data Rates	Service Set ID	Signal Strength
AP1	All	Marketing	50%
AP2	All	Marketing	100%
AP3	All	Sales	20%

Vivian is inclined to communicate with AP2. AP2 has a matching SSID, supports all data rates, and has a signal strength of 100%. AP1 is a close contender, but the signal strength is lower at 50%.

Now that Vivian's station has determined which AP to associate to, she can proceed to the next phase of station connectivity, the authentication process.

The Authentication Process

802.11 authentication consists of two authentication modes: open authentication and shared-key authentication. These two modes are detailed in Chapter 4, "802.11 Wireless LAN Security," which covers wireless security in depth. 802.11 authentication is oriented around device authentication and determines whether the device is allowed on the network. For the purposes of this section, authentication is simplified to an authentication request and an authentication response, as depicted in Figure 2-25.

Figure 2-25 *The Authentication Process*

Vivian
SSID=Marketing

1. Authentication Request →
← 2. Authentication Response

AP 2
SSID=Marketing

The Association Process

The 802.11 association process allows an AP to map a logical port or association identifier (AID) to the wireless station. The association process is initiated by the wireless station with an association request frame containing the capability information of the client and completed by the AP in an association response frame. The association response indicates success or failure as well as a reason code. Figure 2-26 is a protocol decode of an association request frame, and Figure 2-27 is a protocol decode of a association response frame.

Figure 2-26 *An Association Request Frame*

```
DLC: Frame Control Field #1 = 00
DLC:              .... ..00 = 0x0 Protocol Version
DLC:              .... 00.. = 0x0 Management Frame
DLC:              0000 .... = 0x0 Association request (Subtype)
DLC: Frame Control Field #2 = 00
DLC:              .... ...0 = Not to Distribution System
DLC:              .... ..0. = Not from Distribution System
DLC:              .... .0.. = Last fragment
DLC:              .... 0... = Not retry
DLC:              ...0 .... = Active Mode
DLC:              ..0. .... = No more data
DLC:              .0.. .... = Wired Equivalent Privacy is off
DLC:              0... .... = Not ordered
DLC: Duration                  = 314 (in microseconds)
DLC: Destination Address       = Station 00097CAC4391
DLC: Source Address            = Station Airont502F3F
DLC: Basic Service Set ID      = 00097CAC4391
DLC: Sequence Control          = 0x1720
DLC: ...Sequence Number        = 0x172 (370)
DLC: ...Fragment Number        = 0x0  (0)
DLC: Capability information field #1 = 21
DLC:                    .... ...1 = Extended Service Set is on
DLC:                    .... ..0. = Independent Basic Service Set is off
DLC:                    .... 00.. = STA is not Contention Free-Pollable
DLC:                    ...0 .... = No privacy
DLC:                    ..1. .... = Short Preamble option is implemented
DLC:                    .0.. .... = Packet Binary Convolutional Coding Modulation mode option is not implemented
DLC:                    0... .... = Channel agility is not in use
DLC: Capability information field #2 = 00
DLC:                    0000 0000 = Reserved
DLC: Listen interval           = 200
DLC:
DLC: Element ID                = 0 (Service Set Identifier)
DLC: ...Length                 = 5 octet(s)
DLC: ...Service Set Identity   = "cisco"
DLC:
DLC: Element ID                = 1 (Supported Rates)
DLC: ...Length                 = 4 octet(s)
DLC: ...Supported Rates information field = 02
DLC:                    0... .... = Not Basic Service Set Basic Rate
DLC:                    .000 0010 = 1.0 Megabits per second
DLC: ...Supported Rates information field = 04
DLC:                    0... .... = Not Basic Service Set Basic Rate
DLC:                    .000 0100 = 2.0 Megabits per second
DLC: ...Supported Rates information field = 0B
DLC:                    0... .... = Not Basic Service Set Basic Rate
DLC:                    .000 1011 = 5.5 Megabits per second
DLC: ...Supported Rates information field = 16
DLC:                    0... .... = Not Basic Service Set Basic Rate
DLC:                    .001 0110 = 11.0 Megabits per second
DLC:
```

The key fields for the association request frame follow:

- **Listen interval**—The listen interval value is used for a power save operation and is provided by the client station to the AP. It informs the AP of how often the station will "wake up" from low-power mode to receive buffered frames from the AP. This concept is described in detail later in the chapter.

- **SSID element**—The SSID element specifies the client station's SSID to the AP. The AP does not normally accept association requests from stations with SSIDs differing from those configured on the AP.

- **Support rates element**—This element indicates what data rates the client station supports to the AP.

Figure 2-27 *An Association Response Frame*

```
DLC: Frame Control Field #1 = 10
DLC:                .... ..00 = 0x0 Protocol Version
DLC:                .... 00.. = 0x0 Management Frame
DLC:                0001 .... = 0x1 Association response (Subtype)
DLC: Frame Control Field #2 = 00
DLC:                .... ...0 = Not to Distribution System
DLC:                .... ..0. = Not from Distribution System
DLC:                .... .0.. = Last fragment
DLC:                .... 0... = Not retry
DLC:                ...0 .... = Active Mode
DLC:                ..0. .... = No more data
DLC:                .0.. .... = Wired Equivalent Privacy is off
DLC:                0... .... = Not ordered
DLC: Duration                 = 117 (in microseconds)
DLC: Destination Address      = Station Airont502F3F
DLC: Source Address           = Station 00097CAC4391
DLC: Basic Service Set ID     = 00097CAC4391
DLC: Sequence Control         = 0x1150
DLC: ...Sequence Number       = 0x115 (277)
DLC: ...Fragment Number       = 0x0   (0)
DLC: Capability information field #1 = 21
DLC:                .... ...1 = Extended Service Set is on
DLC:                .... ..0. = Independent Basic Service Set is off
DLC:                .... 00.. = No point coordinator at Access Point
DLC:                ...0 .... = No privacy
DLC:                ..1. .... = Short Preamble option is allowed
DLC:                .0.. .... = Packet Binary Convolutional Coding Modulation mode option is not allowed
DLC:                0... .... = Channel agility is not in use
DLC: Capability information field #2 = 00
DLC:                0000 0000 = Reserved
DLC: Status code              = 0 (Successful)
DLC: Association ID           = 29
DLC:
DLC: Element ID               = 1 (Supported Rates)
DLC: ...Length                = 4 octet(s)
DLC: ...Supported Rates information field = 82
DLC:                1... .... = Basic Service Set Basic Rate
DLC:                .000 0010 = 1.0 Megabits per second
DLC: ...Supported Rates information field = 84
DLC:                1... .... = Basic Service Set Basic Rate
DLC:                .000 0100 = 2.0 Megabits per second
DLC: ...Supported Rates information field = 8B
DLC:                1... .... = Basic Service Set Basic Rate
DLC:                .000 1011 = 5.5 Megabits per second
DLC: ...Supported Rates information field = 96
DLC:                1... .... = Basic Service Set Basic Rate
DLC:                .001 0110 = 11.0 Megabits per second
DLC:
```

The key fields from the association response frame follow:

- **Status code**—This element indicates the status code resulting from the association response frame. All status codes are described in the section "802.11 MAC Frame Formats," later in the chapter.

- **Association ID**—You can consider the AID similar to a physical port on an Ethernet hub or switch. The client station needs this value when it operates in power save mode. The AP sends notifications in beacon frames that indicate which AIDs have frames buffered. This concept is described in detail in the section, "Power Save Operation," later in the chapter.

- **Support rates element**—This element indicates what data rates the AP supports.

Power Save Operation

To preserve battery life on portable WLAN clients, the 802.11 specification provides for power save operations on the clients. Power save operations have two categories:

- Unicast frame operation
- Multicast/broadcast frame operation

The premise behind power save (PS) operation is simple. A client station enters low-power mode by turning off its radio. The AP buffers frames destined for the station while the station is in power save mode. At a given interval, the client wakes up and listens for a beacon from the AP indicating whether frames are buffered for the client station.

Unicast power save operation uses a client-specified listen or wake-up interval. In contrast, multicast/broadcast power save operation uses an AP-defined interval, which is advertised in the AP's beacons.

The client wakes up and listens to the beacon frames to determine whether frames are buffered. If the AP does indeed have frames buffered for the client, the client polls the AP for the frames. If the AP does not have frames buffered, the client returns to low-power mode until the next wake-up interval.

Unicast Power Save Operation

When the client associates to the AP, it specifies a listen interval value in the association request frame. The listen interval is the number of beacons the client waits before transitioning to active mode. For example, a listen interval of 200 indicates that the client wakes up every 200 beacons.

The beacon frame includes a traffic indication map (TIM) information element. The element contains a list of all AIDs that have traffic buffered at the AP. There can be up to 2008 unique AIDs, so the TIM element alone can be up to 251 bytes. To minimize network overhead, the TIM utilizes a shorthand method of listing the AIDs. Figure 2-28 is a protocol decode of a beacon with a TIM indicating buffered traffic for a client.

Figure 2-28 *A Protocol Decode of a TIM Element*

```
DLC: Element ID                        = 5 (Traffic Indication Map)
DLC: ...Length                         = 5 octet(s)
DLC: ...Delivery Traffic Indication Message Count  = 5
DLC: ...Delivery Traffic Indication Message Period = 10
DLC: ...Bitmap control field = 03
DLC:                  .... ...1 = Traffic Indicator bit
DLC:                  0000 001. = 1 Bitmap offset
DLC: ...Partial Virtual Bitmap        = 0020
```

Notice that nowhere in the protocol decode is the AID of the client station explicitly stated. To determine the AID of the client station (or stations), you need the following pieces of information:

- The value of the length field
- The value of the bitmap offset field
- The value of the partial virtual bitmap field

802.11 specifies a traffic indication virtual bitmap as a means to indicate which station AIDs have frames buffered. The virtual bitmap starts from AID 1 to AID 2007. AID 0 is reserved for multicast/broadcast. Table 2-2 represents what a traffic indication virtual bitmap might look like. Every station with frames buffered at the AP has a flag value of 1 set for that station's AID. Stations with no frames buffered use a flag value of 0.

Table 2-2 *An Example of the Traffic Indication Virtual Bitmap*

AID	1	2	3	...	15	16	17	18	19	20	21	22	23	24	25	26	27	28	29	30	31	32	...	2007
Flag	0	0	0	...	0	0	0	0	0	0	0	0	0	0	0	0	0	0	1	0	0	0	...	0

Shaded values are included in the partial virtual bitmap.

The partial virtual bitmap eliminates all unnecessary 0 flag values by summarizing them. All client stations that have frames buffered (and therefore have flag values of 1 in the traffic indication virtual bitmap) are included in the partial virtual bitmap. All AIDs with a flag value of 0 leading up to the partial virtual bitmap are summarized by a derived value referred to as X in the following examples. All AIDs with flag values of 0 subsequent to the partial virtual bitmap are summarized by a derived value referred to as Y in the following examples. Referring to Table 2-2, AIDs 1 through 15 are summarized by value X, and AIDs 32 through 2007 are summarized by value Y.

To calculate X and Y, you must first derive N1 and N2. The formulas for deriving N1, N2, X, and Y are as follows:

$$N1 = (\text{bitmap offset} * 2)$$
$$N2 = (\text{length} - 4) + N1$$
$$X = (N1 * 8) - 1$$
$$Y = (N2 + 1) * 8$$

In the sample decode from Figure 2-28, N1 = (1 * 2) = 2 and N2 = (5 − 4) + 2 = 3. The value X is (2 * 8) − 1 or 15, and Y is (3 + 1) * 8 or 32. X indicates that AIDs 1 through 15 all have flag values of 0, and Y indicates that AIDs 32 through 2007 also have flag values of 0.

That leaves AIDs 16 through 31, which is where the partial virtual bitmap comes into play. The partial virtual bitmap in our example is a 2 byte value, 0x0020. The first byte, 0x00 or 00000000 in binary, indicates that the next 8 station AID flags following X (AIDs 16 to 23) are all 0. The second byte is 0x20 or 00100000 in binary. So in the example, AIDs 24 to 28 have a flag value of 0 and AID 29 has a flag value of 1. Because AID 29 is the only AID with a flag value of 1, AID 29 has traffic buffered at the AP.

If the client determines that frames are buffered for it, it sends an 802.11 MAC management frame known as a power save poll (PS-Poll) frame. Figure 2-29 provides a protocol decode of the PS-Poll the client station sent in response to the beacon. Note that the AID field has a value of 29, which is what was determined to be the AID from the partial virtual bitmap in the TIM element.

The AP responds to the PS-Poll frame with one of the client's buffered frames and an indication of whether more frames are buffered. The client must send a PS-Poll frame to the AP to receive each of the buffered frames on the AP. Figure 2-29 is a protocol decode of a PS-Poll frame. Note that the AID field indicated AID 29, as was calculated in the previous example.

Figure 2-29 *A Protocol Decode of a PS-Poll Frame*

```
⊟ DLC: ------ DLC Header ------
  DLC:
  DLC: Frame 58 arrived at  20:37:49.1643; frame size is 16 (0010 hex) bytes.
  DLC: Signal level                   = 100%
  DLC: Channel                        = 1
  DLC: Data rate                      = 2 ( 1.0 Megabits per second)
  DLC:
  DLC: Frame Control Field #1 = A4
  DLC:                 .... ..00 = 0x0 Protocol Version
  DLC:                 .... 01.. = 0x1 Control Frame
  DLC:                 1010 .... = 0xA Power Save (PS)-Poll (Subtype)
  DLC: Frame Control Field #2 = 10
  DLC:                 .... ...0 = Not to Distribution System
  DLC:                 .... ..0. = Not from Distribution System
  DLC:                 .... .0.. = Last fragment
  DLC:                 .... 0... = Not retry
  DLC:                 ...1 .... = Power Save Mode
  DLC:                 ..0. .... = No more data
  DLC:                 .0.. .... = Wired Equivalent Privacy is off
  DLC:                 0... .... = Not ordered
  DLC: Association ID                 = 29
  DLC: Basic Service Set ID           = Station Airont482745
  DLC: Transmitter Address            = Station 0006D7863845
```

Broadcast

A broadcast power save operation has the same basic operation as unicast power save operation. The differences follow:

- The administrator defines the interval for the client to wake up and receive buffered broadcast or multicast traffic on the AP.

- A special TIM information element, known as a DTIM, indicates whether broadcast or multicast traffic is buffered on the AP.

- Broadcast and multicast frames are buffered for all stations (including non-power–save stations) in the BSS, when one or more power save station is associated to the AP.

The TIM has two fields to indicate whether multicast/broadcast traffic is buffered and how long until it is delivered to the BSS:

- **DTIM count field**—This field indicates how many beacons until the delivery of buffered frames. A value of 0 indicates that the TIM is a DTIM, and if there are buffered frames, they will be transmitted immediately following the beacon.

- **DTIM period field**—This field indicates the number of beacons between DTIMs. For example, a value of 10 indicates that every 10th beacon will contain a DTIM.

Figure 2-30 highlights a protocol decode of a beacon containing a DTIM. In Figure 2-31, note that the frames following the beacon are all multicast frames.

Figure 2-30 *A Protocol Decode of a DTIM Element*

```
DLC: Element ID                                  = 5 (Traffic Indication Map)
DLC: ...Length                                   = 4 octet(s)
DLC: ...Delivery Traffic Indication Message Count  = 0
DLC: ...Delivery Traffic Indication Message Period = 10
DLC: ...Bitmap control field = 01
DLC:                    .... ...1 = Traffic Indicator bit
DLC:                    0000 000. = 0 Bitmap offset
DLC: ...Partial Virtual Bitmap      = 00
```

Figure 2-31 *Multicast Frames Following a Beacon Frame with a DTIM Element*

```
[1]   Airont482745   Broadcast        802.11   1.0 Mbps  Signal=100%  Beacon
[1]   [13.1.1.1]     [224.0.0.10]     EIGRP: Hello AS=10
[1]   Airont482745   014096000000     SNAP: ID=Airont Type=0000
[1]   [13.1.1.1]     [224.0.0.10]     EIGRP: Hello AS=10
```

802.11 MAC Frame Formats

There are three categories of frames in the 802.11 MAC:

- **Control frames**—These frames facilitate the data frames during normal 802.11 data exchanges.

- **Management frames**—These frames facilitate WLAN connectivity, authentication, and status.

- **Data frames**—These frames carry station data between the transmitter and receiver.

All 802.11 frames leverage the 802.11 general frame. The three frames types augment and use specific portions of the general MAC frame for their specific purposes. Figure 2-32 illustrates the general MAC frame and its fields.

Figure 2-32 *The General 802.11 MAC Frame*

Frame Control	Duration/ ID	Address 1	Address 2	Address 3	Sequence Control	Address 4	Frame Body	FCS
2 Bytes	2 Bytes	6 Bytes	6 Bytes	6 Bytes	2 Bytes	6 Bytes	0 - 2312 Bytes	4 Bytes

- **Frame control**—The frame control field is a 2 byte value of 11 subfields. Figure 2-33 illustrates the frame control subfields, and Figure 2-34 is a protocol decode of the frame control subfields.

Figure 2-33 *The Frame Control Subfields*

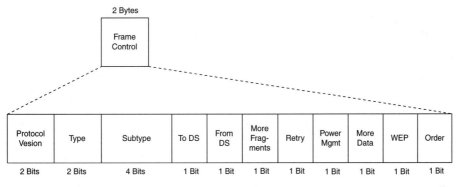

Protocol Vesion	Type	Subtype	To DS	From DS	More Frag- ments	Retry	Power Mgmt	More Data	WEP	Order
2 Bits	2 Bits	4 Bits	1 Bit	1 Bit	1 Bit	1 Bit	1 Bit	1 Bit	1 Bit	1 Bit

Figure 2-34 *A Protocol Decode of the Frame Control Subfields*

```
DLC:  Frame Control Field #1 = B0
DLC:                   .... ..00 = 0x0 Protocol Version
DLC:                   .... 00.. = 0x0 Management Frame
DLC:                   1011 .... = 0xB Authentication (Subtype)
DLC:  Frame Control Field #2 = 00
DLC:                   .... ...0 = Not to Distribution System
DLC:                   .... ..0. = Not from Distribution System
DLC:                   .... .0.. = Last fragment
DLC:                   .... 0... = Not retry
DLC:                   ...0 .... = Active Mode
DLC:                   ..0. .... = No more data
DLC:                   .0.. .... = Wired Equivalent Privacy is off
DLC:                   0... .... = Not ordered
```

The list that follows describes the 11 frame control subfields:

— **Protocol version**—This field specifies the version of 802.11 MAC protocol. To date, there is only one version, so the only valid value is 0. All other values are reserved.

— **Type**—This field specifies the type of MAC frame: control, management, or data. The fourth value is reserved.

— **Subtype**—This field specifies the frame subtype. These values are listed in Table 2-3.

Table 2-3   *Frame Types and Subtypes*

Type Value (Bit 3, Bit 2)	Type Description	Subtype Value (Bit 7, Bit 6, Bit 5, Bit 4)	Subtype Description
00	Management	0000	Association request
00	Management	0001	Association response
00	Management	0010	Reassociation request
00	Management	0011	Reassociation response
00	Management	0100	Probe request
00	Management	0101	Probe response
00	Management	0110–0111	Reserved
00	Management	1000	Beacon
00	Management	1001	Announcement traffic indication frame (ATIM)
00	Management	1010	Disassociation
00	Management	1011	Authentication
00	Management	1100	Deauthentication
00	Management	1101–1111	Reserved
01	Control	0000–1001	Reserved
01	Control	1010	PS-Poll
01	Control	1011	RTS
01	Control	1100	CTS
01	Control	1101	Acknowledgment (ACK)
01	Control	1110	CF-End
01	Control	1111	CF-End+CF-Ack
10	Data	0000	Data
10	Data	0001	Data+CF-Ack
10	Data	0010	Data+CF-Poll
10	Data	0011	Data+CF-Ack+CF-Poll
10	Data	0100	Null function (no data)
10	Data	0101	CF-Ack (no data)
10	Data	0110	CF-Poll (no data)
10	Data	0111	CF-Ack+CF-Poll (no data)
10	Data	1000–1111	Reserved
11	Reserved	0000–1111	Reserved

- **To DS**—This field indicates whether the frame is destined for the DS.

- **From DS**—This field indicates whether the frame is sourced from the DS.

- **More fragments**—This field indicates whether this frame is the only management or data frame or whether other fragments should be expected.

- **Retry**—This field indicates whether this frame is being retransmitted. It allows the receiver to discard duplicate frames.

- **Power management**—Indicates the power save mode of the station. A value of 1 indicates the station is in power save mode, and a value of 0 indicates the station is in active mode. Frames from the AP always have a value of 0.

- **More data**—When the bit for this field is set, the receiving station is notified that it has data destined for it buffered at the AP.

- **WEP**—This field indicates whether Wired Equivalent Privacy (WEP) encryption is used to encrypt the frame body.

- **Order**—This field is set to 1 if the data frame is using the StrictlyOrdered service class; otherwise, it is set to 0.

- **Duration/ID**—This field is used differently depending on whether a power save station is accessing the medium, the medium is in a PCF mode CFP, and a DCF station is accessing the medium. Table 2-4 describes the bit values for the various situations.

Table 2-4 *Values for the Duration Field*

Bit 15	Bit 14	Bit 13–0	Usage
0	0–32,767		Duration of frame exchange (in microseconds) for DCF stations
1	0	0	Values used during CFP frame exchanges
1	0	1–1683	Reserved
1	1	0	Reserved
1	1	1–2007	Association ID for use in PS-Poll frames
1	1	2008–16,383	Reserved

- **Address 1, 2, 3, and 4**—These fields vary depending on frame type and subtype.

- **Sequence control**—This field is the sequence number and fragment number of the frame.

- **FCS**—This field is a 32-bit cyclic redundancy check (CRC) value calculated over all fields in the MAC header and frame body.

Figure 2-35 is a protocol decode of the remaining fields in the general MAC frame.

Figure 2-35 *A Protocol Decode of the Duration, Address, and Sequence Control Subfields*

```
DLC: Duration                    = 314 (in microseconds)
DLC: Destination Address         = Station Airont31669C
DLC: Source Address              = Station Airont500292
DLC: Basic Service Set ID        = Airont31669C
DLC: Sequence Control            = 0x0A40
DLC: ...Sequence Number          = 0x0A4 (164)
DLC: ...Fragment Number          = 0x0   (0)
```

802.11 Control Frames

The 802.11 specification stipulates six unique control frames:

- Power save poll (PS-Poll)
- RTS
- CTS
- ACK
- Contention-free End (CF-End)
- CF-End + contention-free acknowledgment (CF-End+CF-ACK)

The first four are the primary frames to focus on. The CF-End and CF-End+CF-ACK are part of the PCF, which is not widely deployed.

The PS-Poll Frame

The PS-Poll frame is an indicator to the AP that a wireless station in power save mode is requesting that any frames buffered on the AP be delivered. The PS-Poll frame contains the following variation of the generic MAC frame:

- **AID**—The AID of the wireless client, with the two most significant bits set to 1
- **The BSS identifier (BSSID)**—The MAC address of the AP in an infrastructure network
- **Transmitter address (SA)**—The MAC address of the power save wireless station

Figure 2-36 shows the frame format of the PS-Poll frame, and Figure 2-37 shows a protocol decode of the PS-Poll frame.

Figure 2-36 *Frame Format of the PS-Poll Frame*

Frame Control	AID	BSSID	TA	FCS
2 Bytes	2 Bytes	6 Bytes	6 Bytes	4 Bytes

Figure 2-37 *A Protocol Decode of PS-Poll Frame*

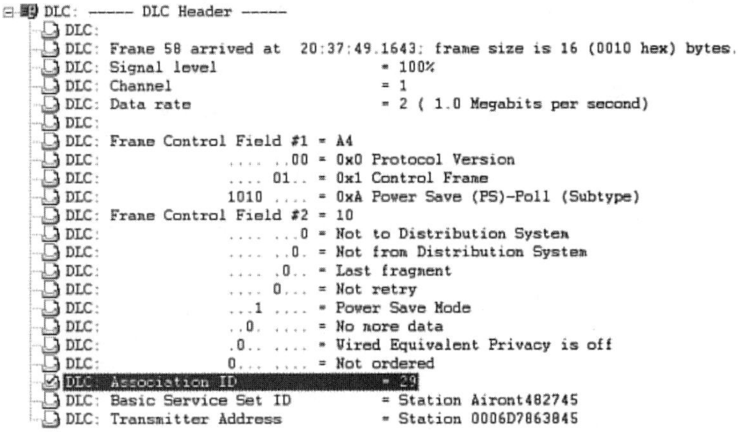

```
⊟-📳 DLC: ------ DLC Header ------
   -📄 DLC:
   -📄 DLC: Frame 58 arrived at  20:37:49.1643; frame size is 16 (0010 hex) bytes.
   -📄 DLC: Signal level              = 100%
   -📄 DLC: Channel                   = 1
   -📄 DLC: Data rate                 = 2 ( 1.0 Megabits per second)
   -📄 DLC:
   -📄 DLC: Frame Control Field #1 = A4
   -📄 DLC:                .... ..00 = 0x0 Protocol Version
   -📄 DLC:                .... 01.. = 0x1 Control Frame
   -📄 DLC:                1010 .... = 0xA Power Save (PS)-Poll (Subtype)
   -📄 DLC: Frame Control Field #2 = 10
   -📄 DLC:                .... ...0 = Not to Distribution System
   -📄 DLC:                .... ..0. = Not from Distribution System
   -📄 DLC:                .... .0.. = Last fragment
   -📄 DLC:                .... 0... = Not retry
   -📄 DLC:                ...1 .... = Power Save Mode
   -📄 DLC:                ..0. .... = No more data
   -📄 DLC:                .0.. .... = Wired Equivalent Privacy is off
   -📄 DLC:                0... .... = Not ordered
   -☑ DLC: Association ID             = 39
   -📄 DLC: Basic Service Set ID       = Station Airont482745
   -📄 DLC: Transmitter Address        = Station 0006D7863845
```

The RTS Frame

The RTS frame is the request to reserve the wireless medium as a part of the 802.11 medium access mechanism:

- **Duration**—The time required for the station's frame exchange to take place. It includes the time to transmit the RTS frame, the time to receive the CTS frame (including the SIFS interval), the time to transmit the data frame (including the SIFS interval), and the time to receive the ACK frame (including the SIFS interval). Duration time is measured in microseconds.

- **Receiver address**—The MAC address of the intended recipient of the frame.

- **Transmitter address**—The MAC address of the transmitter of the frame sender.

Figure 2-38 shows the frame format of the RTS frame and Figure 2-39 shows a protocol decode of the RTS frame.

Figure 2-38 *Frame Format for the RTS Frame*

Frame Control	Duration	RA	TA	FCS
2 Bytes	2 Bytes	6 Bytes	6 Bytes	4 Bytes

Figure 2-39 *A Protocol Decode of the RTS Frame*

```
DLC: Frame Control Field #1 = B4
DLC:                 .... ..00 = 0x0 Protocol Version
DLC:                 .... 01.. = 0x1 Control Frame
DLC:                 1011 .... = 0xB Request To Send (RTS) (Subtype)
DLC: Frame Control Field #2 = 00
DLC:                 .... ...0 = Not to Distribution System
DLC:                 .... ..0. = Not from Distribution System
DLC:                 .... .0.. = Last fragment
DLC:                 .... 0... = Not retry
DLC:                 ...0 .... = Active Mode
DLC:                 ..0. .... = No more data
DLC:                 .0.. .... = Wired Equivalent Privacy is off
DLC:                 0... .... = Not ordered
DLC: Duration                 = 1054 (in microseconds)
DLC: Receiver Address         = Station 00097CAC4391
DLC: Transmitter Address      = Station Airont502F3F
```

The CTS Frame

The CTS frame is the response to an RTS frame. It is an indication to the receiving station that the medium has been reserved for the specified duration:

- **Duration**—The value obtained from the Duration field of the immediately previous RTS frame, minus the time required to transmit the CTS frame and its SIFS interval.

- **Receiver address**—The MAC address of the intended recipient of the frame.

Figure 2-40 shows the frame format of the CTS frame, and Figure 2-41 shows a protocol decode of the CTS frame.

Figure 2-40 *Frame Format for the CTS Frame*

Frame Control	Duration	RA	FCS
2 Bytes	2 Bytes	6 Bytes	4 Bytes

Figure 2-41 *A Protocol Decode of the CTS Frame*

```
DLC: Frame Control Field #1 = C4
DLC:                 .... ..00 = 0x0 Protocol Version
DLC:                 .... 01.. = 0x1 Control Frame
DLC:                 1100 .... = 0xC Clear To Send (CTS) (Subtype)
DLC: Frame Control Field #2 = 00
DLC:                 .... ...0 = Not to Distribution System
DLC:                 .... ..0. = Not from Distribution System
DLC:                 .... .0.. = Last fragment
DLC:                 .... 0... = Not retry
DLC:                 ...0 .... = Active Mode
DLC:                 ..0. .... = No more data
DLC:                 .0.. .... = Wired Equivalent Privacy is off
DLC:                 0... .... = Not ordered
DLC: Duration                 = 836 (in microseconds)
DLC: Receiver Address         = Station Airont502F3F
DLC: Implied Transmitter Address = Station 00097CAC4391
```

The ACK Frame

The ACK frame acknowledges frame transmission. The receiver of a frame sends an ACK frame to the sender to indicate successful frame receipt:

- **Duration**—The duration for ACK frames is usually 0 because the frame it is acknowledging includes the transmission time for the SIFS interval and the ACK frame in its duration field.

- **Receiver address**—The MAC address of the intended recipient of the frame.

Figure 2-42 shows the frame format of the ACK frame, and Figure 2-43 shows a protocol decode of the ACK frame.

Figure 2-42 *Frame Format for the ACK Frame*

Frame Control	Duration	RA	FCS
2 Bytes	2 Bytes	6 Bytes	4 Bytes

Figure 2-43 *A Protocol Decode of the ACK Frame*

```
DLC: Frame Control Field #1 = D4
DLC:                 .... ..00 = 0x0 Protocol Version
DLC:                 .... 01.. = 0x1 Control Frame
DLC:                 1101 .... = 0xD Acknovledgment (ACK) (Subtype)
DLC: Frame Control Field #2 = 00
DLC:                 .... ...0 = Not to Distribution System
DLC:                 .... ..0. = Not from Distribution System
DLC:                 .... .0.. = Last fragment
DLC:                 .... 0... = Not retry
DLC:                 ...0 .... = Active Mode
DLC:                 ..0. .... = No more data
DLC:                 .0.. .... = Wired Equivalent Privacy is off
DLC:                 0... .... = Not ordered
DLC: Duration                 = 0 (in microseconds)
DLC: Receiver Address         = Station Airont502F3F
DLC: Implied Transmitter Address = Station 00097CAC4391
```

The CF-End and CF-End+CF-ACK Frames

The CF-End and CF-End+CF-ACK frames are specific to PCF operation. They indicate the end of the contention-free period, and the CF-End+CF-ACK also includes an acknowledgment of the last frame received by the PC. Figure 2-44 shows the format for the CF-End and CF-End+CF-ACK frames and the list that follows describes the key fields.

Figure 2-44 *Frame Format for the CF-End and CF-End+CF-ACK Frames*

Frame Control	Duration	RA	BSSID	FCS
2 Bytes	2 Bytes	6 Bytes	6 Bytes	4 Bytes

- **Duration**—Set to 0.

- **Receiver address**—The destination MAC address of the intended recipient of the frame. In the case of the CF-End frames, it is the broadcast MAC address because every station in the service set should receive the notification.

- **BSSID**—The MAC address of the AP.

802.11 Management Frame Fields and Elements

802.11 management frames leverage fields from the generic MAC frame detailed earlier and also utilize data structures known as information elements (IE) and fixed fields.

Figure 2-45 shows the format of an IE. The purpose of the IE and the fixed fields is to give flexible capability definitions to existing frames and to provide a scalable method of expanding the functionality of the MAC management frames. The 802.11 management frames are constructed by using relevant fields from the general MAC frame format and adding the appropriate IEs and fixed fields (see Figure 2-46).

Figure 2-45 *Format of an IE*

Frame Control	Length	Information
1 Byte	1 Byte	

Figure 2-46 *Management Frame Construction using IEs and Fixed Fields*

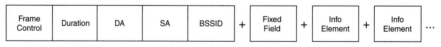

| Frame Control | Duration | DA | SA | BSSID | + | Fixed Field | + | Info Element | + | Info Element | ... |

Table 2-5 lists the 802.11-defined IEs.

Table 2-5 *802.11 IEs*

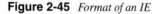

IE	Element ID
SSID	0
Supported rates	1
Frequency hop (FH) parameter set	2
DS parameter set	3

Table 2-5   *802.11 IEs (Continued)*

IE	Element ID
CF parameter set	4
TIM	5
IBSS parameter set	6
Reserved	7–15
Challenge text	16
Reserved for challenge text extension	17–31
Reserved	32–255

The SSID IE

The SSID can be up to 32 bytes in length, and if the length is 0, the SSID is a broadcast SSID.

Figure 2-47 shows the frame format of the SSID IE, and Figure 2-48 shows a protocol decode of the SSID IE.

Figure 2-47   *Format of the SSID IE*

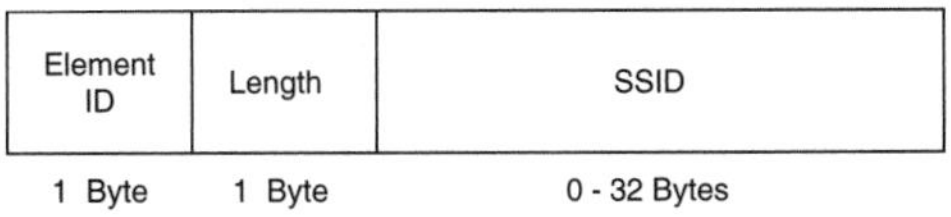

Element ID	Length	SSID
1 Byte	1 Byte	0 - 32 Bytes

Figure 2-48   *A Protocol Decode of an SSID IE*

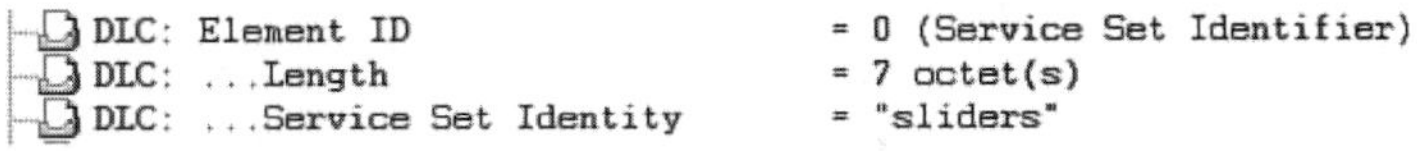

```
DLC: Element ID                    = 0 (Service Set Identifier)
DLC: ...Length                     = 7 octet(s)
DLC: ...Service Set Identity       = "sliders"
```

The Supported Rates IE

The supported rates IE specifies what rates the wireless station is capable of supporting. The binary values are in increments of 500 kbps. For example, a supported rate of 11 Mbps is represented by 0x16, which is equal to decimal 22. 22/500 kbps (or .5 Mbps) = 11 Mbps.

Figure 2-49 shows the frame format of the supported rates IE, and Figure 2-50 shows a protocol decode of the supported rates IE.

Figure 2-49   *Format of the Supported Rates IE*

Figure 2-50   *A Protocol Decode of the Supported Rates IE*

```
DLC: Element ID                        = 1 (Supported Rates)
DLC: ...Length                         = 4 octet(s)
DLC: ...Supported Rates information field = 02
DLC:                          0... .... = Not Basic Service Set Basic Rate
DLC:                          .000 0010 = 1.0 Megabits per second
DLC: ...Supported Rates information field = 04
DLC:                          0... .... = Not Basic Service Set Basic Rate
DLC:                          .000 0100 = 2.0 Megabits per second
DLC: ...Supported Rates information field = 0B
DLC:                          0... .... = Not Basic Service Set Basic Rate
DLC:                          .000 1011 = 5.5 Megabits per second
DLC: ...Supported Rates information field = 16
DLC:                          0... .... = Not Basic Service Set Basic Rate
DLC:                          .001 0110 = 11.0 Megabits per second
```

FH Parameter Set IE

Figure 2-51 shows the format of the FH parameter set IE, and the list that follows describes the key fields:

- **Dwell time**—The FH dwell time in TU
- **Hop set**—The FH hopping pattern set
- **Hop pattern**—The individual FH hopping pattern
- **Hop index**—The current channel index from within the hopping pattern

Figure 2-51   *Format of the FH Parameter Set IE*

The DS Parameter Set IE

Figure 2-52 shows the format of the DS parameter set IE. The current channel field indicates the channel in use by the direct-sequencing wireless station.

Figure 2-52 *Format of the DS Parameter Set IE*

The CF Parameter Set IE

Figure 2-53 shows the format of the CF parameter set IE, and the list that follows describes the key fields:

- **CFP count**—A count of remaining DTIMs (including the current frame) before the start of the next CFP

- **CFP period**—The number of DTIM intervals between the CFPs

- **CFP MaxDuration**—The maximum duration of the CFP in TUs

- **CFP DurationRemaining**—The duration remaining in TUs for the current CFP

Figure 2-53 *Format of the CF Parameter Set IE*

The TIM IE

Figure 2-54 shows the frame format of the TIM IE, and Figure 2-55 shows a protocol decode of the TIM IE. The list that follows describes the key fields of the TIM IE frame:

- **DTIM count**—A count of how many beacon frames (including the current frame) appear before the next DTIM. A value of 0 indicates this frame is the DTIM.

- **DTIM period**—The number of DTIM intervals between DTIM frames. A value of 1 indicates all TIMs are DTIMs. The value of 0 is reserved.

- **Bitmap control**—Bit 0 of the field contains the traffic indicator bit associated with AID 0. This bit is set to 1 in TIM elements with a value of 0 in the DTIM count field when one or more broadcast or multicast frames are buffered at the AP. The remaining 7 bits of the field form the bitmap offset.

- **Partial virtual bitmap**—A per-station indication of AP frame buffer status. An indication for AID 0 indicates that broadcast/multicast frames are buffered.

Figure 2-54 *Format of the TIM IE*

Element ID	Length	DTIM Count	DTIM Period	Bitmap Control	Partial Virtual Bitmap
1 Byte	1 Byte	1 Byte	1 Byte	1 Byte	1 – 251 Bytes

Figure 2-55 *A Protocol Decode of the TIM IE*

```
DLC:  Element ID                          = 5 (Traffic Indication Map)
DLC:  ...Length                           = 5 octet(s)
DLC:  ...Delivery Traffic Indication Message Count  = 5
DLC:  ...Delivery Traffic Indication Message Period = 10
DLC:  ...Bitmap control field = 03
DLC:                   .... ...1 = Traffic Indicator bit
DLC:             0000 001. = 1 Bitmap offset
DLC:  ...Partial Virtual Bitmap     = 0020
```

The IBSS Parameter Set IE

Figure 2-56 shows the format of the IBSS parameter set IE.

Figure 2-56 *Format of the IBSS Parameter Set IE*

Element ID	Length	ATIM Window
1 Byte	1 Byte	2 Bytes

The ATIM window field indicates the ATIM window length in TU.

The Challenge Text IE

Figure 2-57 shows the format of the challenge text IE.

Figure 2-57 *Format of the Challenge Text IE*

Element ID	Length	Challenge Text
1 Byte	1 Byte	1 – 253 Bytes

The challenge text field indicates the challenge text for use in authentication frames.

802.11 Fixed Field Elements

In addition to IEs, the 802.11 specification also defines 10 fixed-field elements for use in management frames, as listed in Table 2-6.

Table 2-6   *802.11 Fixed Fields*

Fixed Field Element	Length (Bits)
Authentication algorithm number	16
Authentication transaction sequence number	16
Beacon interval	16
Capability information	16
Current AP address	48
Listen interval	16
Reason code	16
AID	16
Status code	16
Timestamp	64

The Authentication Algorithm Number Field

For this field, a value of o indicates open authentication. A value of 1 indicates shared-key authentication. All other values are reserved.

The Authentication Transaction Sequence Number Field

This field indicates the current step in a multistep authentication process.

The Beacon Interval Field

This field indicates the number of TUs between beacon transmissions.

The Capability Information Field

The capability information field only includes subfields relevant for the management frames for which the transmission rules are defined. Figure 2-58 illustrates the capability information field format, and the list that follows describes the key subfields:

- **ESS**—The AP sets this value to 1 and the IBSS subfield to 0 in beacon and probe response frames.

- **IBSS**—Stations in an IBSS set this field to 1 and the ESS subfield to 0 in beacon and probe response frames.

- **CF-Pollable**—APs and wireless stations use this subfield.

- **CF-Poll request**—APs and wireless stations use this subfield. Tables 2-7 and 2-8 describe the subfield settings and corresponding meanings.

- **Privacy**—This subfield is set to 1 if WEP encryption is required for data frames. It is included in beacon, probe response, association, and reassociation response frames. If WEP encryption is not required, this subfield is set to 0.

Figure 2-58   *Format of the Capability Information Field*

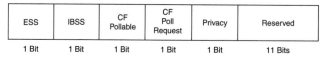

Table 2-7   *CF-Poll Request Field in Frames Sourced by the Client Station*

CF-Pollable	CF-Poll Request	Meaning
0	0	Station is not CF-Pollable.
1	0	Station is CF-Pollable and is requesting to be placed on the polling list.
0	1	Station is CF-Pollable and is not requesting to be placed on the polling list.
1	1	Station is CF-Pollable and is requesting to never be placed on the polling list.

Table 2-8   *CF-Poll Request Field in Frames Sourced by the AP*

CF-Pollable	CF-Poll Request	Meaning
0	0	AP does not support PCF; no PC.
1	0	PC supports frame delivery only.
0	1	PC supports frame delivery and polling.
1	1	Reserved.

The Current AP Address Field

This field indicates the MAC address of the AP the wireless station is currently associated to.

The Listen Interval Field

This field indicates the number of beacon intervals when power save station wakes up to listen for a beacon frame.

The Reason Code Field

This field indicates the reason for the transmission of an unsolicited deauthentication or dissociation frame. Table 2-9 lists all reason codes and their meanings.

Table 2-9   *802.11 Reason Codes*

Reason Code	Meaning
0	Reserved
1	Unspecified reason
2	Previous authentication no longer valid
3	Deauthenticated because sending station is leaving (has left) IBSS or ESS
4	Disassociated due to inactivity
5	Disassociated because AP is unable to handle all currently associated stations
6	Class 2 frame received from nonauthenticated station
7	Class 3 frame received from nonassociation station
8	Disassociated because sending station is leaving (has left) BSS
9	Station requesting (re)association is not authenticated with responding station
10–65,535	Reserved

The AID Field

This field indicates the value assigned by the AP to represent the 16-bit ID for the wireless station. This value is a logical port for the wireless station.

The Status Code Field

This field indicates a value in management response frames representing success or failure of a management frame request. Table 2-10 lists all the 802.11 status codes and their meanings.

Table 2-10 *802.11 Status Codes*

Status Code	Meaning
0	Successful
1	Unspecified failure
2–9	Reserved
10	Cannot support all requested capabilities in the capability information field
11	Reassociation denied due to inability to confirm that association exists
12	Association denied due to reason outside the scope of this standard
13	Responding station does not support the specified authentication algorithm
14	Received an authentication frame with authentication transaction sequence number out of expected sequence
15	Authentication rejected because of challenge failure
16	Authentication rejected due to timeout waiting for next frame in sequence
17	Association denied because AP is unable to handle additional associated stations
18	Association denied due to requesting station not supporting all of the data rates in the BSSBasicRateSet parameter
19–65,535	Reserved

The Timestamp Field

This field indicates the value of the TSFTIMER of the frame sender.

802.11 Management Frames

802.11 management frames consist of the following:

- Beacon frame
- Probe request frame
- Probe response frame

- Authentication frame
- Deauthentication frame
- Association request frame
- Association response frame
- Reassociation request frame
- Reassociation response frame
- Disassociation frame
- Announcement traffic indication frame

The following sections give more details on each management frame.

The Beacon Frame

The beacon frame is a management frame that the AP (or beacon sender in an IBSS) transmits at the beacon interval rate. The beacon provides time synchronization between the AP and the wireless stations as well as PHY-specific parameters. In addition, power save stations are alerted if the AP has frames buffered. In addition to the 802.11 defined fields and IEs, vendor-specific IEs can also be included in the beacon frames.

Figure 2-59 shows the frame format of a beacon frame, and Figure 2-60 shows a protocol decode of the beacon frame.

Figure 2-59 *Frame Format of a Beacon Frame*

Frame Control	Duration	DA	SA	BSSID	Sequence Control	Time-stamp Field	Beacon Interval Field	Capability Information Field	SSID IE	Supported Rates IE	FH/DS Parameter Set IE	CF Parameter Set IE (Optional)	IBSS Parameter Set IE (Optional)	TIM IE (Optional)

The Probe Request Frame

Figure 2-61 shows the frame format of a probe request frame, and Figure 2-62 shows a protocol decode of the probe request frame.

Figure 2-60 *A Protocol Decode of a Beacon Frame*

```
DLC: Frame Control Field #1 = 80
DLC:                  .... ..00 = 0x0 Protocol Version
DLC:                  .... 00.. = 0x0 Management Frame
DLC:                  1000 .... = 0x8 Beacon (Subtype)
DLC: Frame Control Field #2 = 00
DLC:                  .... ...0 = Not to Distribution System
DLC:                  .... ..0. = Not from Distribution System
DLC:                  .... .0.. = Last fragment
DLC:                  .... 0... = Not retry
DLC:                  ...0 .... = Active Mode
DLC:                  ..0. .... = No more data
DLC:                  .0.. .... = Wired Equivalent Privacy is off
DLC:                  0... .... = Not ordered
DLC: Duration                  = 0 (in microseconds)
DLC: Destination Address       = BROADCAST FFFFFFFFFFFF, Broadcast
DLC: Source Address            = Station Airont482745
DLC: Basic Service Set ID      = Airont482745
DLC: Sequence Control          = 0x0070
DLC: ...Sequence Number        = 0x007 (7)
DLC: ...Fragment Number        = 0x0   (0)
DLC: Timestamp                 = 16385154 (in microseconds)
DLC: Beacon Interval           = 2000
DLC: Capability information field #1 = 21
DLC:                  .... ...1 = Extended Service Set is on
DLC:                  .... ..0. = Independent Basic Service Set is off
DLC:                  .... 00.. = No point coordinator at Access Point
DLC:                  ...0 .... = No privacy
DLC:                  ..1. .... = Short Preamble option is allowed
DLC:                  .0.. .... = Packet Binary Convolutional Coding Modulation mode option is not allowed
DLC:                  0... .... = Channel agility is not in use
DLC: Capability information field #2 = 00
DLC:                  0000 0000 = Reserved
DLC:
DLC: Element ID                = 0 (Service Set Identifier)
DLC: ...Length                 = 9 octet(s)
DLC: ...Service Set Identity   = "powersave"
DLC:
DLC: Element ID                = 1 (Supported Rates)
DLC: ...Length                 = 4 octet(s)
DLC: ...Supported Rates information field = 82
DLC:                  1... .... = Basic Service Set Basic Rate
DLC:                  .000 0010 = 1.0 Megabits per second
DLC: ...Supported Rates information field = 84
DLC:                  1... .... = Basic Service Set Basic Rate
DLC:                  .000 0100 = 2.0 Megabits per second
DLC: ...Supported Rates information field = 8B
DLC:                  1... .... = Basic Service Set Basic Rate
DLC:                  .000 1011 = 5.5 Megabits per second
DLC: ...Supported Rates information field = 96
DLC:                  1... .... = Basic Service Set Basic Rate
DLC:                  .001 0110 = 11.0 Megabits per second
DLC:
DLC: Element ID                = 3 (Direct Sequence Parameter set)
DLC: ...Length                 = 1 octet(s)
DLC: ...dot11CurrentChannelNumber = 1
DLC:
DLC: Element ID                = 5 (Traffic Indication Map)
DLC: ...Length                 = 4 octet(s)
DLC: ...Delivery Traffic Indication Message Count  = 2
DLC: ...Delivery Traffic Indication Message Period = 10
DLC: ...Bitmap control field = 00
DLC:                  .... ...0 = Traffic Indicator bit
DLC:                  0000 000. = 0 Bitmap offset
DLC: ...Partial Virtual Bitmap    = 00
```

Figure 2-61 *Frame Format of the Probe Request Frame*

Frame Control	Duration	DA	SA	BSSID	Sequence Control	SSID IE	Supported Rates IE

Figure 2-62 *A Protocol Decode of the Probe Request Frame*

```
DLC: Frame Control Field #1 = 40
DLC:              .... ..00 = 0x0 Protocol Version
DLC:              .... 00.. = 0x0 Management Frame
DLC:              0100 .... = 0x4 Probe request (Subtype)
DLC: Frame Control Field #2 = 00
DLC:              .... ...0 = Not to Distribution System
DLC:              .... ..0. = Not from Distribution System
DLC:              .... .0.. = Last fragment
DLC:              .... 0... = Not retry
DLC:              ...0 .... = Active Mode
DLC:              ..0. .... = No more data
DLC:              .0.. .... = Wired Equivalent Privacy is off
DLC:              0... .... = Not ordered
DLC: Duration              = 0 (in microseconds)
DLC: Destination Address   = BROADCAST FFFFFFFFFFFF, Broadcast
DLC: Source Address        = Station Airont500292
DLC: Basic Service Set ID  = BROADCAST FFFFFFFFFFFF, Broadcast
DLC: Sequence Control      = 0x6F30
DLC: ...Sequence Number    = 0x6F3 (1779)
DLC: ...Fragment Number    = 0x0  (0)
DLC: Element ID            = 0 (Service Set Identifier)
DLC: ...Length             = 7 octet(s)
DLC: ...Service Set Identity = "sliders"
DLC:
DLC: Element ID            = 1 (Supported Rates)
DLC: ...Length             = 4 octet(s)
DLC: ...Supported Rates information field = 02
DLC:              0... .... = Not Basic Service Set Basic Rate
DLC:              .000 0010 = 1.0 Megabits per second
DLC: ...Supported Rates information field = 04
DLC:              0... .... = Not Basic Service Set Basic Rate
DLC:              .000 0100 = 2.0 Megabits per second
DLC: ...Supported Rates information field = 0B
DLC:              0... .... = Not Basic Service Set Basic Rate
DLC:              .000 1011 = 5.5 Megabits per second
DLC: ...Supported Rates information field = 16
DLC:              0... .... = Not Basic Service Set Basic Rate
DLC:              .001 0110 = 11.0 Megabits per second
```

The Probe Response Frame

Figure 2-63 shows the frame format of a probe response frame, and Figure 2-64 shows a protocol decode of the probe response frame.

Figure 2-63 *Frame Format of the Probe Response Frame*

Frame Control	Duration	DA	SA	BSSID	Sequence Control	Time-stamp Field	Beacon Interval Field	Capability Information Field	SSID IE	Supported Rates IE	FH/DS Parameter Set IE	CF Parameter Set IE (Optional)	IBSS Parameter Set IE (Optional)

Figure 2-64 *A Protocol Decode of the Probe Response Frame*

```
DLC: Frame Control Field #1 = 50
DLC:                  .... ..00 = 0x0 Protocol Version
DLC:                  .... 00.. = 0x0 Management Frame
DLC:                  0101 .... = 0x5 Probe response (Subtype)
DLC: Frame Control Field #2 = 00
DLC:                  .... ...0 = Not to Distribution System
DLC:                  .... ..0. = Not from Distribution System
DLC:                  .... .0.. = Last fragment
DLC:                  .... 0... = Not retry
DLC:                  ...0 .... = Active Mode
DLC:                  ..0. .... = No more data
DLC:                  .0.. .... = Wired Equivalent Privacy is off
DLC:                  0... .... = Not ordered
DLC: Duration                  = 213 (in microseconds)
DLC: Destination Address       = Station Airont502F3F
DLC: Source Address            = Station 00097CAC4391
DLC: Basic Service Set ID      = 00097CAC4391
DLC: Sequence Control          = 0x2C30
DLC: ...Sequence Number        = 0x2C3 (707)
DLC: ...Fragment Number        = 0x0  (0)
DLC: Timestamp                 = 72298844
DLC: Beacon Interval           = 100
DLC: Capability information field #1 = 21
DLC:                  .... ...1 = Extended Service Set is on
DLC:                  .... ..0. = Independent Basic Service Set is off
DLC:                  .... 00.. = No point coordinator at Access Point
DLC:                  ...0 .... = No privacy
DLC:                  ..1. .... = Short Preamble option is allowed
DLC:                  .0.. .... = Packet Binary Convolutional Coding Modulation mode option is not allowed
DLC:                  0... .... = Channel agility is not in use
DLC: Capability information field #2 = 00
DLC:                  0000 0000 = Reserved
DLC:
DLC: Element ID                = 0 (Service Set Identifier)
DLC: ...Length                 = 9 octet(s)
DLC: ...Service Set Identity   = "marketing"
DLC:
DLC: Element ID                = 1 (Supported Rates)
DLC: ...Length                 = 4 octet(s)
DLC: ...Supported Rates information field = 82
DLC:                  1... .... = Basic Service Set Basic Rate
DLC:                  .000 0010 = 1.0 Megabits per second
DLC: ...Supported Rates information field = 84
DLC:                  1... .... = Basic Service Set Basic Rate
DLC:                  .000 0100 = 2.0 Megabits per second
DLC: ...Supported Rates information field = 8B
DLC:                  1... .... = Basic Service Set Basic Rate
DLC:                  .000 1011 = 5.5 Megabits per second
DLC: ...Supported Rates information field = 96
DLC:                  1... .... = Basic Service Set Basic Rate
DLC:                  .001 0110 = 11.0 Megabits per second
DLC:
DLC: Element ID                = 3 (Direct Sequence Parameter set)
DLC: ...Length                 = 1 octet(s)
DLC: ...dot11CurrentChannelNumber = 1
```

The Authentication Frame

Figure 2-65 shows the frame format of an authentication frame, and Figure 2-66 shows a protocol decode of the authentication frame.

Figure 2-65 *Frame Format of the Authentication Frame*

Frame Control	Duration	DA	SA	BSSID	Sequence Control	Authentication Algorithm Numer Field	Authentication Transaction Sequence Numer Field	Status Code Field	Challenge Text IE (Optional)

Figure 2-66 *A Protocol Decode of the Authentication Frame*

```
DLC: Frame Control Field #1 = B0
DLC:                .... ..00 = 0x0 Protocol Version
DLC:                .... 00.. = 0x0 Management Frame
DLC:                1011 .... = 0xB Authentication (Subtype)
DLC: Frame Control Field #2 = 00
DLC:                .... ...0 = Not to Distribution System
DLC:                .... ..0. = Not from Distribution System
DLC:                .... .0.. = Last fragment
DLC:                .... 0... = Not retry
DLC:                ...0 .... = Active Mode
DLC:                ..0. .... = No more data
DLC:                .0.. .... = Wired Equivalent Privacy is off
DLC:                0... .... = Not ordered
DLC: Duration                 = 213 (in microseconds)
DLC: Destination Address      = Station 0006D7863845
DLC: Source Address           = Station Airont482745
DLC: Basic Service Set ID     = Airont482745
DLC: Sequence Control         = 0x00B0
DLC: ...Sequence Number       = 0x00B (11)
DLC: ...Fragment Number       = 0x0  (0)
DLC: Authentication algorithm number = 0 (Open System)
DLC: Authentication transaction sequence number = 2
DLC: Status code              = 0 (Successful)
```

The Deauthentication Frame

Figure 2-67 shows the frame format of a deauthentication frame, and Figure 2-68 shows a protocol decode of the Deauthentication frame.

Figure 2-67 *Frame Format of the Deauthentication Frame*

Frame Control	Duration	DA	SA	BSSID	Sequence Control	Reason Code Field

Figure 2-68 *A Protocol Decode of Deauthentication Frame*

```
DLC: Frame Control Field #1 = C0
DLC:                .... ..00 = 0x0 Protocol Version
DLC:                .... 00.. = 0x0 Management Frame
DLC:                1100 .... = 0xC Deauthentication (Subtype)
DLC: Frame Control Field #2 = 00
DLC:                .... ...0 = Not to Distribution System
DLC:                .... ..0. = Not from Distribution System
DLC:                .... .0.. = Last fragment
DLC:                .... 0... = Not retry
DLC:                ...0 .... = Active Mode
DLC:                ..0. .... = No more data
DLC:                .0.. .... = Wired Equivalent Privacy is off
DLC:                0... .... = Not ordered
DLC: Duration                 = 213 (in microseconds)
DLC: Destination Address      = Station Airont502F3F
DLC: Source Address           = Station 00097CAC4391
DLC: Basic Service Set ID     = 00097CAC4391
DLC: Sequence Control         = 0x2530
DLC: ...Sequence Number       = 0x253 (595)
DLC: ...Fragment Number       = 0x0  (0)
DLC: Reason code              = 1 (Unspecified reason)
```

The Association Request Frame

Figure 2-69 shows the frame format of an association request frame, and Figure 2-70 shows a protocol decode of the association request frame.

Figure 2-69 *Frame Format of the Association Request Frame*

Frame Control	Duration	DA	SA	BSSID	Sequence Control	Capability Information Field	Listen Interval Field	SSID IE	Supported Rates IE

Figure 2-70 *A Protocol Decode of Association Request Frame*

```
DLC: Frame Control Field #1 = C0
DLC:                    .... ..00 = 0x0 Protocol Version
DLC:                    .... 00.. = 0x0 Management Frame
DLC:                    1100 .... = 0xC Deauthentication (Subtype)
DLC: Frame Control Field #2 = 00
DLC:                    .... ...0 = Not to Distribution System
DLC:                    .... ..0. = Not from Distribution System
DLC:                    .... .0.. = Last fragment
DLC:                    .... 0... = Not retry
DLC:                    ...0 .... = Active Mode
DLC:                    ..0. .... = No more data
DLC:                    .0.. .... = Wired Equivalent Privacy is off
DLC:                    0... .... = Not ordered
DLC: Duration                    = 213 (in microseconds)
DLC: Destination Address         = Station Airont502F3F
DLC: Source Address              = Station 00097CAC4391
DLC: Basic Service Set ID        = 00097CAC4391
DLC: Sequence Control            = 0x2530
DLC: ...Sequence Number          = 0x253 (595)
DLC: ...Fragment Number          = 0x0  (0)
DLC: Reason code                 = 1 (Unspecified reason)
```

The Association Response Frame

Figure 2-71 shows the frame format of an association response frame, and Figure 2-72 shows a protocol decode of the association response frame.

Figure 2-71 *Frame Format of the Association Response Frame*

Frame Control	Duration	DA	SA	BSSID	Sequence Control	Capability Information Field	Status Code Field	AID Field	Supported Rates IE

Figure 2-72 *A Protocol Decode of Association Response Frame*

```
DLC: Frame Control Field #1 = 10
DLC:                 .... ..00 = 0x0 Protocol Version
DLC:                 .... 00.. = 0x0 Management Frame
DLC:                 0001 .... = 0x1 Association response (Subtype)
DLC: Frame Control Field #2 = 00
DLC:                 .... ...0 = Not to Distribution System
DLC:                 .... ..0. = Not from Distribution System
DLC:                 .... .0.. = Last fragment
DLC:                 .... 0... = Not retry
DLC:                 ...0 .... = Active Mode
DLC:                 ..0. .... = No more data
DLC:                 .0.. .... = Wired Equivalent Privacy is off
DLC:                 0... .... = Not ordered
DLC: Duration                  = 117 (in microseconds)
DLC: Destination Address       = Station Airont502F3F
DLC: Source Address            = Station 00097CAC4391
DLC: Basic Service Set ID      = 00097CAC4391
DLC: Sequence Control          = 0x1150
DLC: ...Sequence Number        = 0x115 (277)
DLC: ...Fragment Number        = 0x0   (0)
DLC: Capability information field #1 = 21
DLC:                 .... ...1 = Extended Service Set is on
DLC:                 .... ..0. = Independent Basic Service Set is off
DLC:                 .... 00.. = No point coordinator at Access Point
DLC:                 ...0 .... = No privacy
DLC:                 ..1. .... = Short Preamble option is allowed
DLC:                 .0.. .... = Packet Binary Convolutional Coding Modulation mode option is not allowed
DLC:                 0... .... = Channel agility is not in use
DLC: Capability information field #2 = 00
DLC:                 0000 0000 = Reserved
DLC: Status code               = 0 (Successful)
DLC: Association ID            = 29
DLC:
DLC: Element ID                = 1 (Supported Rates)
DLC: ...Length                 = 4 octet(s)
DLC: ...Supported Rates information field = 82
DLC:                 1... .... = Basic Service Set Basic Rate
DLC:                 .000 0010 = 1.0 Megabits per second
DLC: ...Supported Rates information field = 84
DLC:                 1... .... = Basic Service Set Basic Rate
DLC:                 .000 0100 = 2.0 Megabits per second
DLC: ...Supported Rates information field = 8B
DLC:                 1... .... = Basic Service Set Basic Rate
DLC:                 .000 1011 = 5.5 Megabits per second
DLC: ...Supported Rates information field = 96
DLC:                 1... .... = Basic Service Set Basic Rate
DLC:                 .001 0110 = 11.0 Megabits per second
DLC:
```

The Reassociation Request Frame

Figure 2-73 shows the frame format of a reassociation request frame, and Figure 2-74 shows a protocol decode of the reassociation request frame.

Figure 2-73 *Frame Format of the Reassociation Request Frame*

Frame Control	Duration	DA	SA	BSSID	Sequence Control	Capability Information Field	Listen Interval Field	Current AP Address Field	SSID IE	Supported Rates IE

Figure 2-74 *A Protocol Decode of Reassociation Request Frame*

```
DLC: Frame Control Field #1 = 20
DLC:                   .... ..00 = 0x0 Protocol Version
DLC:                   .... 00.. = 0x0 Management Frame
DLC:                   0010 .... = 0x2 Reassociation request (Subtype)
DLC: Frame Control Field #2 = 00
DLC:                   .... ...0 = Not to Distribution System
DLC:                   .... ..0. = Not from Distribution System
DLC:                   .... .0.. = Last fragment
DLC:                   .... 0... = Not retry
DLC:                   ...0 .... = Active Mode
DLC:                   ..0. .... = No more data
DLC:                   .0.. .... = Wired Equivalent Privacy is off
DLC:                   0... .... = Not ordered
DLC: Duration                       = 314 (in microseconds)
DLC: Destination Address            = Station 00097CAC4391
DLC: Source Address                 = Station Airont502F3F
DLC: Basic Service Set ID           = 00097CAC4391
DLC: Sequence Control               = 0x1FB0
DLC: ...Sequence Number             = 0x1FB (507)
DLC: ...Fragment Number             = 0x0   (0)
DLC: Capability information field #1 = 21
DLC:                   .... ...1 = Extended Service Set is on
DLC:                   .... ..0. = Independent Basic Service Set is off
DLC:                   .... 00.. = STA is not Contention Free-Pollable
DLC:                   ...0 .... = No privacy
DLC:                   ..1. .... = Short Preamble option is implemented
DLC:                   .0.. .... = Packet Binary Convolutional Coding Modulation mode option is not implemented
DLC:                   0... .... = Channel agility is not in use
DLC: Capability information field #2 = 00
DLC:                   0000 0000 = Reserved
DLC: Listen interval                = 200
DLC: Current Access Point address   = Station 00097CAC4391
DLC:
DLC: Element ID                     = 0 (Service Set Identifier)
DLC: ...Length                      = 9 octet(s)
DLC: ...Service Set Identity        = "marketing"
DLC:
DLC: Element ID                     = 1 (Supported Rates)
DLC: ...Length                      = 4 octet(s)
DLC: ...Supported Rates information field = 02
DLC:                   0... .... = Not Basic Service Set Basic Rate
DLC:                   .000 0010 = 1.0 Megabits per second
DLC: ...Supported Rates information field = 04
DLC:                   0... .... = Not Basic Service Set Basic Rate
DLC:                   .000 0100 = 2.0 Megabits per second
DLC: ...Supported Rates information field = 0B
DLC:                   0... .... = Not Basic Service Set Basic Rate
DLC:                   .000 1011 = 5.5 Megabits per second
DLC: ...Supported Rates information field = 16
DLC:                   0... .... = Not Basic Service Set Basic Rate
DLC:                   .001 0110 = 11.0 Megabits per second
```

The reassociation request frame is nearly identical to the association request frame, with the addition of the current AP address field. The key purpose of this frame is to alert the AP that the station is associating to that it had a previous association. The new AP can query the old AP for buffered frames for the roaming client, but it is a vendor-specific implementation and not defined in the 802.11 specification.

The Reassociation Response Frame

Figure 2-75 shows the frame format of a reassociation response frame, and Figure 2-76 shows a protocol decode of the reassociation response frame.

Figure 2-75 *Frame Format of the Reassociation Response Frame*

Frame Control	Duration	DA	SA	BSSID	Sequence Control	Capability Information Field	Status Code Field	AID Field	Supported Rates IE

Figure 2-76 *A Protocol Decode of Reassociation Response Frame*

```
DLC: Frame Control Field #1 = 30
DLC:                .... ..00 = 0x0 Protocol Version
DLC:                .... 00.. = 0x0 Management Frame
DLC:                0011 .... = 0x3 Reassociation response (Subtype)
DLC: Frame Control Field #2 = 00
DLC:                .... ...0 = Not to Distribution System
DLC:                .... ..0. = Not from Distribution System
DLC:                .... .0.. = Last fragment
DLC:                .... 0... = Not retry
DLC:                ...0 .... = Active Mode
DLC:                ..0. .... = No more data
DLC:                .0.. .... = Wired Equivalent Privacy is off
DLC:                0... .... = Not ordered
DLC: Duration                 = 117 (in microseconds)
DLC: Destination Address      = Station Airont502F3F
DLC: Source Address           = Station 00097CAC4391
DLC: Basic Service Set ID     = 00097CAC4391
DLC: Sequence Control         = 0x25E0
DLC: ...Sequence Number       = 0x25E (606)
DLC: ...Fragment Number       = 0x0  (0)
DLC: Capability information field #1 = 21
DLC:                .... ...1 = Extended Service Set is on
DLC:                .... ..0. = Independent Basic Service Set is off
DLC:                .... 00.. = No point coordinator at Access Point
DLC:                ...0 .... = No privacy
DLC:                ..1. .... = Short Preamble option is allowed
DLC:                .0.. .... = Packet Binary Convolutional Coding Modulation node option is not allowed
DLC:                0... .... = Channel agility is not in use
DLC: Capability information field #2 = 00
DLC:                0000 0000 = Reserved
DLC: Status code              = 0 (Successful)
DLC: Association ID           = 29
DLC:
DLC: Element ID               = 1 (Supported Rates)
DLC: ...Length                = 4 octet(s)
DLC: ...Supported Rates information field = 82
DLC:                1... .... = Basic Service Set Basic Rate
DLC:                .000 0010 = 1.0 Megabits per second
DLC: ...Supported Rates information field = 84
DLC:                1... .... = Basic Service Set Basic Rate
DLC:                .000 0100 = 2.0 Megabits per second
DLC: ...Supported Rates information field = 8B
DLC:                1... .... = Basic Service Set Basic Rate
DLC:                .000 1011 = 5.5 Megabits per second
DLC: ...Supported Rates information field = 96
DLC:                1... .... = Basic Service Set Basic Rate
DLC:                .001 0110 = 11.0 Megabits per second
```

The reassociation response frame is identical to the association response frame.

The Disassociation Frame

Figure 2-77 shows the frame format of a disassociation frame, and Figure 2-77 shows a protocol decode of the disassociation frame.

Figure 2-77 *Frame Format of the Disassociation Frame*

Frame Control	Duration	DA	SA	BSSID	Sequence Control	Reason Code Field

Figure 2-78 *A Protocol Decode of Disassociation Frame*

```
DLC: Frame Control Field #1 = A0
DLC:                    .... ..00 = 0x0 Protocol Version
DLC:                    .... 00.. = 0x0 Management Frame
DLC:                    1010 .... = 0xA Disassociation (Subtype)
DLC: Frame Control Field #2 = 00
DLC:                    .... ...0 = Not to Distribution System
DLC:                    .... ..0. = Not from Distribution System
DLC:                    .... .0.. = Last fragment
DLC:                    .... 0... = Not retry
DLC:                    ...0 .... = Active Mode
DLC:                    ..0. .... = No more data
DLC:                    .0.. .... = Wired Equivalent Privacy is off
DLC:                    0... .... = Not ordered
DLC: Duration                     = 213 (in microseconds)
DLC: Destination Address          = Station Airont502F3F
DLC: Source Address               = Station 00097CAC4391
DLC: Basic Service Set ID         = 00097CAC4391
DLC: Sequence Control             = 0x3AF0
DLC: ...Sequence Number           = 0x3AF (943)
DLC: ...Fragment Number           = 0x0  (0)
DLC: Reason code                  = 1 (Unspecified reason)
DLC:
```

The ATIM

The ATIM frame has no fixed fields or IEs.

802.11 Data Frames

The 802.11 specification stipulates eight unique data frames:

- Data
- Null data
- Data+CF-Ack
- Data+CF-Poll
- Data+CF-Ack+CF-Poll
- CF-Ack
- CF-Poll
- CF-Ack+CF-Poll

The Data Frame

Figure 2-79 shows the frame format of the data frame, and Figure 2-80 shows a protocol decode of the data frame.

Figure 2-79 *Frame Format of a Data Frame (AP to Client Station)*

Frame Control	Duration	DA	BSSID	SA	Sequence Control	Payload	FCS
2 Bytes	2 Bytes	6 Bytes	6 Bytes	6 Bytes	2 Bytes	0-2312 Bytes	4 Bytes

Figure 2-80 *A Protocol Decode of a Data Frame*

```
DLC: Frame Control Field #1 = 08
DLC:                 .... ..00 = 0x0 Protocol Version
DLC:                 .... 10.. = 0x2 Data Frame
DLC:                 0000 .... = 0x0 Data (Subtype)
DLC: Frame Control Field #2 = 11
DLC:                 .... ...1 = To Distribution System
DLC:                 .... ..0. = Not from Distribution System
DLC:                 .... .0.. = Last fragment
DLC:                 .... 0... = Not retry
DLC:                 ...1 .... = Power Save Mode
DLC:                 ..0. .... = No more data
DLC:                 .0.. .... = Wired Equivalent Privacy is off
DLC:                 0... .... = Not ordered
DLC: Duration                 = 117 (in microseconds)
DLC: Basic Service Set ID     = Station Aironт482745
DLC: Source Address           = Station 0006D7863845
DLC: Destination Address      = Station Cisco 588400
DLC: Sequence Control         = 0x02F0
DLC: ...Sequence Number       = 0x02F (47)
DLC: ...Fragment Number       = 0x0   (0)
DLC:
LLC: C D=AA S=AA UI
SNAP: Ethernet Type=0800 (IP)
IP:  D=[13.1.1.1] S=[13.1.1.58] LEN=13 ID=28705
ICMP: Echo
DLC: Frame padding= 13 bytes
```

The Data+CF-Ack, Data+CF-Poll, and Data+CF-Ack+CF-Poll Frames

These data frames have the same frame body as the standard data frame. The subtype value is different to provide the CF-Ack and or CF-Poll functionality required in PCF operation.

The Null Data

Figure 2-81 shows the frame format of the null data frame, and Figure 2-82 shows a protocol decode of the null data frame.

Figure 2-81 *Frame Format of a Null Data Frame*

Frame Control	Duration	DA	BSSID	SA	Sequence Control	FCS
2 Bytes	2 Bytes	6 Bytes	6 Bytes	6 Bytes	2 Bytes	4 Bytes

Figure 2-82 *A Protocol Decode of a Data Frame*

```
DLC: Frame Control Field #1 = 48
DLC:              .... ..00 = 0x0 Protocol Version
DLC:              .... 10.. = 0x2 Data Frame
DLC:              0100 .... = 0x4 Null function (no data) (Subtype)
DLC: Frame Control Field #2 = 02
DLC:              .... ...0 = Not to Distribution System
DLC:              .... ..1. = From Distribution System
DLC:              .... .0.. = Last fragment
DLC:              .... 0... = Not retry
DLC:              ...0 .... = Active Mode
DLC:              ..0. .... = No more data
DLC:              .0.. .... = Wired Equivalent Privacy is off
DLC:              0... .... = Not ordered
DLC: Duration               = 117 (in microseconds)
DLC: Destination Address    = Station 0006D7863845
DLC: Basic Service Set ID   = Station Airont482745
DLC: Source address         = Station Airont482745
DLC: Sequence Control       = 0x00E0
DLC: ...Sequence Number     = 0x00E (14)
DLC: ...Fragment Number     = 0x0  (0)
```

A null data frame is so named because it has no payload field. Its purpose is to indicate a change in the power save mode bit in the frame control field.

The CF-Ack, CF-Poll, and CF-Ack+CF-Poll Frames

The frames have the same frame body as a standard null data frame. The subtype value is different to provide the CF-Ack and or CF-Poll functionality required in PCF operation.

Summary

The 802.11 MAC layer is more complicated than the 802.3 MAC layer, as this chapter shows. The wireless medium presents new challenges in the area of medium access, and as a result, you need a more robust MAC layer.

This chapter gave you a good understanding of basic MAC layer operations. As you progress through the book, you should be able to understand more complicated 802.11 MAC layer issues, such as MAC layer security, QoS or channel access prioritization, and mobility. These topics are covered in subsequent chapters in great detail and leverage the information contained within this chapter.

CHAPTER 3

802.11 Physical Layer Technologies

The ratification of the 1999 802.11a and 802.11b standards transformed wireless LAN (WLAN) technology from a niche solution for the likes of barcode scanners to a generalized solution for portable, low-priced, interoperable network access. Today, many vendors offer 802.11a and 802.11b clients and access points that provide performance comparable to wired Ethernet. The lack of a wired network connection gives users the freedom to be mobile as they use their devices. Although standardization has been key, the use of unlicensed frequencies, where a costly and time-consuming licensing process is not required, has also contributed to a rapid and pervasive spread of the technology.

802.11 as a standards body actually defined a number of different physical layer (PHY) technologies to be used with the 802.11 MAC. This chapter examines each of these 802.11 PHYs, including the following:

- The 802.11 2.4 GHz frequency hopping PHY
- The 802.11 2.4 GHz direct sequencing PHY
- The 802.11b 2.4 GHz direct sequencing PHY
- The 802.11a 5 GHz Orthogonal Frequency Division Multiplexing (OFDM) PHY
- The 802.11g 2.4 GHz extended rate physical (ERP) layer

802.3 Ethernet has evolved over the years to include 802.3u Fast Ethernet and 802.3z/802.3ab Gigabit Ethernet. In much the same way, 802.11 wireless Ethernet is evolving with 802.11b high-rate direct sequence spread spectrum (HR-DSSS) and 802.11a OFDM standards and the recent addition of the 802.11g ERP. In fact, the physical layer for each 802.11 type is the main differentiator between them.

Wireless Physical Layer Concepts

The 802.11 PHYs essentially provide wireless transmission mechanisms for the MAC, in addition to supporting secondary functions such as assessing the state of the wireless medium and reporting it to the MAC. By providing these transmission mechanisms independently of the MAC, 802.11 has developed advances in both the MAC and the PHY, as long as the interface is maintained. This independence between the MAC and PHY is what has enabled the addition of the higher data rate 802.11b, 802.11a, and 802.11g PHYs. In fact, the MAC layer for each of the 802.11 PHYs is the same.

Each of the 802.11 physical layers has two sublayers:

- Physical Layer Convergence Procedure (PLCP)
- Physical Medium Dependant (PMD)

Figure 3-1 shows how the sublayers are oriented with respect to each other and the upper layers.

Figure 3-1 *PHY Sublayers in the Open System Interconnection (OSI) Model*

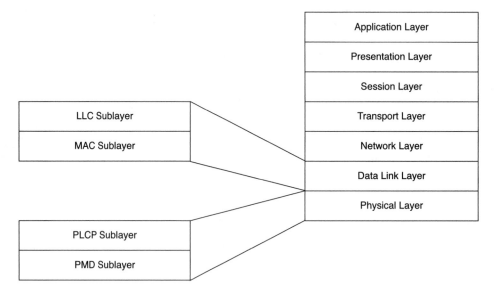

The PLCP is essentially a handshaking layer that enables MAC protocol data units (MPDUs) to be transferred between MAC stations over the PMD, which is the method of transmitting and receiving data through the wireless medium. In a sense, you can think of the PMD as a wireless transmission service function that is interfaced via the PLCP. The PLCP and PMD sublayers vary based on 802.11 types.

All PLCPs, regardless of 802.11 PHY type, have data primitives that provide the interface for the transfer of data octets between the MAC and the PMD. In addition, they provide primitives that enable the MAC to tell the PHY when to commence transmission and the PHY to tell the MAC when it has completed its transmission. On the receive side, PLCP primitives from the PHY to the MAC indicate when it has started to receive a transmission from another station and when that transmission is complete. To support the clear channel assessment (CCA) function, all PLCPs provide a mechanism for the MAC to reset the PHY CCA engine and for the PHY to report the current status of the wireless medium.

In general, the 802.11 PLCPs operate according to the state diagram in Figure 3-2. Their basic operating state is the carrier sense/clear channel assessment (CS/CCA) procedure. This procedure detects the start of a signal from a different station and determines whether the channel is clear for transmitting. Upon receiving a Tx Start request, it transitions to the Transmit state by switching the PMD from receive to transmit and sends the PLCP protocol data unit (PPDU). Then, it issues a Tx End and returns to the CA/CCA state. The PLCP invokes the Receive state when the CS/CCA procedure detects the PLCP preamble and valid PLCP header. If the PLCP detects an error, it indicates the error to the MAC and proceeds to the CS/CCA procedure. A number of different CCA mechanisms are discussed later in this chapter.

Figure 3-2   *PLCP State Diagram*

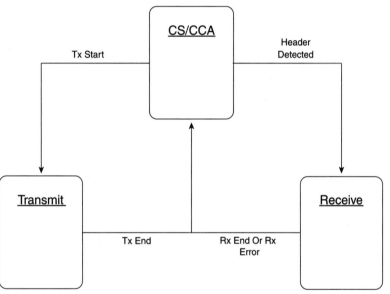

Physical Layer Building Blocks

To understand the different PMDs that each 802.11 PHY provides, you must first understand the following basic PHY concepts and building blocks:

- Scrambling
- Coding
- Interleaving
- Symbol mapping and modulation

Scrambling

One of the foundations of modern transmitter design that enables the transfer of data at high speeds is the assumption that the data you provide appears to be random from the transmitter's perspective. Without this assumption, many of the gains made from the other building blocks would not be realized. However, it is conceivable and actually common for you to receive data that is not at all random and might, in fact, contain repeatable patterns or long sequences of 1s or 0s. *Scrambling* is a method for making the data you receive look more random by performing a mapping between bit sequences, from structured to seemingly random sequences. It is also referred to as *whitening* the data stream. The receiver descrambler then remaps these random sequences into their original structured sequence. Most scrambling methods are self-synchronizing, meaning that the descrambler is able to sync itself to the state of the scrambler.

Coding

Although scrambling is an important tool that has allowed engineers to develop communications systems with higher spectral efficiency, *coding* is the mechanism that has enabled the high-speed transmission of data over noisy channels. All transmission channels are noisy, which introduces errors in the form of corrupted or modified bits. Coding allows you to maximize the amount of data that you send over a noisy communication medium. You can do so by replacing sequences of bits with longer sequences that allow you to recognize and correct a corrupted bit. For example, as shown in Figure 3-3, if you want to communicate the sequence 01101 over the telephone to your friend, you might instead agree with your friend that you will repeat each bit three times, resulting in the sequence 000111111000111. Even if your friend mistook some of the bits at his end—resulting in the sequence 100111111000101, with the second to last bit being corrupted—he would recognize that the original sequence was 01101 via a majority voting scheme. Although this coder is rather simple and not efficient, you now understand the concept behind coding.

Figure 3-3   *Simple Coding Example*

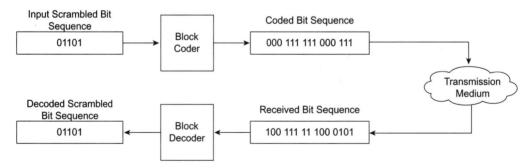

The most common type of coding in communications systems today is the convolutional coder because it can be implemented rather easily in hardware with delays and adders. In contrast to the preceding code, which is a memory-less block code, the convolutional code is a finite memory code, meaning that the output is a function not just of the current input, but also of several of the past inputs. The constraint length of a code indicates how long it takes in output units for an input to fall out of the system. Codes are often described through their rate. You might see a rate 1/2 convolutional coder. This rate indicates that for every one input bit, two output bits are produced. When comparing coders, note that although higher rate codes support communication at higher data rates, they are also correspondingly more sensitive to noise.

Interleaving

One of the base assumptions of coding is that errors introduced in the transmission of information are independent events. This assumption is the case in the earlier example where you were communicating a sequence of bits over the phone to your friend and bits 1 and 9 were corrupted. However, you might often find that bit errors are not independent and that they occur in batches. In the previous example, suppose a dump truck drove by during the first part of your conversation, thereby interfering with your friend's ability to hear you correctly. The sequence your friend received might look like 011001111000111, as shown in Figure 3-4. He would erroneously conclude that the original sequence was 10101.

Figure 3-4   *Correlated Error Events*

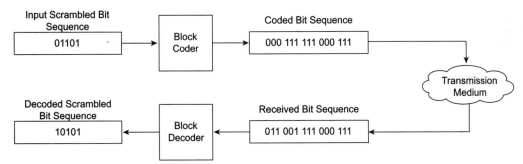

For this reason, *interleavers* were introduced to spread out the bits in block errors that might occur, thus making them look more independent. An interleaver can be either a software or hardware construct; regardless, its main purpose is to spread out adjacent bits by placing nonadjacent bits between them. Working with the same example, instead of just reading the 16-bit sequence to your friend, you might enter the bits five at a time into the rows of a matrix and then read them out as columns three bits at a time, as shown in Figure 3-5. Your friend would then write them into a matrix in columns three bits at a time, read them out in rows five bits at a time, and apply the coding rule to retrieve the original sequence.

Figure 3-5   *Coding with Block Interleaver*

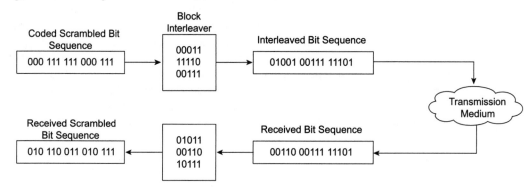

Symbol Mapping and Modulation

The modulation process applies the bit stream to a carrier at the operating frequency band. Think of the carrier as a simple sine wave; the modulation process can be applied to the amplitude, the frequency, or the phase. Figure 3-6 provides an example of each of these techniques.

Figure 3-6   *Modulation Example*

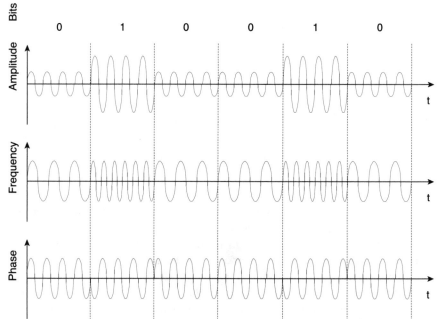

NOTE   The idea of applying the data bits to the amplitude or frequency of the carrier has a parallel in the broadcast AM and FM radio world. Rather than apply data bits to a sinusoid, you apply the voice or music waveform to either the amplitude or the frequency of the sinusoid, resulting in amplitude modulation (AM) or frequency modulation (FM). The concept really is the same, with the only difference being the format of information to be transmitted.

Often, instead of using just a single sinusoid, you employ two sinusoids that are 90 degrees out of phase. The two are referred to as the *in-phase* and *quadrature* components.

Although you could directly modulate the bit sequence onto a carrier using one of the amplitude, frequency, or phase methodologies, you can transmit more bits in the available bandwidth of the carrier by mapping groups of bits into symbols. *Symbol mapping* is the process by which you group bits together and map them into quadrature and in-phase components. It is often represented in a Cartesian coordinate system with the in-phase component on the x axis and the quadrature component on the y axis to yield what is called a *constellation*. Sometimes, it is also referred to as the *complex plane*, with the imaginary number, j, which equals the square root of –1, on the quadrature or y axis and the real component on the in-phase or x axis.

If you have a bit rate of 11 Mbps, but map two bits per symbol, the resulting symbol rate, or baud rate, is 5.5 Mbps. Taking the output sequence from the interleaver described in Figure 3-5, we can use quadrature phase shift keying (QPSK), which maps two bits at a time into symbols. The symbol mapping is depicted in Figure 3-7 with the input bits and resulting waveform, with the in-phase signal in blue and quadrature signal in red, next to each point on the constellation. This process results in a complex time domain baseband signal that is then shifted in frequency to become a real passband signal. Demodulation is merely the reverse process at the receiver.

Figure 3-7   *QPSK Constellation and Resulting In-Phase and Quadrature Waveforms*

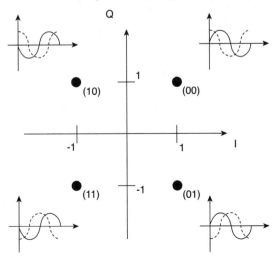

802.11 Wireless LANs

The original 802.11 standard defined two WLAN PHY methods:

- 2.4 GHz frequency hopping spread spectrum (FHSS)
- 2.4 GHz direct sequence spread spectrum (DSSS)

As noted, both of these operate at 2.4 GHz, where the FCC allocated 82 MHz of spectrum in the U.S. for the Industrial, Scientific, and Medical (ISM) band. These and other bands are discussed in Chapter 8, "Deploying Wireless LANs." Each PHY has its own PLCP and PMD sublayers, which are described in the next sections.

Frequency Hopping WLANs

FHSS WLANs support 1 Mbps and 2 Mbps data rates. As the name implies, a FHSS device changes or "hops" frequencies with a predetermined hopping pattern and a set rate, as depicted in Figure 3-8. FHSS devices split the available spectrum into 79 nonoverlapping channels (for North America and most of Europe) across the 2.402 to 2.480 GHz frequency range. Each of the 79 channels is 1 MHz wide, so FHSS WLANs use a relatively fast 1 MHz symbol rate and hop among the 79 channels at a much slower rate.

Figure 3-8   *Frequency Hopping Example*

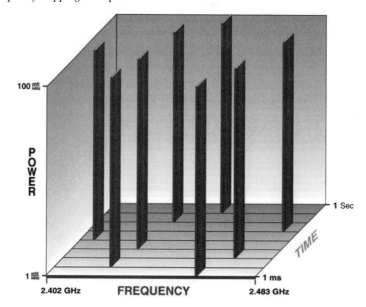

The hopping sequence must hop at a minimum rate of 2.5 times per second and must contain a minimum of six channels (6 MHz). To minimize the collisions between overlapping coverage areas, the possible hopping sequences can be broken down into three sets of length, 26 for use in North America and most of Europe. Tables 3-1 through 3-4 show the minimum overlap hopping patterns for different countries, including the U.S., Japan, Spain, and France.

Table 3-1   *FHSS Hopping Pattern for North America and Europe*

Set	Hopping Pattern
1	{0,3,6,9,12,15,18,21,24,27,30,33,36,39,42,45,48,51,54,57,60,63,66,69,72,75}
2	{1,4,7,10,13,16,19,22,25,28,31,34,37,40,43,46,49,52,55,58,61,64,67,70,73,76}
3	{2,5,8,11,14,17,20,23,26,29,32,35,38,41,44,47,50,53,56,59,62,65,68,71,72,77}

Table 3-2   *FHSS Hopping Pattern for Japan*

Set	Hopping Pattern
1	{6,9,12,15}
2	{7,10,13,16}
3	{8,11,14,17}

Table 3-3   *FHSS Hopping Pattern for Spain*

Set	Hopping Pattern
1	{0,3,6,9,12,15,18,21,24}
2	{1,4,7,10,13,16,19,22,25}
3	{2,5,8,11,14,17,20,23,26}

Table 3-4   *FHSS Hopping Pattern for France*

Set	Hopping Pattern
1	{0,3,6,9,12,15,18,21,24,27,30}
2	{1,4,7,10,13,16,19,22,25,28,31}
3	{2,5,8,11,14,17,20,23,26,29,32}

In essence, the hopping patterns provide a slow path through the possible channels in such a way that each hop covers at least 6 MHz and, when considering a multicell deployment, minimizes the probability of a collision. The reduced set length for countries such as Japan, Spain, and France results from the smaller ISM band frequency allocation at 2.4 GHz.

FHSS PLCP

After the MAC layer passes a MAC frame, also known as a PLCP service data unit (PSDU) in FHSS WLANs, to the PLCP sublayer, the PLCP adds two fields to the beginning of the frame to form a PPDU frame. Figure 3-9 shows the FHSS PLCP frame format.

Figure 3-9   *FHSS PPDU*

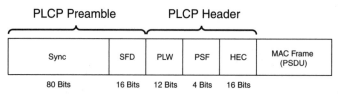

The PLCP preamble consists of two subfields:

- The SYNC subfield is 80 bits long and is a string of alternating 0s and 1s, starting with 0. The receiving station uses the field to make an antenna-selection decision in diversity deployments, to correct any frequency offset, and to synchronize packet timing.

- The start of frame delimiter (SFD) subfield is 16 bits long and consists of a specific bit string (0000 1100 1011 1101, leftmost bit first) to provide frame timing to the receiving station.

The PLCP header consists of three subfields:

- The PSDU length word (PLW) is 12 bits long and specifies the size of the MAC frame (PSDU) in octets.

- The PLCP signaling field (PSF) is 4 bits long and indicates the data rate of the frame. Table 3-5 shows the decoding of the data rate.

- The header error control (HEC) is an International Telecommunications Union Telecommunication Standardization Sector (ITU-T) Cyclic Redundancy Check (CRC-16) value for the PLCP header field. The transmitter generates the checksum and then the receiver uses it to detect errors in the received PLW and PSF.

Table 3-5   *PSF Decoding*

b1	b2	b3	Data Rate
0	0	0	1.0 Mbps
0	0	1	1.5 Mbps
0	1	0	2.0 Mbps
0	1	1	2.5 Mbps
1	0	0	3.0 Mbps
1	0	1	3.5 Mbps
1	1	0	4.0 Mbps
1	1	1	4.5 Mbps

The PSDU is passed through a scrambler to whiten or randomize the input bit sequence, as described earlier in the section, "Physical Layer Building Blocks." The resulting PSDU appears in Figure 3-10. Stuff symbols are also inserted between each 32-symbol block. These stuff symbols remove any bias in the data, more 1s than 0s or more 0s than 1s, which could have an undesirable effect upon later processing modules.

Figure 3-10 *FHSS Scrambled PSDU*

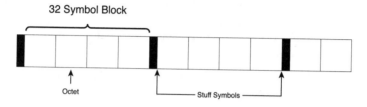

32 Symbol Block

Octet

Stuff Symbols

FHSS PMD-GFSK Modulation

The PLCP converts the frame into a binary bit stream and passes this bit stream to the PMD sublayer. The FHSS PMD sublayer modulates the data stream by using Gaussian frequency shift keying (GFSK).

To understand GFSK modulation, you must first grasp the basic concepts of Frequency Shift Keying (FSK). Unlike the QPSK modulation described earlier, FSK operates by representing each symbol with a different frequency. For example, if you want to convey the binary value 0, you transmit a sinusoid with a frequency of f_1; you transmit a frequency of f_2 for a binary value of 1. You agree upon the symbol period with your friend on the other side, and that would govern how long each sinusoid is transmitted. Often, rather than express the two frequencies in absolutes, you give them relative to the carrier frequency, f_c, specified in the hopping sequence. Figure 3-11 depicts a frequency domain of the frequencies with the magnitude given by the height of the vector, $f_1 = f_c - f_d$ and $f_2 = f_c + f_d$.

Figure 3-11 *FSK Frequency Domain Example*

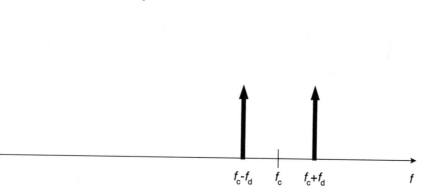

Some of the advantages of FSK are that you can fairly easily design a transmitter and receiver; in fact, FSK operates under the same principles as your FM radio receiver in your automobile. As you shall see in Chapter 8, FSK also greatly simplifies your radio-frequency design because it is a constant modulus signal, meaning that no information is carried by the amplitude of the signal, allowing you to transmit at a higher average power for a set peak power. However, FSK also has some significant disadvantages, not the least of which is that it is spectrally inefficient: It does not convey as much information per quantum of spectrum as other methods. In addition, the modulator is not a linear process, which means that it is difficult for you to correct the signal for channel impairments or to analytically determine the performance.

You can understand one of the great challenges for an FSK modulator by examining the transmission of a 0 followed by a 1. It requires the signal to instantaneously jump from a sinusoid of frequency $f_c - f_d$ to a frequency of $f_c + f_d$, which introduces a discontinuous change in the transmitter output that creates significant amounts of out-of-band energy. Figure 3-12 shows an example of this challenge at baseband, meaning that the carrier component is removed.

Figure 3-12 *FSK Frequency Transition*

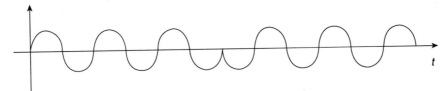

To combat this problem, you can filter the input to the frequency modulator to smooth the transition from $f_c - f_d$ to $f_c + f_d$. For GFSK, you use a Gaussian filter, hence the name. f_d is referred to as the frequency deviation, and 802.11 specifies that it must be at least 110 kHz. For 2 Mbps operation, you use 4GFSK, which modulates two bits at a time using two deviation frequencies, as shown in Table 3-6, where f_{d1} is roughly 3 times f_{d2}.

Table 3-6   *4 GFSK Symbol to Frequency Mapping*

Symbol	Frequency
10	$f_c + f_{d2}$
11	$f_c + f_{d1}$
01	$f_c - f_{d1}$
00	$f_c - f_{d2}$

Although FHSS was fairly widely deployed in applications such as warehousing and manufacturing in the early days of WLAN, it does come with its own set of problems. The first and most basic is that it doesn't provide the kind of high data rates that are achievable in the wired LAN space and that the new WLAN standards offer. The second and slightly less obvious problem is that although up to 79 channels are available for use in the hopping sequence and each of the three standard hopping sets, as described in the beginning of this section, your signal will be hopping all over the ISM band, regardless of other energy and signals that might be in the band. As discussed in Chapter 8 and Chapter 9, "The Future of Wireless LANs," no standardized method exists for you to eliminate those frequencies where there is known interference. If interference occurs in half of the band and you are operating at 1 Mbps, 50 percent of the time, you will be hopping to a channel that does not support communication because of the interference. So, your effective throughput will be 500 Kbps at most.

Even more interesting is that no mechanism exists to coordinate or synchronize the hopping sequences of adjacent access points. Their hopping sequences could overlap, causing more interference. If your bandwidth requirements are low and you do not need to scale to multiple access points, you can still deploy a limited network using FHSS.

Direct Sequence Spread Spectrum WLANs

DSSS is another physical layer for the 802.11 specifications. As defined in the 1997 802.11 standard, DSSS supports data rates of 1 and 2 Mbps. In 1999, the 802.11 Working Group ratified the 802.11b standard to support data rates of 5.5 and 11 Mbps. The 802.11b DSSS physical layer is compatible with existing 802.11 DSSS WLANs. The PLCP for 802.11b DSSS is the same as that for 802.11 DSSS, with the addition of an optional short preamble and short header.

DSSS WLANs use 22 MHz channels, which allows multiple WLANs to operate in the same coverage area. In North America and most of Europe, the use of 22 MHz channels allows for three nonoverlapping channels in 2.4 to 2.483 GHz range. Figure 3-13 shows these channels, which are discussed in more detail in Chapter 8.

802.11 DSSS

Similar to the PLCP sublayer for FHSS, the PLCP for 802.11 DSSS adds two fields to the MAC frame to form the PPDU: the PLCP preamble and PLCP header. The frame format appears in Figure 3-14.

Figure 3-13 *DSSS Channelization*

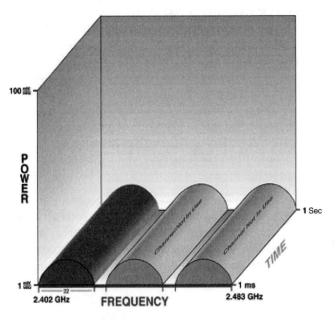

Figure 3-14 *802.11 DSSS PPDU*

PLCP Preamble		PLCP Header				MAC Frame
Sync	SFD	Signal	Service	Length	CRC	MAC Frame
128 Bits	16 Bits	8 Bits	8 Bits	16 Bits	16 Bits	

The PLCP preamble comprises two subfields:

- The SYNC subfield is 128 bits long and is a string of binary 1s. The function of the field is to provide synchronization for the receiving station.

- The SFD subfield is 16 bits long and consists of a specific bit string, 0xF3A0, to provide timing to the receiving station.

The PLCP header comprises four subfields:

- The Signal subfield is 8 bits long and specifies the modulation and data rate for the frame. Table 3-7 gives the mapping.

- The Service subfield is 8 bits long and is a reserved subfield, meaning that it was left undefined at the time the spec was written but also kept reserved so that future changes to the standard could use the subfield.

- The Length subfield is 16 bits long and contains the number of microseconds, ranging from 16 to $2^{16} - 1$, that is required to transmit the MAC portion of the frame.

- The CRC subfield is 16 bits long and provides the resulting value of the same ITU-T CRC-16 used in FHSS as applied to the PLCP header subfields.

Table 3-7   *Signal to Data Rate Mapping*

Signal	Data Rate
0x0A	1 Mbps
0x14	2 Mbps

The PLCP converts the frame into a bit stream and passes the data to the PMD sublayer. The entire PPDU is passed through a scrambler to randomized the data.

The scrambled PLCP preamble is always transmitted at the 1 Mbps data rate, whereas the scrambled MPDU frame is transmitted at the data rate specified in the Signal subfield. The PMD sublayer modulates the whitened bit stream using one of the following modulation techniques:

- Differential binary phase shift keying (DBPSK) for 1 Mbps operation

- Differential quadrature phase shift keying (DQPSK) for 2 Mbps operation

The next section describes the DSSS PMD modulation process.

DSSS Basics

Spread-spectrum techniques take a modulation approach that uses a much higher than necessary spectrum bandwidth to communicate information at a much lower rate. Each bit is replaced or spread by a wideband spreading code. Much like coding, because the information is spread into many more information bits, it has the ability to operate in low signal-to-noise ratio (SNR) conditions, either because of interference or low transmitter power. With DSSS, the transmitted signal is directly multiplied by a spreading sequence, shared by the transmitter and receiver.

WLAN DSSS specifically encodes data by taking a 1 Mbps data stream from the data link layer and converting it to an 11 MHz chip stream. The spreading sequence (or chipping sequence or Barker sequence), which converts a data bit into chips, is an 11-bit value. In the case of 1 and 2 Mbps operation, one data bit is expanded to an 11-bit value. (A binary 1 expands to 1111111111 and 0 to 0000000000.) The expanded data bit is then exclusive ORed (XORed) with the spreading sequence, and the resulting chips are mapped to symbols and modulated. Figures 3-15 and 3-16 show this process.

Figure 3-15 *Spreading a Data Bit with Value 1*

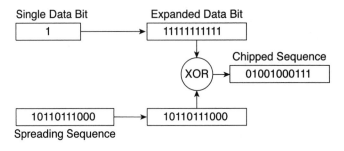

Figure 3-16 *Spreading a Data Bit with Value 0*

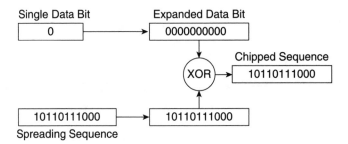

You might wonder what good it does for WLANs to increase transmission overhead from 1 Mbps to 11 Mbps. The 11-chip sequence represents a single data bit. For example, suppose a chipped sequence is transmitted across the wireless medium. During the transmission, some interference occurs in a few of the channel's frequencies. Because the transmitter spreads the sequence across the 22-MHz–wide channel, only a few chips of the sequence should be impacted by the interference. The receiver is capable of rebuilding the original sequence by examining the received chips. Contrast this process to sending raw data bits, which incur data loss because of the interference and require subsequent retransmission. Direct sequencing can use the frequencies in a channel to increase throughput and reduce latency.

DBPSK Modulation

You might recall that we described QPSK symbol mapping or modulation onto the complex plane earlier in the section, "Physical Layer Building Blocks." BPSK uses a similar technique, but each symbol has only an in-phase component because both constellation points reside on the I axis. Figure 3-17 shows the BPSK constellation.

To ensure that the receiver does not need to remove the phase component of any frequency offset, the keying uses differential encoding, resulting in DBPSK. Differential encoding works as follows: Each chip maps into a single symbol. A 0 tells the symbol mapper to transmit the same symbol as in the previous symbol period, and a 1 tells the symbol mapper to rotate the phase by 180 degrees, or π in radians. BPSK also results in a constant modulus signal, thereby simplifying the radio design.

Figure 3-17 *BPSK Constellation*

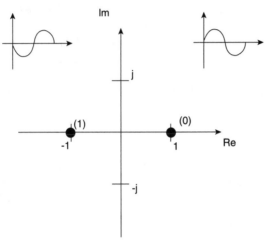

DQPSK Modulation

To achieve a 2 Mbps data rate, a QPSK constellation maps two chips per symbol, like the one shown in Figure 3-6. You use differential encoding once again, with the two chip symbols mapping into the phase rotation indicated in Table 3-8 to achieve DQPSK modulation.

Table 3-8 *DQPSK Mapping*

Chip Input	Phase Change (Degrees)
00	0
01	90
11	180
10	270 (-90)

Both DBPSK and DQPSK transmissions result in an 11 MHz symbol rate, but for DQPSK, each symbol contains two chips, resulting in a 22 MHz chip rate or a 2 Mbps bit rate.

DSSS achieved a fair amount of success in the marketplace because of its resilience, especially in the presence of interference. However, it shares the same handicap as FHSS did with its low data rates. This limit opened the door for the ensuing higher rate standards 802.11a and 802.11b.

802.11b WLANs

The 802.11b 1999 draft introduced high-rate DSSS (HR-DSSS), which enables you to operate your WLAN at data rates up to and including 5.5 Mbps and 11 Mbps in the 2.4 GHz ISM band, using complementary code keying (CCK) or optionally packet binary convolutional coding (PBCC). HR-DSSS uses the same channelization scheme as DSSS with a 22 MHz bandwidth and 11 channels, 3 nonoverlapping, in the 2.4 GHz ISM band. This section provides you with the details to understand how these higher rates are supported.

802.11b HR-DSSS PLCP

The PLCP sublayer for HR-DSSS has two PPDU frame types: long and short. The preamble and header in the 802.11b HR-DSSS long PLCP are always transmitted at 1 Mbps to maintain backward compatibility with DSSS. In fact, the HR-DSSS long PLCP is the same as the DSSS PLCP but with some extensions to support the higher data rates. These extensions are as follows:

- The Signal subfield has the additional data rates specified in Table 3-9.
- The Service subfield defines the previously reserved bits specified in Table 3-10.
- The Length subfield still provides the number of microseconds to transmit the PSDU.

At data rates greater than 8 Mbps, ambiguity exists in the number of octets because the Length subfield is rounded up to the nearest integer. For example, if you have 517 octets to transmit, that equates to 376 microseconds (Ceiling(517 ∗ 8/11)). But 516 octets also require 376 microseconds, so in the latter case, you are forced to round up by more than 1 octet. You can flag this rounding to the receiver by placing a 1 in the Length Extension bit of the Service subfield. This way, the receiver knows to subtract 1 from the number of Rx octets he is expecting. Note that if you are using PBCC, the protocol uses an extra octet, so you can add the value of the modulation selection bit to the number of octets before multiplying by 8/11 to get the time in microseconds.

Table 3-9   *Additional Signal Subfield Mappings*

Signal	Data Rate
0x37	5.5 Mbps
0x6E	11 Mbps

Table 3-10   *Service Subfield Bit Definitions*

Bit	Name	Decode
B2	Locked clocks	0 = not locked, 1 = Tx frequency and symbol clocks are locked
B3	Modulation selection	0 = CCK, 1 = PBCC
B7	Length extension	Used by the length subfield

The short PLCP PPDU provides a means to minimize overhead while still enabling transmitters and receivers to communicate appropriately. The 802.11b HR-DSSS short header, which is shown in Figure 3-18, still uses the same preamble, header, and PSDU format, but the PLCP header is transmitted at 2 Mbps, whereas the PSDU is transmitted at 2, 5.5, or 11 Mbps. In addition, the subfields are modified as follows:

- The SYNC field is shortened from 128 bits to 56 bits long and is a string of 0s.

- The SFD field is 16 bits long and has the same function of indicating the start of the frame but also indicates the use of short headers or long headers. With short headers, the 16 bits are transmitted in the reverse time order relative to long headers, so they use 0x05CF instead of 0xF3A0.

Figure 3-18   *HR-DSSS Short PPDU*

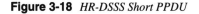

Just like the 802.11 PHY, the PLCP converts the entire PPDU through the same scrambler used throughout 802.11 to the PMD. Within the PMD, the various subfields are transmitted at the appropriate data rate and modulation technique: CCK or PBCC.

802.11b PMD—CCK Modulation

Although the spreading mechanism to achieve 5.5 Mbps and 11 Mbps with CCK is related to the techniques you employ for 1 and 2 Mbps, it is still unique. In both cases, you employ a spreading technique, but for CCK, the spreading code is actually an 8 complex chip code, where a 1 and 2 Mbps operation uses an 11-bit code. The 8-chip code is determined by either four or eight bits, depending upon the data rate. The chip rate is 11 Mchips/second, so with 8 complex chips per symbol and 4 or 8 bits per symbol, you achieve the data rates 5.5 Mbps and 11 Mbps.

To transmit at 5.5 Mbps, you take the scrambled PSDU bit stream and group it into symbols of 4 bits each: (b_0, b_1, b_2, and b_3). You use the latter two bits (b_2, b_3) to determine an 8 complex chip sequence, as shown in Table 3-11, where $\{c_1, c_2, c_3, c_4, c_5, c_6, c_7, c_8\}$ represent the chips in the sequence. In Table 3-11, j represents the imaginary number, sqrt(-1), and appears on the imaginary or quadrature axis in the complex plane.

Table 3-11   *CCK Chip Sequence*

(b2, b3)	C1	C2	C3	C4	C5	C6	C7	C8
00	j	1	j	-1	j	1	-1	1
01	-j	-1	-j	1	j	1	-j	1
10	-j	1	-j	-1	-j	1	j	1
11	j	-1	j	1	-j	1	j	1

Now with the chip sequence determined by (b_2, b_3), you use the first two bits (b_0, b_1) to determine a DQPSK phase rotation that is applied to the sequence. Table 3-12 shows this process. You must also number each 4-bit symbol of the PSDU, starting with 0, so that you can determine whether you are mapping an odd or an even symbol according to the table. You will also note that you use DQPSK, not QPSK, and as such, these represent phase changes relative to the previous symbol or, in the case of the first symbol of the PSDU, relative to the last symbol of the preceding 2 Mbps DQPSK symbol.

Table 3-12   *CCK Phase Rotation*

(b0, b1)	Even Symbols Phase Change	Odd Symbols Phase Change
00	0 (0 degrees)	π (180 degrees)
01	$\pi/2$ (90 degrees)	$-\pi/2$ (-90 degrees)
11	π (180 degrees)	0 (0 degrees)
10	$-\pi/2$ (-90 degrees)	$\pi/2$ (90 degrees)

Apply this phase rotation to the 8 complex chip symbol and then modulate that to the appropriate carrier frequency.

To transmit at an 11 Mbps data rate, you group the scrambled PSDU bit sequence into 8 bit symbols. The latter 6 bits select one 8 complex chip sequence, out of 64 possible sequences, much the same way that bits (b2, b3) were used to select one sequence from four possible. You use bits (b0, b1) in the same manner as 5.5 Mbps CCK to rotate the sequence and then modulate it to the appropriate carrier frequency.

PBCC Modulation

As already indicated, the HR-DSSS standard also defines an optional PBCC modulation mechanism for generating 5.5 Mbps and 11 Mbps data rates. This scheme is a bit different from both CCK and 802.11 DSSS. You first pass the scrambled PSDU bits through a half-rate binary convolution encoder, which was first introduced in the section, "Physical Layer Building Blocks." The particular half-rate encoder has six delay, or memory elements, and outputs 2 bits for every 1 input bit. Because 802.11 works under a frame structure and convolutional encoders have memory, you must zero all the delay elements at the beginning of a frame and append one octet of zeros at the end of the frame to ensure all bits are equally protected. This final octet explains why the length calculation, discussed in the section, "802.11b HR-DSSS PLCP," is slightly different for CCK and PLCC. You then pass the encoded bit stream through a BPSK symbol mapper to achieve the 5.5 Mbps data rate or through a QPSK symbol mapper to achieve the 11 Mbps data rate. (You do not employ differential encoding here.) The particular symbol mapping you use depends upon the binary value, s, coming out of a 256-bit pseudo-random cover sequence. The two QPSK symbol mappings appear in Figure 3-19, and the two BPSK symbol mappings appear in Figure 3-20. For PSDUs longer than 256 bits, the pseudo-random sequence is merely repeated.

Figure 3-19 *PBCC QPSK Symbol Mapping*

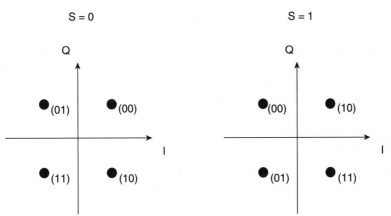

Figure 3-20 *PBCC BPSK Symbol Mapping*

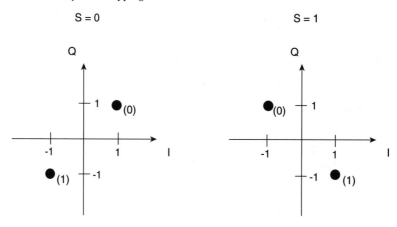

802.11a WLANs

At the same time that the 802.11b 1999 draft introduced HR-DSSS PHY, the 802.11a-1999 draft introduced the Orthogonal Frequency Division Multiplexing (OFDM) PHY for the 5 GHz band. It provided mandatory data rates up to 24 Mbps and optional rates up to 54 Mbps in the Unlicensed National Information Infrastructure (U-NII) bands of 5.15 to 5.25 GHz, 5.25 to 5.35 GHz, and 5.725 to 5.825 GHz. 802.11a utilizes 20 MHz channels and defines four channels in each of the three U-NII bands. (These are discussed in further detail in Chapter 8.) This section provides you with the details to understand how to support OFDM.

802.11j

The IEEE 802.11j draft amendment for LAN/metropolitan-area networks (MAN) requirements provides for 802.11a type operation in the 4.9 GHz band allocated in Japan and in the U.S. for public safety applications as well as in the 5.03 to 5.091 GHz Japanese allocation. A channel numbering scheme uses channels 240 to 255 to cover these frequencies in 5 MHz channel increments.

802.11a OFDM PLCP

The PLCP sublayer for the 802.11a PHY has its own unique PPDU frame format, which is shown in Figure 3-21.

Figure 3-21 *802.11a PPDU Frame Format*

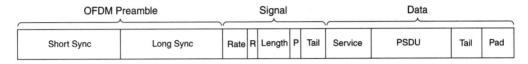

Three basic pieces make up the PPDU: OFDM preamble, Signal, and Data. The OFDM preamble consists of short SYNC training sequences and a long sync training symbol. The receiver uses the former for automatic gain control (AGC), timing, and initial frequency offset estimation, whereas it uses the latter for channel, timing, and fine frequency offset estimation. The mechanism for constructing this is discussed later in this section.

You compose the Signal field with five subfields:

- The four-bit RATE subfield specifies the data rate for the DATA part of the frame. Table 3-13 gives the mapping of these bits (R1–R4) to the data rate.

- The bit R is reserved for future use.

- The Length subfield, which is an unsigned 12-bit integer, specifies the number of octets in the PSDU.

- The bit P is an even parity bit for the 17 bits in the Rate, R, and Length subfields.

- The Signal Tail field provides six nonscrambled 0 bits.

Table 3-13 *Rate Subfield Mapping*

R1–R4	Rate (Mbps)
1101	6
1111	9
0101	12
0111	18
1001	24
1011	36
0001	48
0011	54

The Data field contains four subfields:

- The Service subfield provides 7 bits that are set to 0, followed by 7 reserved bits that are also currently set to 0. This subfield allows the receiver to synchronize its descrambler.

- The PSDU subfield contains the actual data bits to be transmitted.
- The TAIL subfield replaces the final 6 scrambled 0s with unscrambled 0s to re-initialize the finite memory convolutional encoder.
- The PAD Bits subfield adds the number of bits needed to achieve the appropriate number of coded bits in the OFDM symbol. The section, "OFDM Basics" explains this area in more detail.

OFDM Basics

To understand the "how" and "why" of the 802.11a OFDM PMD, you first need to understand the basics of OFDM, which is unlike any modulation technique discussed so far. OFDM is part of a family of multichannel modulation schemes that were invented to transmit data under severe intersymbol interference (ISI). Consider the simple QPSK symbol first introduced in the section, "Physical Layer Building Blocks," and then consider the transmission of two consecutive symbols. As these symbols travel through the transmission medium from the transmitter to the receiver, they experience distortions, and various parts of the signal can be delayed. If these delays are long enough, the first symbol might overlap in time with the second symbol. This overlapping is ISI. The time delay from the reception of the first instance of the signal until the last instance is referred to as the *delay spread* of the channel. You can also think of it as the amount of time that the first symbol spreads into the second. Traditionally, designers address ISI in one of two ways: employing symbols that are long enough to be decoded correctly in the presence of ISI or by equalizing to remove the distortion caused by the ISI. The former method limits the symbol rate to something less than the bandwidth of the channel, which is inversely proportional to the delay spread. As the bandwidth of the channel increases, you can increase the symbol rate, thereby achieving a higher end data rate. The latter method, often used in conjunction with the former, requires the use of ever more complicated and expensive methods to implement channel-equalization schemes to maximize the usable bandwidth of the channel.

Multichannel modulation schemes take a completely different approach. As a multichannel modulation designer, you break up the channel into small, independent, parallel or orthogonal transmission channels upon which narrowband signals, with a low symbol rate, are modulated, usually in the frequency domain, onto individual subcarriers. Similar to how you can modulate FHSS signal onto the appropriate carrier, you break the channel into N independent channels. For a given channel bandwidth, the larger the N that you choose, the longer the symbol period and the narrower the subchannel, so you can see that as the number of subchannels goes to infinity, the ISI goes to zero.

To build these independent symbols, a useful tool is the Fast Fourier Transform (FFT), which is an efficient implementation of a Discrete Fourier transform (DFT) and can convert a time domain signal to the frequency domain and vice versa. In the frequency domain, you generate N 4-QAM (Quadrature Amplitude Modulation) symbols, which are then converted to the time domain using an inverse FFT (IFFT). You should also know that making the size of the FFT a power of two allows for simple and efficient implementations. For that reason, OFDM systems usually pick N such that it is a power of two.

Without going into the intricacies of mathematics that are beyond the scope of this book, it simplifies the processing greatly if everything is done in the frequency domain using FFTs. To enable this processing at the receiver, however, the received signal must be a circular convolution of the input with the channel, as opposed to just a convolution. *Convolution* is a mathematical mechanism for passing a signal through a channel and determining the output. To ensure this property, you must take the time domain representation of an OFTM symbol and create a cyclic prefix by repeating the final v samples at the beginning. Figure 3-22 shows this process, where v is the length of the cyclic prefix and N is the size of the FFT in use.

Figure 3-22 *OFDM Cyclic Prefix Formation*

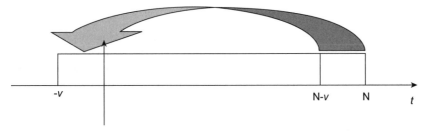

The length of the cyclic prefix must be longer than the delay spread of the channel to ensure that each OFDM symbol received is a circular convolution of the channel with the transmitted symbol. Another way to think about it is that you want a guard time between symbols, which ensures that any residual signal from the previous OFDM symbol has died off before you perform your processing on the current symbol. This time allows for symbol-by-symbol processing, and when it happens in the frequency domain, it allows for subchannel-by-subchannel processing.

To allow the receiver to estimate the channel, you often either intersperse known training symbols on some of the N subcarriers or transmit a separate known OFDM symbol that the receiver can use to estimate the channel. You also often fill the subchannels at the band edges with 0s to aid the transmitter because the filters in the transmitter and receiver will most likely attenuate them to the point where no information could be carrier over them anyway.

Unlike some other multichannel modulation techniques, OFDM places an equal number of bits in all subchannels. In nonwireless applications such as asynchronous digital subscriber line (ADSL), where the channel is not as time varying, the transmitter uses knowledge of the channel and transmits more bits, or information, on those subcarriers that are less distorted or attenuated.

OFDM Training

As previously mentioned, the SYNC consists of long and short symbols, as depicted in Figure 3-23. Ten short training symbols exist, each of which is a short OFDM symbol that fills 12 of the 52 usable subchannels with a specified QPSK symbol in multiples of 4. It results in a periodic time domain sequence that you can use for detecting the start of the frame, performing automatic gain control, selecting the appropriate antenna if selection diversity is in use, estimating coarse frequency offset, and synchronizing the timing.

Figure 3-23 *SYNC Field*

Short Training Symbols										Long Training Symbols		
t1	t2	t3	t4	t5	t6	t7	t8	t9	t10	G	T1	T2

The two long training symbols are identical and modulate the subcarriers by a specific sequence. The long training sequences allow you to perform channel estimation and fine frequency offset estimation. Because they are designed to be processed together, they require only a single guard interval, indicated by G in Figure 3-23.

802.11a OFDM PMD

Figure 3-24 depicts the generalized OFDM transmitter used by the 802.11a OFDM PMD. As in other PHY schemes, you pass the data bits through the scrambler and then through a convolution encoder to create coded bits. The rate is determined by the data rate in use. Next, you interleave the coded bits in groups that are equal in size to the number of coded bits per OFDM symbol. The interleaved coded bits are then mapped into 48 symbols with the number of bits per symbol determined by the data rate. These are placed into 48 of the subcarriers of the OFDM symbol, and pilot tones are placed into 4 of the subcarriers. An IFFT is performed and is followed by the formation of the cyclic prefix. The resulting sequence is modulated to the appropriate carrier.

Figure 3-24 *802.11a Generalized OFDM Transmitter*

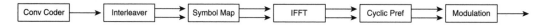

Table 3-14 shows how the data rate is mapped to the appropriate parameters for the components of the OFDM transmitter.

Table 3-14 *802.11a Transmitter Parameters*

Data Rate (Mbps)	Constellation Scheme	Convolutional Coding Rate	Coded Bits per Subcarrier	Coded Bits per OFDM Symbol	Data Bits per OFDM Symbol
6	BPSK	1/2	1	48	24
9	BPSK	3/4	1	48	36
12	QPSK	1/2	2	96	48
18	QPSK	3/4	2	96	72
24	16-QAM	1/2	4	192	96
36	16-QAM	3/4	4	192	144
48	64-QAM	2/3	6	288	192
54	64-QAM	3/4	6	288	216

The Signal field described earlier is transmitted in a single OFDM symbol at the 6 Mbps data rate, which allows the transmission of 24 data bits. This explains why there are 6 Tail bits at the end of the field. The Data field is transmitted as a number of sequential OFDM symbols, at the data rate specified in the Rate subfield of the Signal field. You can determine the number of pad bits required to make the length of the Data field a multiple of the number of coded bits per OFDM symbol once you know the length of the PSDU.

Examining the details of the 802.11a transmitter, the scrambler uses the same generator polynomial that is used in all the other 802.11 modulation schemes. The convolutional encoder uses a slightly different base rate 1/2 encoder than you would use for the optional 802.11b PBCC. The rate 2/3 and 3/4 encoders are formed by puncturing or omitting some of the encoded bits at the transmitter and then replacing them with 0 bits at the receiver. This replacement has the end effect of increasing the coding rate because there are fewer coded bits transmitted per input bits. The puncturing is performed in a known and systematic manner.

The interleaver is a block interleaver with the block size given by the number of coded bits per OFDM symbol. The interleaving actually occurs in two steps.

The first step ensures that adjacent coded bits are mapped into nonadjacent subcarriers, whereas the second step ensures the adjacent coded bits are mapped in an alternating pattern into less and more significant bits of the constellation symbol mapping. This process is important because in higher order constellations, the least significant bits (LSBs) are often less reliable. The issues is more evident when you examine the constellations, where constellation points that are close together and more easily confused or mistaken tend to only differ in their LSBs.

The mappings of groups of bits into symbols in the complex plane appear in Figures 3-25, 3-26, 3-27, and 3-28 for BPSK, QPSK, 16-QAM, and 64-QAM, respectively.

NOTE	QAM encodes information onto both the amplitude and phase portions of the sinusoid. 16-QAM has 4 amplitude levels in each dimension, whereas 64-QAM has 8 levels. You can think of the phase determining 2 bits, like QPSK, and the amplitude determining 2 or 3 bits.

To make sure that all data rates statistically have the same average power, each symbol is multiplied by a scaling factor that is a function of the modulation type. Table 3-15 gives the scale factor.

Table 3-15 *Power Normalizing Scale Factor*

Modulation Type	Scale Factor
BPSK	1
QPSK	1/sqrt (2)
16-QAM	1/sqrt (10)
64-QAM	1/sqrt (42)

Figure 3-25 *802.11a BPSK Constellation*

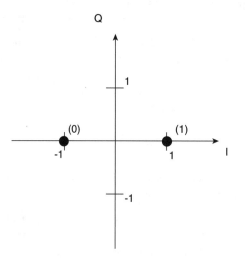

Figure 3-26   *802.11a QPSK Constellation*

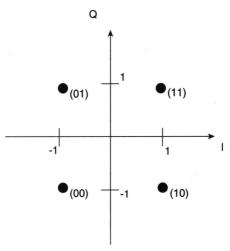

Figure 3-27   *802.11a 16-QAM Constellation*

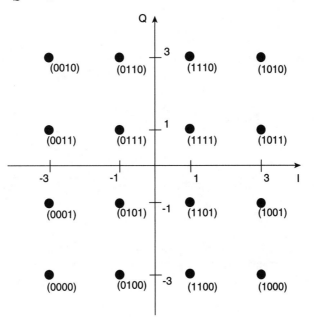

Figure 3-28 *802.11a 64-QAM Constellation*

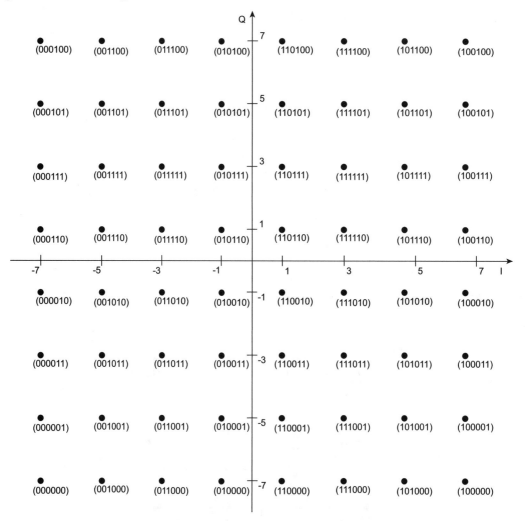

Within each OFDM symbol, four pilot signals are also added at regular intervals in the IFFT for use by the receiver. These pilot subcarriers are BPSK encoded and modulated by a pseudo binary sequence.

802.11g WLANs

The IEEE 802.11g standard, approved in June 2003, introduces an ERP to provide support for data rates up to 54 Mbps in the 2.4 GHz ISM band by borrowing from the OFDM techniques introduced by 802.11a. In contrast to 802.11a, it provides backward compatibility to 802.11b because 802.11g devices can fall back in data rate to the slower 802.11b speeds. Three modulation schemes are defined: ERP-ORFM, ERP-PBCC, and DSSS-OFDM. The ERP-OFDM form specifically provides mechanisms for 6, 9, 12, 18, 24, 36, 48, and 54 Mbps, with the 6, 12, and 24 Mbps data rates being mandatory, in addition to the 1, 2, 5.5, and 11 Mbps data rates. The standard also allows for optional PBCC modes at 22 and 33 Mbps as well as optional DSSS-OFDM modes at 6, 9, 12, 18, 24, 36, 48, and 54 Mbps. This section describes the changes necessary to form the ERP-OFDM, ERP-PBCC, and DSSS-OFDM.

802.11g PLCP

The 802.11g standard defines five PPDU formats: long preamble, short preamble, ERP-OFDM preamble, a long DSSS-OFDM preamble, and a short DSSS-OFDM preamble. Support for the first three is mandatory, but support for the latter two is optional. Table 3-16 summarizes the different preambles and the modulation schemes and data rates they support or are interoperable with.

Table 3-16 *Preambles*

Preamble Type	Data Rates Supported/Interoperable
Long	1, 2, 5.5, and 11 Mbps DSSS-OFDM at all OFDM rates ERP-PBCC at all ERP-PBCC rates
Short	2, 5.5, and 11 Mbps DSSS-OFDM at all OFDM rates ERP-PBCC at all ERP-PBCC rates
ERP-OFDM	ERP-OFDM at all rates
Long DSSS-OFDM	DSSS-OFDM at all rates
Short DSSS-OFDM	DSSS-OFDM at all rates

The long preamble uses the same long preamble defined in the HR-DSSS but with the Service field modified as shown in Table 3-17.

Table 3-17 *ERP SERVICE Field Definitions*

Bit	Name	Decode
b0	Reserved	0
b1	Reserved	0
b2	Locked clocks	0 = not locked; 1 = Tx frequency and symbol clocks are locked
b3	Modulation selection	0 = not ERP-PBCC 1 = ERP-PBCC
b4	Reserved	0
b5	Length extension	For ERP-PBCC
b6	Length extension	For ERP-PBCC
b7	Length extension	For PBCC

The length extension bits determine the number of octets, when the 11 Mbps PBCC and 22 and 33 Mbps ERP-PBCC modes are in use.

The short preamble makes the same modifications to the HR-DSSS short preamble that are summarized in Table 3-16.

The ERP-OFDM preamble takes the 802.11a preamble and adds an extra 6 microsecond signal extension, during which no transmission occurs, to make the packet longer to align it with the longer 16 microsecond SIFS timing of 802.11a versus the 10 microsecond SIFS timing of 802.11b.

The CCK-OFDM Long Preamble PPDU format appears in Figure 3-29. You set the rate subfield in the Signal to 3 Mbps. This setting ensures compatibility with non-ERP stations because they still read the length field and defer, despite not being able to demodulate the payload. The PLCP header matches that of the previously defined long preamble, but the preamble is the same as for the HR-DSSS. Both the preamble and the header are transmitted at 1 Mbps using DBPSK, and the PSDU is transmitted using the appropriate OFDM data rate. The header is scrambled using the HR-DSSS scrambler, and the data symbols are scrambled utilizing the 802.11a scrambler.

Figure 3-29 *CCK-OFDM Long and Short Preamble PPDU Format*

Sync	SFD	Signal	Service	Length	CRC	OFDM Sync	OFDM Signal	OFDM Data Symbols	OFDM Signal Extension

PLCP Preamble — PLCP Header — PSDU

Much like the DSSS-OFDM long preamble, the short preamble DSSS-OFDM PPDU format uses the HR-DSSS short preamble and header at a 2 Mbps data rate. With the HR-DSSS scrambler and the data symbols, the short preamble and header are transmitted with OFDM and use the 802.11a scrambler.

ERP-OFDM

As previously stated, the ERP-OFDM provides a mechanism to use the 802.11a data rates in the ISM band in a manner that is backward compatible with DSSS and HR-DSSS. In addition to utilizing the 802.11a OFDM modulation under the 2.4 GHz frequency plan, ERP-OFDM also mandates that the transmit center frequency and symbol clock frequency are locked to the same oscillator, which was an option for DSSS. It utilizes a 20 microsecond slot time, but this time can be dropped to 9 microseconds if only ERP devices are found in the BSS.

ERP-PBCC

The higher data 22 and 33 Mbps PBCC data rates use the same mechanism as the lower rate 5.5 and 11 Mbps PBCC, but with 8-PSK instead of QPSK and BPSK to get 22 Mbps. 33 Mbps is achieved by using a 16.5 MHz clock instead of 11 MHz. The symbol mapping, as governed by the cover sequence, appears in Figure 3-30.

Figure 3-30 *802.11g ERP-PBCC Constellation*

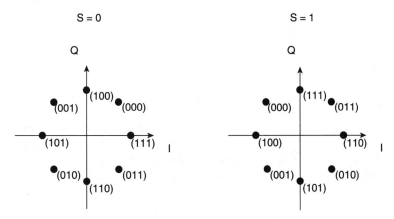

802.11g Summary

The key item to remember about 802.11g: It extends the data rates supported at 2.4 GHz up to 54 Mbps in a manner that ensures backward compatibility with older 802.11b devices. In an environment with only 802.11g devices operating, all transmissions take place at the highest data rates available. However, as soon as an 802.11b device is introduced, the header information needs to back down to the 802.11b rates that this older device can understand. This backing down occurs on all transmissions regardless of whether they are between 802.11g or 802.11b devices. The end effect is an overall increase in overhead, so a small price is paid for the backward compatibility that 802.11g affords.

CCA

The different 802.11 standards define five different CCA modes for use in the 2.4 GHz band:

- Energy detection bases the CCA decision only on whether energy was detected over a threshold.

- Carrier sense bases the CCA decision purely upon whether an 802.11 signal is detected.

- Carrier sense with energy detection uses a combination of modes 1 and 2.

- Carrier sense with timer reports that the medium is idle if no 802.11 signal is detected for 3.65 milliseconds.

- Extended rate PHY energy detection and carrier sense is much the same as mode 3 but applied to the ERP.

It is mandatory that the CCA process employ at least one of these modes.

Summary

Table 3-18 summarizes the different PHY technologies discussed in this chapter. Although FHSS experienced a fairly high adoption rate, it was quickly overtaken by DSSS and HR-DSSS as the most common. At the time of this writing, the industry is on the cusp of another technology revolution as users migrate to 802.11a and 802.11g.

Table 3-18   *802.11 PHY Standards*

Characteristic	802.11 FHSS	802.11 DSSS	802.11b HR-DSSS	802.11a OFDM	802.11g ERP	802.11j
Frequency Band (GHz)	2.4	2.4	2.4	5	2.4	4.9
Max Data Rate (Mbps)	2	2	11	54	54	54
Modulation	QPSK	GFSK	CCK	OFDM	OFDM	OFDM

This chapter provided an introduction to the basic physical layer building blocks and how you can use them together to form a full physical layer system. The chapter discussed the distinct parameters of each of the different physical layers, along with the trade-offs involved in deciding upon a technology to use.

This chapter covers the following topics:

- **Security as defined in the 1997 802.11 specification**—Why was Wired Equivalent Privacy (WEP) selected as the encryption algorithm and Open and Shared Key selected as the authentication algorithms?

- **Security vulnerabilities in the 1997 802.11 standard**—Why is WEP ineffective for encryption and Open and Shared Key ineffective for authentication?

- **Next generation wireless LAN (WLAN) security enhancements**—What are the new technologies being used to secure 802.11 WLANs?

802.11 Wireless LAN Security

For developers who have implemented or are currently implementing 802.11 wireless, an alphabet soup of acronyms describe enhanced 802.11 WLAN security. Abbreviations such as 802.1X, EAP, LEAP, PEAP, EAP-TLS, WEP, TKIP, WPA, and AES are common terms in describing 802.11 security. For the network administrator accustomed to dealing with IP and connectivity-oriented technologies, these new security-focused protocols can prove confusing.

Wireless Security

Imagine extending a long Ethernet cable from your internal network outside your office and laying it on the ground in the parking lot. Anyone who wants to use your network can simply plug into that network cable. Connecting unsecured WLANs to your internal network has the potential to offer the same opportunity.

802.11-based devices communicate with one another using radio frequencies (RFs) as the carrier signal for data. The data is broadcast from the sender in the hopes that the receiver is within RF range. The drawback to this mechanism is that any other station within range of the RF also receives the data.

Without a security mechanism of some sort, any 802.11 station can process the data sent on a WLAN, as long as that receiver is in RF range. To provide a minimum level of security in a WLAN, you need two components:

- **A means to decide who or what can use a WLAN**—This requirement is satisfied by authentication mechanisms for LAN access control.

- **A means to provide privacy for the wireless data**—The requirement is satisfied by encryption algorithms.

As Figure 4-1 depicts, wireless security consists of both authentication and encryption. Neither mechanism alone is enough to secure a wireless network.

Figure 4-1 *Wireless Security Requires Authentication and Encryption*

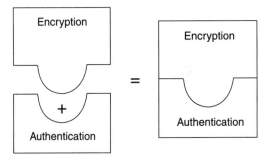

The 802.11 specification defines Open and Shared Key authentication and WEP to provide device authentication and data privacy, respectively. The Open and Shared Key algorithms both rely on WEP encryption and possession of the WEP keys for access control. Because of the importance of WEP in 802.11 security, the following section focuses on the basics of encryption and ciphers in general.

Overview of Encryption

Data encryption mechanisms are based on cipher algorithms that give data a randomized appearance. Two type of ciphers exist:

- Stream ciphers
- Block ciphers

Both cipher types operate by generating a key stream from a secret key value. The key stream is mixed with the data, or plaintext, to produce the encrypted output, or ciphertext. The two cipher types differ in the size of the data they operate on at a time.

A stream cipher generates a continuous key stream based on the key value. For example, a stream cipher can generate a 15-byte key stream to encrypt one frame and a 200-byte key stream to encrypt another. Figure 4-2 illustrates stream cipher operation. Stream ciphers are small and efficient encryption algorithms and as a result do not incur extensive CPU usage. A commonly used stream cipher is RC4, which is the basis of the WEP algorithm.

A block cipher, in contrast, generates a single encryption key stream of a fixed size. The plaintext is fragmented into blocks, and each block is mixed with the key stream independently. If the plaintext block is smaller than the key stream block, padding is added to the plaintext block to make it the appropriate size. Figure 4-3 illustrates block cipher operation. The fragmentation process, in addition to other aspects of block cipher encryption, causes the block cipher to incur a larger CPU processing penalty than would a stream cipher. As a result, block cipher operation decreases the effective throughput of a device.

Figure 4-2   *Stream Cipher Operation*

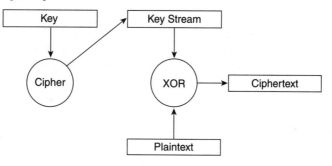

Figure 4-3   *Block Cipher Operation*

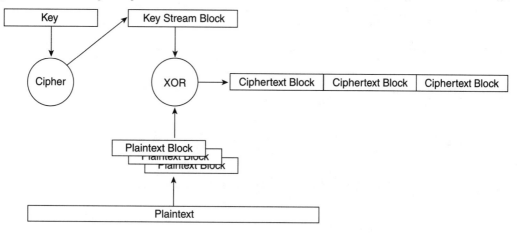

The process of encryption described here for stream ciphers and block ciphers is known as Electronic Code Book (ECB) encryption mode. ECB mode encryption has the characteristic that the same plaintext input always generates the same ciphertext output. The input plaintext always produces the same ciphertext. This factor is a potential security threat because eavesdroppers can see patterns in the ciphertext and start making educated guesses about the original plaintext.

Some encryption techniques can overcome this issue:

- Initialization vectors
- Feedback modes

Initialization Vectors

An initialization vector (IV) is a number added to the key, which has the end result of altering the key stream. The IV is concatenated to the key before the key stream is generated. Every time the IV changes, so does the key stream. Figure 4-4 shows two scenarios. The first is stream cipher encryption without the use of an IV. In this case, the plain text DATA when mixed with the key stream 12345 always produces the ciphertext AHGHE. The second scenario shows the same plaintext mixed with the IV augmented key stream to generate different ciphertext. Note that the ciphertext output in the second scenario is different from the ciphertext output from the first. The 802.11 world recommends that you change the IV on a per-frame basis. This way, if the same frame is transmitted twice, it's highly probable that the resulting ciphertext is different for each frame.

Figure 4-4   *Encryption and Initialization Vectors*

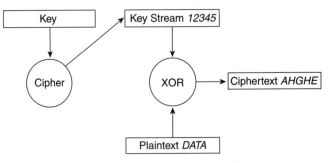

1. Stream Cipher Encryption Without an Initialization Vector

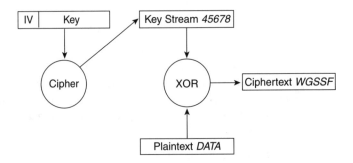

2. Stream Cipher Encryption with an Initialization Vector

Feedback Modes

Feedback modes are modifications to the encryption process to avoid a plaintext generating the same ciphertext during encryption. Feedback modes are generally used with block ciphers. Feedback modes are discussed later in this chapter.

Encryption in the 802.11 Standard

The 802.11 specification provides data privacy with the WEP algorithm. WEP is based on the RC4 symmetric stream cipher. The symmetric nature of RC4 requires that matching WEP keys, either 40 or 104 bits in length, must be statically configured on client devices and access points (APs). WEP was chosen primarily because of its low computational overhead. Although 802.11-enabled PCs are common today, this situation was not the case back in 1997. The majority of WLAN devices were application-specific devices (ASDs). Examples of ASDs include barcode scanners, tablet PCs, and 802.11-based phones. The applications that run on ASDs generally do not require much computational power, so as a result, ASDs have meager CPUs. WEP is a simple-to-implement algorithm that you can write in as few as 30 lines of code, in some cases. The low overhead incurred by WEP made it an ideal encryption algorithm to use on ASDs.

To avoid the ECB mode of encryption, WEP uses a 24-bit IV, which is concatenated to the key before being processed by the RC4 cipher. Figure 4-5 shows a WEP-encrypted frame, including the IV.

Figure 4-5   *A WEP-Encrypted Frame*

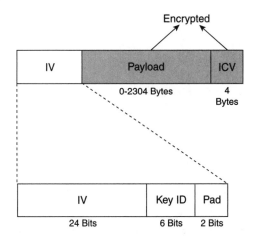

The IV must change on a per-frame basis to avoid IV collisions. *IV collisions* occur when the same IV and WEP key are used, resulting in the same key stream being used to encrypt a frame. This collision gives attackers a better opportunity to guess the plaintext data by seeing similarities in the ciphertext. The point of using an IV is to prevent this scenario, so it is important to change the IV often. Most vendors offer per-frame IVs on their WLAN devices.

The 802.11 specification requires that matching WEP keys be statically configured on both client and infrastructure devices. You can define up to four keys on a device, but you can use only one at a time for encrypting outbound frames. Figure 4-6 shows a Cisco Aironet client configuration screen for WEP configuration.

Figure 4-6   *WEP Configuration*

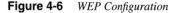

WEP encryption is used only on data frames and during Shared Key authentication. WEP encrypts the following fields of an 802.11 data frame:

- The data or payload
- The integrity check value (ICV)

All other fields are transmitted without encryption. The IV must be sent unencrypted within the frame so that the receiving station can use it to properly decrypt the payload and ICV. Figure 4-7 details the process for encryption, transmission, receipt, and decryption of a WEP encrypted data frame.

In addition to data encryption, the 802.11 specification provides for a 32-bit value that functions as an integrity check for the frame. This check tells the receiver that the frame has arrived without being corrupted during transmission. It augments the Layer 1 and Layer 2 frame check sequences (FCSs), which are designed to check for transmission-related errors.

Figure 4-7   *The WEP Encryption and Decryption Process*

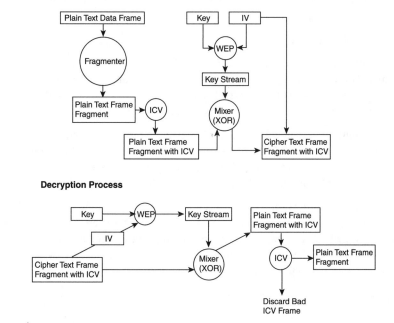

The ICV is calculated against all fields in the frame using a cyclic redundancy check (CRC)-32 polynomial function. The sender calculates the values and places the result in the ICV field. The ICV is included in the WEP-encrypted portion of the frame, so it is not plainly visible to eavesdroppers. The frame receiver decrypts the frame, calculates an ICV value, and compares what it calculates against what has arrived in the ICV field. If the values match, the frame is considered to be genuine and untampered with. If they don't match, the frame is discarded. Figure 4-8 diagrams the ICV operation.

Figure 4-8   *ICV Operation*

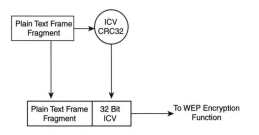

Authentication Mechanisms in the 802.11 Standard

The 802.11 specification stipulates two mechanisms for authentication of WLAN clients:

- Open authentication
- Shared Key authentication

Open authentication is a null authentication algorithm. The AP grants any request for authentication. It might sound pointless at first to have such an algorithm defined, but Open authentication has its place in 802.11 network authentication. The requirements for authentication allow devices to quickly gain access to the network.

Access control in Open authentication relies on the preconfigured WEP key on the client and AP. The client and AP must have matching WEP keys to enable them to communicate. If the client and AP do not have WEP enabled, there is no security in the BSS. Any device can join the BSS and all data frames are transmitted unencrypted.

After Open authentication and the association process, the client can begin transmitting and receiving data. If the client is configured with a key that differs from the key on the AP, the client will be unable to encrypt or decrypt data frames correctly, and the frames will be discarded by both the client and the AP. This process essentially provides a means of controlling access to the BSS. It is illustrated in Figure 4-9.

Figure 4-9 *Open Authentication with Differing WEP Keys*

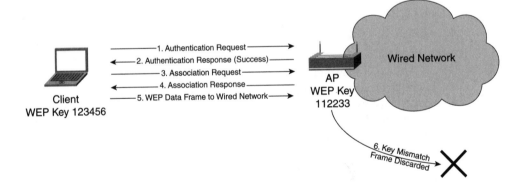

Unlike Open authentication, Shared Key authentication requires that the client station and the AP have WEP enabled and have matching WEP keys. The following summarizes the Shared Key authentication process:

1 The client sends an authentication request for Shared Key authentication to the AP.

2 The AP responds with a cleartext challenge frame.

3 The client encrypts the challenge and responds back to the AP.

4 If the AP can correctly decrypt the frame and retrieve the original challenge, the client is sent a success message.

5 The client can access the WLAN.

The premise behind Shared Key authentication is similar to that of Open authentication with WEP keys as the access control means. The client and AP must have matching keys. The difference between the two schemes is that the client cannot associate in Shared Key authentication unless the correct key is configured. Figure 4-10 shows the Shared Key authentication process.

Figure 4-10 *Shared Key Authentication Process*

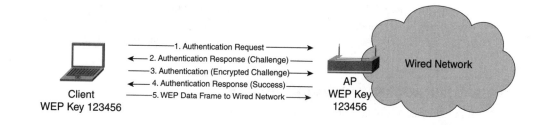

MAC Address Authentication

MAC address authentication is not specified in the 802.11 specification, but it is supported by many vendors. MAC address authentication verifies the client's MAC address against a locally configured list of allowed addresses or against an external authentication server, as shown in Figure 4-11. MAC authentication augments the Open and Shared Key authentications provided by 802.11, potentially reducing the likelihood of unauthorized devices accessing the network. For example, a network administrator might want to limit a particular AP to just three specific devices. If all stations and APs in the BSS have the same WEP keys, it is difficult to use Open or Shared Key authentication to facilitate this scenario. The administrator can configure MAC address authentication to augment 802.11 authentication.

Figure 4-11 *MAC Address Authentication Process*

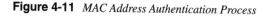

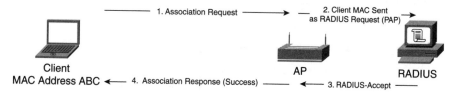

Security Vulnerabilities in the 802.11 Standard

The prior section detailed how 802.11 authentication and encryption operates. It is no secret that security in the 802.11 specification is flawed. Not long after the ratification of 802.11, a number of published papers pinpointed vulnerabilities in 802.11 authentication and WEP encryption.

Open Authentication Vulnerabilities

Open authentication provides no way for the AP to determine whether a client is valid. This lack is a security vulnerability if WEP encryption is not implemented in a WLAN. Even with static WEP enabled on the client and AP, Open authentication provides no means of determining who is using the WLAN device. An authorized device in the hands of an unauthorized user is just as much a network security threat as providing no security at all!

Shared Key Authentication Vulnerabilities

Shared key authentication requires the client to use a preshared WEP key to encrypt challenge text sent from the AP. The AP authenticates the client by decrypting the shared-key response and validating that the challenge text is the same.

The process of exchanging the challenge text occurs over the wireless link and is vulnerable to a known plaintext attack. This vulnerability with Shared Key authentication relies on the mathematical principal behind encryption. Earlier in this chapter, encryption was defined as plaintext mixed with a key stream to produce ciphertext. The mixing process is a binary mathematical function known as an exclusive OR (XOR). If plaintext is mixed with corresponding ciphertext, the result of the function is the key stream for the WEP key and IV pair, as shown in Figure 4-12.

An eavesdropper can capture both the plaintext challenge text and the ciphertext response. By simply running the values through an XOR function, an eavesdropper has a valid key stream. The eavesdropper can then use the key stream to decrypt frames matching the same size as the key stream, given that the IV used to derive the key stream is the same as the encrypted frame. Figure 4-13 illustrates how an attacker can eavesdrop on a Shared Key authentication and derive the key stream.

MAC Address Authentication Vulnerabilities

MAC addresses are sent unencrypted in all 802.11 frames, as required by the 802.11 specification. As a result, WLANs that use MAC authentication are vulnerable to an attacker undermining the MAC authentication process by spoofing a valid MAC address.

MAC address spoofing is possible in 802.11 network interface cards (NICs) that allow the universally administered address (UAA) to be overwritten with a locally administered address (LAA). The UAA is the MAC address that is hard-coded on the NIC by the manufacturer. An attacker can use a protocol analyzer to determine a valid MAC address in the BSS and an LAA-compliant NIC to spoof the valid MAC address.

Figure 4-12 *Deriving a Key Stream*

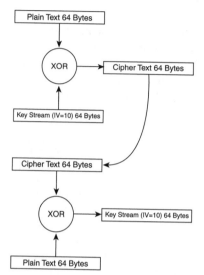

Figure 4-13 *Shared Key Authentication Vulnerability*

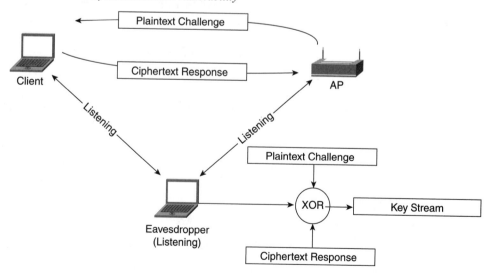

WEP Encryption Vulnerabilities

The most compelling and damaging vulnerability to 802.11 was delivered by three crypt-analysts, Fluhrer, Mantin, and Shamir. In their paper, they determined that you could derive a WEP key by passively collecting particular frames from a WLAN.

The vulnerability surrounds how WEP has implemented the key scheduling algorithm (KSA) from the RC4 stream cipher. A number of IVs (referred to as *weak IVs*) can reveal key bytes after statistical analysis. Researchers at AT&T and Rice University as well as the developers of the AirSnort application implemented this vulnerability and verified that you can derive WEP keys of either 40- or 104-bit key length after as few as 4 million frames. For high usage 802.11b WLANs, that can translate to roughly one hour until a 104-bit WEP key is derived. This vulnerability renders WEP ineffective as a mechanism to provide data privacy.

The attack is a passive attack, where an attacker simply eavesdrops on a BSS and collects transmitted frames. Unlike the Shared Key authentication vulnerability, the Fluhrer, Mantin, and Shamir attack can derive the actual WEP key, not just the key stream. This information allows the attacker to access the BSS as an authenticated device, unbeknownst to network administrators.

As if this attack was not enough, a second class of attacks on WEP have been theorized but never practically implemented. These inductive attacks leverage the same principle used for the Shared Key authentication vulnerability: a known plaintext and corresponding ciphertext used to derive a key stream.

As stated previously, a derived key stream is only useful to decrypt frames for a given IV and WEP key pair and for a specific length. Ideally, an attacker endeavors to collect as many of these key streams as possible to build a key-stream database to subvert the network and decrypt frames. In WLANs where Shared Key authentication is not used, frame bit flipping attacks allow an attacker to derive large numbers of key streams in a short amount of time.

Frame bit flipping attacks rely on the weakness of the ICV. The ICV is based on the CRC-32 polynomial function. This function is ineffective as a means of message integrity. Mathematical properties of the CRC-32 function allow a frame to be tampered with and the ICV value to be modified without the original contents of the frame being known.

Although the data payload size can vary by frame, many elements in 802.11 data frames remain constant and in the same bit position. The attacker leverages this fact and tampers with the payload portion of the frame to modify the higher-layer packet. The process for a bit flipping attack follows (see also Figure 4-14):

1 The attacker captures a frame from the WLAN.

2 The attacker flips random bits in the data payload of the frame.

3 The attacker modifies the ICV (detailed later).

4 The attacker transmits the modified frame.

5 The receiver (either a client or the AP) receives the frame and calculates the ICV based on the frame contents.

6 The receiver compares the calculated ICV with the value in the ICV field of the frame.

7 The receiver accepts the modified frame.

8 The receiver forwards the frame to an upper-layer device (a router or host PC).

9 Because bits are flipped in the Layer 3 packet, the Layer 3 checksum fails.

10 The receiver IP stack generates a predictable error.

11 The attacker sniffs the WLAN looking for the encrypted error message.

12 Upon receiving the error message, the attacker derives the key stream, as with the IV replay attack.

Figure 4-14 *Bit Flipping Attack*

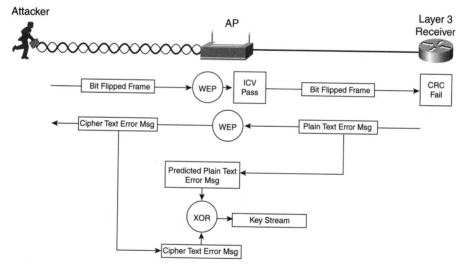

The basis for this attack is the failure of the ICV. The ICV is in the WEP-encrypted portion of the frame, so how is the attacker able to modify it to match the bit flipped changes to the frame? Figure 4-15 illustrates the process of actually flipping bits and changing the ICV:

1 A given frame (F1) has an ICV (C1). (See Figure 4-15.)

2 A new frame is generated (F2) with the same length as F1 with bits set.

3 Frame F3 is created by XORing F1 and F2.

4 The ICV for F3 is calculated (C2).

5 ICV C3 is generated by XORing C1 and C2.

Figure 4-15 *Modifying the ICV with Bit Flipping*

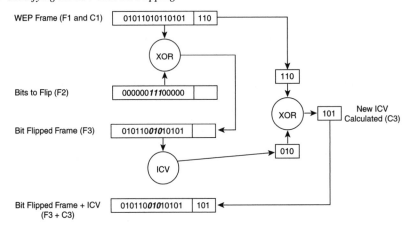

Static WEP Key Management Issues

The 802.11 specification does not specify key-management mechanisms. Although not a specific vulnerability, WEP is defined to support only static, preshared keys. Because 802.11 authentication authenticates a device and not the user of the device, the loss or theft of a wireless adapter becomes a security issue for the network. This issue presents network administrators with the tedious task of manually rekeying all wireless devices in the network when the existing key is compromised because an adapter was lost or stolen.

This risk might be acceptable for small deployments where managing user devices is a simple task. Such a prospect is not scalable for medium and large deployments where the number of wireless users can reach into the thousands. Without a mechanism to distribute or generate keys, administrators must keep close tabs on wireless NIC whereabouts.

Secure 802.11 WLANs

The WLAN industry recognized the vulnerabilities in 802.11 authentication and data privacy. To provide users with a secure WLAN solution that is scalable and manageable, the IEEE has augmented 802.11 security by developing enhancements to 802.11 authentication and encryption. The changes are being incorporated into the 802.11i draft standard. To date, the 802.11i draft has not been passed as a standard, so the Wi-Fi Alliance has put together an subset of the components of 802.11i called Wi-Fi Protected Access (WPA). This section details and explains 802.11i and WPA components.

Although this chapter has detailed 802.11 security as a combination of Open/Shared Key authentication and WEP encryption so far, many mistakenly believe WEP to be the only component to WLAN security. Wireless security actually consists of four facets:

- **The authentication framework**—This facet is the mechanism that accommodates the authentication algorithm by securely communicating messages between the client, AP, and authentication server.

- **The authentication algorithm**—This facet is the algorithm that validates the user credentials.

- **The data privacy algorithm**—This facet provides data privacy across the wireless medium for data frames.

- **The data integrity algorithm**—This facet provides data integrity across the wireless medium to ensure to the receiver that the data frame was not tampered with.

These facets are illustrated in Figure 4-16.

Figure 4-16 *The Four Facets of Wireless Security*

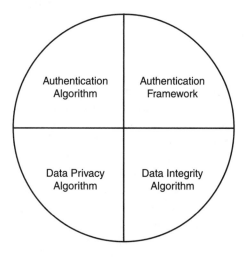

Facet 1: The Authentication Framework

The authentication framework in 802.11 is the 802.11 authentication management frame. The authentication frame facilitates Open and Shared Key authentication algorithms, yet the frame itself does not possess the ability to authenticate a client. Because the shortcomings of 802.11 authentication have already been highlighted, it is important to understand what is needed to provide secure authentication in a WLAN.

802.11 is missing some key components to provide effective authentication:

- Centralized, user-based authentication
- Dynamic encryption keys
- Encryption key management
- Mutual authentication

User-based authentication is critical for network security. Device-based authentication, such as Open or Shared Key authentication, does not prevent unauthorized users from using authorized devices. Also, logistical issues, such as lost or stolen devices and employee termination, can force network administrators to manually rekey all 802.11 APs and clients. Centralized, user-based management via an authentication, authorization, and accounting (AAA) server, such as a RADIUS, lets you allow or disallow specific users, regardless of the specific devices they use.

The requirement for user-based authentication has a positive side effect: user-specific encryption keys. Authentication types that support the creation of dynamic encryption keys fit well into the WLAN security and management model. Per user, dynamic keys relieve the network administrator from having to statically manage keys. Encryption keys are dynamically derived and discarded as the user authenticates and disconnects from the network. Should you need to remove a user from the network, you only need to disable her account to prevent her access.

Mutual authentication is two-way authentication. The "two-way" nature comes from not only the network authenticating the client, but also the client authenticating the network. In Open and Shared Key authentication, the AP or network authenticates the client. The client does not know for sure that the AP or network is valid because no mechanism is defined in the 802.11 specification to allow the client to authenticate the network. As a result, a rogue AP or rogue client station can pose as a valid AP and subvert the data on the client's machine. Figure 4-17 diagrams one-way authentication versus mutual authentication.

802.11 WLAN vendors and the IEEE understand the need to augment and replace existing security mechanisms, both in authentication and encryption. Work is currently underway in task group I of the 802.11 working group, and after the changes are complete, the security specifications will be ratified as the 802.11i specification.

The IEEE has addressed the shortcomings of 802.11 authentication by incorporating the 802.1X authentication framework. 802.1X itself is an IEEE standard that provides all 802 link layer topologies with extensible authentication, normally seen in higher layers. 802.1X is based on a Point-to-Point Protocol (PPP) authentication framework known as the Extensible Authentication Protocol (EAP). In oversimplified terms, 802.1X encapsulates EAP messages for use at Layer 2. 802.11i incorporates the 802.1X authentication framework requiring its use for user-based authentication. Figure 4-18 illustrates 802.1X with respect to authentication algorithms and 802 link layer topologies.

Figure 4-17 *One-Way Authentication Versus Mutual Authentication*

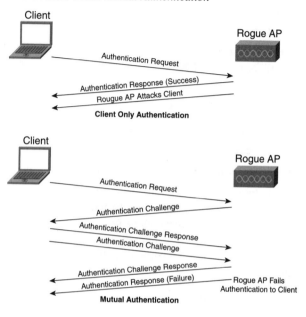

Figure 4-18 *802.1X in Contrast to 802 Link Layer Topologies*

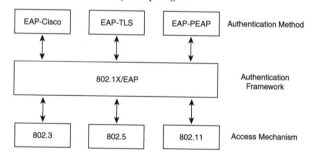

EAP (RFC 2284) and 802.1X do not mandate the use of any specific authentication algorithm. The network administrator can use any EAP-compliant authentication type for either 802.1X or EAP authentication. The only requirement is that both the 802.11 client (known as the supplicant) and the authentication server support the EAP authentication algorithm. This open and extensible architecture lets you use one authentication framework in differing environments, where each environment may use a different authentication type. Examples of EAP authentication types include the following:

- **EAP-Transport Layer Security (EAP-PEAP)**—Operates similar to Secure Sockets Layer (SSL) at the link layer. Mutual authentication is accomplished via server-side digital certificates used to create a SSL tunnel for the client to securely authenticate to the network.

- **EAP-Message Digest 5 (EAP-MD5)**—Similar to the Challenge Handshake Authentication Protocol (CHAP), EAP-MD5 provides a password based, one-way authentication algorithm.

- **EAP-Cisco**—Also known as LEAP, EAP-Cisco was the first EAP type defined specifically for use in WLANs. EAP-Cisco is a password-based, mutually authenticating algorithm.

802.1X authentication requires three entities:

- **The supplicant**—Resides on the WLAN client
- **The authenticator**—Resides on the AP
- **The authentication server**—Resides on the RADIUS server

These entities are logical software components on network devices. With respect to 802.11, the authenticator creates a logical port per client device, based on the client's association ID (AID). This logical port has two data paths: uncontrolled and controlled. The uncontrolled data path allows all 802.1X authentication traffic through to the network. The controlled data path blocks normal network traffic until successful client authentication occurs. Figure 4-19 shows the logical ports of an 802.1X authenticator.

Figure 4-19   *802.1X Logical Authenticator Ports*

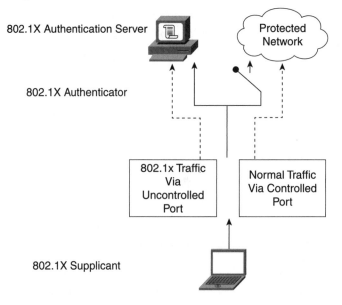

802.1X message exchanges vary, depending on the authentication algorithm, but the general message exchange is as follows:

1 The client supplicant becomes active on the medium and associates to the AP authenticator.

2 The authenticator detects the client association and enables the supplicant's port. It forces the port into an unauthorized state so only 802.1X traffic is forwarded. All other traffic is blocked.

3 The client may send an EAP-Start message, although client initiation is not required. Figure 4-20 diagrams the 802.1X message exchange.

4 The authenticator replies with an EAP-Request Identity message back to the supplicant to obtain the client's identity.

5 The supplicant's EAP-Response packet containing the client's identity is forwarded to the authentication server. The value of the identity response varies by EAP type, but in general, only the username or equivalent is sent, not any form of shared secret, such as a password.

6 The authentication server is configured to authenticate clients with a specific authentication algorithm. Currently, 802.1X for 802.11 LANs does not stipulate a specific algorithm to use.

7 Depending on the EAP authentication algorithm-specific credential exchange outcome, the last 802.1X-specific message is a RADIUS-ACCEPT or RADIUS-REJECT packet from the authentication server to the AP.

8 Upon receiving the ACCEPT packet, the authenticator transitions the client's port to an authorized state, and traffic may be forwarded.

Figure 4-20   *The 802.1X Message Exchange*

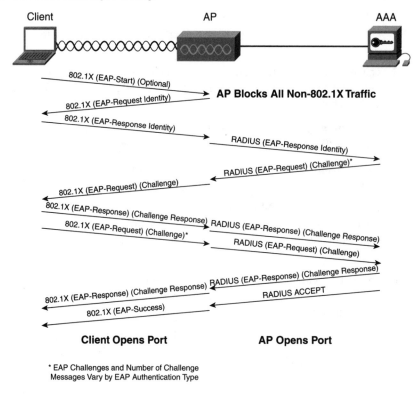

* EAP Challenges and Number of Challenge
Messages Vary by EAP Authentication Type

802.1X does not specify nor mandate any particular EAP authentication algorithm.

Facet 2: The Authentication Algorithm

802.11i and WPA provide a mechanism for authentication algorithms to communicate between client, AP, and authentication server, via the 802.1X authentication framework. Neither 802.11i nor WPA mandate the use of specific authentication algorithm, but both recommend the use of an algorithm that supports mutual authentication, dynamic encryption key generation, and user-based authentication. Figure 4-21 highlights the messages exchanged between the client, AP, and AAA server, but it might be easier to conceptualize the process with a specific example. This section highlights the operation of EAP-Cisco. EAP-Cisco (more commonly known as Cisco LEAP) is a simple and effective algorithm that is specifically designed for use in WLANs.

Figure 4-21 depicts EAP-Cisco operation. The following list describes each transaction in greater detail.

Figure 4-21   *EAP-Cisco Authentication*

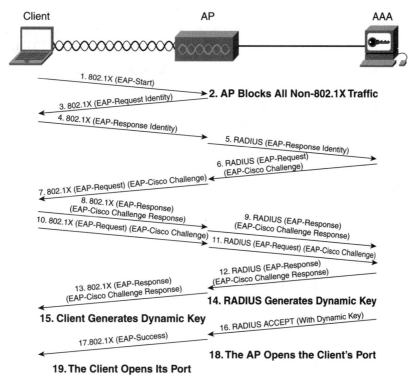

1 The client becomes active on the medium and sends an 802.1X-encapsulated EAP-Start message to the AP.

2 The AP blocks the client's port, allowing only 802.1X traffic through to the network.

3 The AP sends an 802.1X-encapsulated EAP-Request Identity message to the client.

4 The client replies with an 802.1X-encapsulated EAP-Response containing the username of the client.

5 The AP forwards the username to the authentication server encapsulated in a RADIUS ACCESS-REQUEST packet.

6 The RADIUS server generates an EAP-Cisco challenge message and sends it to the client (via the AP) encapsulated in a RADIUS ACCESS-RESPONSE packet.

7 The AP forwards the EAP-Cisco challenge to the client encapsulated in an 802.1X frame.

8 The client processes the challenge through the EAP-Cisco algorithm and sends a challenge response back to the RADIUS server via the AP.

9 The AP encapsulates the EAP-Cisco challenge response in a RADIUS ACCESS-REQUEST packet and forwards it to the RADIUS server.

10 The client sends an EAP-Cisco challenge to the RADIUS server (via the AP) to authenticate the network. The challenge is encapsulated in an 802.1X frame.

11 The AP encapsulates the EAP-Cisco challenge in a RADIUS ACCESS-REQUEST packet.

12 The RADIUS server sends the EAP-Cisco challenge response back to the client (via the AP) encapsulated in a RADIUS ACCESS-RESPONSE packet.

13 The AP encapsulates the EAP-Cisco challenge response in an 802.1X frame and sends it to the client.

14 The RADIUS server generates a dynamic encryption key based on the user's password and some session-specific information.

15 The client generates the same dynamic encryption key. The client is capable of locally generating the same key because it has access to the same information.

16 The RADIUS server sends the key to the AP encapsulated in a RADIUS ACCEPT packet. The RADIUS ACCEPT packet indicates to the AP that authentication was successful.

17 The AP installs the dynamic key for the specific client, encapsulates an EAP-Success message in an 802.1X frame, and forwards the message to the client.

18 The AP transitions the client's port into a forwarding state.

19 The client opens its port (assuming successful mutual authentication).

EAP-Cisco is a proprietary authentication algorithm that runs atop an open authentication framework. For this reason, details of the EAP-Cisco algorithm (such as challenge generation and challenge response contents, as well as encryption key derivation) are unavailable for public consumption. EAP-Cisco covers the requirements set forth for secure user authentication in WLAN by including the following:

- User-based authentication
- Mutual authentication
- Dynamic encryption keys

Should you need to remove a specific user from the network, you disable only his account from the centralized authentication server. This process prevents the user from successfully authenticating and generating a valid dynamic encryption key.

Facet 3: Data Privacy

The encryption vulnerabilities in WEP present 802.11 vendors and the IEEE with a predicament: How can you fix 802.11 encryption without requiring a complete replacement of AP hardware or client NICs?

The IEEE answered this question with the Temporal Key Integrity Protocol (TKIP) as part of 802.11i (and WPA). TKIP uses many key functions of WEP to maintain client investment in existing 802.11 equipment and infrastructure but fixes several of the vulnerabilities to provide effective data-frame encryption. The key enhancements contained with TKIP are

- **Per-frame keying**—The WEP key is quickly changed on a per-frame basis.

- **Message integrity check (MIC)**—A check provides effective data-frame integrity to prevent frame tampering and frame replay (discussed later).

The Fluhrer, Mantin, and Shamir paper describes the vulnerability of RC4 as it is implemented in WEP. Attacks that leverage this weak IV vulnerability, such as AirSnort, rely on collecting several data frames with encrypted data using weak IVs. The easiest way to mitigate these attacks is to change the WEP key used between the client and AP before an attacker can collect enough frames to derive key bytes.

The IEEE has adopted a scheme known as *per-frame keying*. (It is also known as per-packet keying and fast packet keying.) The premise behind per-frame keying is that the IV, the transmitter MAC address, and the WEP key are processed together via a two-phase mixing function. The output of the function matches the standard 104-bit WEP key and 24-bit IV.

The IEEE is also proposing that the 24-bit IV be increased to a 48-bit IV. Subsequent sections detail why the IV expansion is necessary. Figure 4-22 depicts a sample 48-bit IV and how the IV is broken apart for use in per-frame keying.

Figure 4-22 *48-Bit IV Broken Apart for Per-Frame Keying*

The following steps outline the process for per-frame keying:

1 The base WEP key (derived from 802.1X authentication) is mixed with the most significant 32 bits (a 32-bit number ranges from 0 to 4,294,967,295) of the 48-bit IV and the MAC address of the transmitter. The output is called a phase 1 key. This process allows the phase 1 key to be cached and also places directionality into the key (see Figure 4-23).

2 The phase 1 key is again mixed with the IV and the transmitter MAC address to yield the per-frame key.

3 The IV used for frame transmission is only 16 bits (a 16-bit number ranges from 0 to 65,535). The remaining 8 bits is a fixed value used as a placeholder.

4 The per-frame key is used to WEP-encrypt the data frame.

5 When the 16-bit IV space is exhausted, the phase 1 key is discarded, and the 32 most significant bits are incremented by 1. (If the phase 1 IV was 12, it increments to 13.)

6 The per-frame key is recalculated as in Step 2.

Figure 4-23 *The Per-Frame Keying Operation*

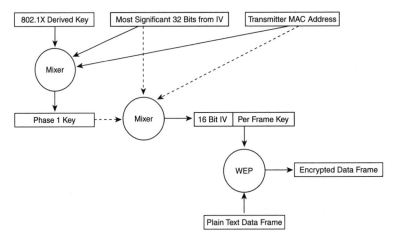

The per-frame key is only valid when the 16-bit IV values have not been used. If an IV value is used twice, an IV collision occurs, which gives attacks an opportunity to derive the key stream. To avoid IV collision, the phase 1 key is recalculated by incrementing the most significant 32 bits of the IV by 1 and recalculating the per-frame key.

NOTE   Per-frame keying mitigates statistical attacks (such as the AirSnort) against the per-frame key as long as the per-frame key/IV pair remain unique.

The following steps illustrate the per-frame keying operation in detail:

1 The device initialized the IV to 0. The binary representation of the IV is 0000000000000000000000000000000000000000000000000.

2 The first (most significant) 32 bits of the IV (in this case, the first 32 0), is mixed with 802.1X-derived key (a 128-bit value) and the transmitter MAC address (a 48-bit value) to produce the phase 1 key (an 80-bit value).

3 The phase 1 key is mixed with the first (most significant) 32 bits of the IV and the transmitter MAC address again to yield a 128-bit per-frame key output, of which is the first 16 bits is the IV (16 0s).

4 The IV for the per-frame key increments by 1. (The first IV is 16 0s, the subsequent is 15 0s and a 1, and so on, until all 16 bits are 1.)

5 After the per-frame IV is exhausted, the phase 1 IV (32 bits) is incremented by 1. (It is now 31 0s and a 1, 00000000000000000000000000000001.)

The next logical questions is "Will this mechanism ever cause an IV collision?" The answer is yes, but the real issue is when. Given that the maximum forwarding rate for an 802.11b device is roughly 1000 frames per second, the 16-bit frame IV exhausts after 65 seconds (2^{16} frames/1000 frame per second).

There are 2^{32} possible phase 1 IVs (the first 32 bits of the 48-bit IV), which is 4,294,967,296 possible values. Each one of these values increments after the 16-bit frame IV exhausts (which is every 65 seconds), so the entire 48-bit IV exhausts after 65 seconds * 4,294,967,296, about 8852 years. Unless the administrator forces a reauthentication, a rekey is not realistically required to avoid IV collisions.

This algorithm strengthens WEP to the point that most known attacks are mitigated without having to replace existing hardware. It is important to note that this algorithm (and TKIP as a whole) is designed to patch the holes in WEP and 802.11 authentication. It offers weak algorithms in lieu of hardware replacement. The next generation of 802.11 equipment should support TKIP, but WEP/TKIP should be phased out in favor of an algorithm with a higher degree of cryptographic strength, such as Advanced Encryption Standard (AES) (discussed later).

Data Integrity

The MIC is a feature used to augment the ineffective ICV of the 802.11 standard. The MIC solves vulnerabilities such as the frame tampering/bit flipping attacks discussed earlier in the chapter. The IEEE has proposed a specific algorithm, known as *Michael*, to augment the ICV function in the encryption of 802.11 data frames.

The MIC has a unique key that differs from the key used to encrypt data frames. This unique key is mixed with the destination MAC address and the source MAC address from the frame as well as the entire unencrypted data payload portion of the frame. Figure 4-24 illustrates the Michael MIC algorithm.

Figure 4-24 *The Michael MIC Algorithm*

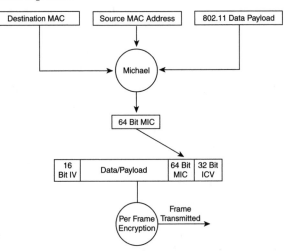

The entire TKIP encryption mechanism is detailed in the following steps:

1 The per-frame keying algorithm derives a per-frame key (see Figure 4-25).

2 The MIC algorithm generates a MIC for the entire frame.

3 The frame is fragmented according to MAC settings for fragmentation.

4 The per-frame key encrypts the frame fragments.

5 The encrypted fragments are transmitted.

Figure 4-25 *The TKIP Encryption Process*

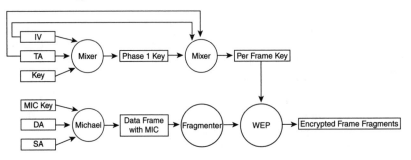

Similar to the TKIP encryption process (see Figure 4-26), the following steps detail the TKIP decryption process:

1 The phase 1 key is precomputed.

2 The phase 2 per-frame key is calculated based on the IV from the incoming WEP frame fragment.

3 If the IV arrives out of order, the frame is discarded.

4 The frame fragment is decrypted and the ICV check is done.

5 If the ICV fails, the frame is discarded.

6 The decrypted frame fragments are reassembled into the original data frame.

7 The receiver calculates the MIC value and compares it to what is in the MIC field of the frame.

8 If the values match, the frame is processed by the receiver.

9 If the values do not match, the frame has a MIC failure and the receiver initiates MIC countermeasures.

Figure 4-26 *The TKIP Decryption Process*

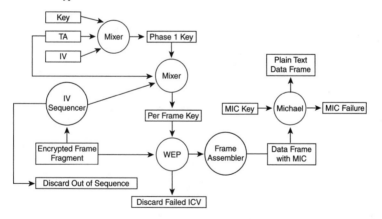

The MIC countermeasures consist of the following tasks performed by the receiver:

1 The receiver deletes the existing keys for the association.

2 The receiver logs the issue as a security-relevant matter.

3 The associated client from which the faulty frame was received cannot associate and authenticate for a period of 60 seconds to slow down the attacker.

4 If the client received the faulty frame, the client drops any non-802.1X frames.

5 The client also requests a new key.

The per-frame keying and MIC discussion has mentioned two primary keys: the encryption key and the MIC key. No discussion covered how the keys are generated or sent from client to AP and vice versa. The next section deals with proposed 802.11 key management.

Enhanced Key Management

802.1X and EAP authentication algorithms can provide the RADIUS server and client with dynamic, user-based keys. But the key that is derived during authentication is not the key used for frame encryption or for message integrity. In 802.11i and WPA, it is known as the *master key*, used to derive these other keys. Figure 4-27 depicts the 802.11 unicast key hierarchy.

Figure 4-27 *802.11 Unicast Key Hierarchy*

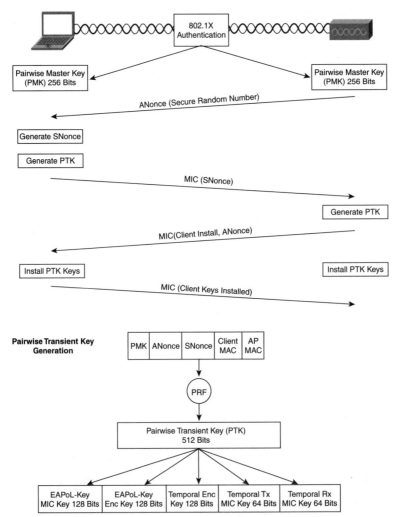

The mechanism for generating the encryption keys is known as the *four-way handshake*. The following steps summarize the four-way handshake:

1 The client and AP install the dynamic key (known as the pairwise master key or PMK) derived from 802.1X authentication.

2 The AP sends the client a secure random number, known as the authenticator nonce (ANonce) via an 802.1X EAPoL-Key message.

3 The client locally generates a secure random number, known as the supplicant nonce (SNonce).

4 The client generates the pairwise transient key (PTK) by combining the PMK, SNonce, ANonce, Client MAC, AP MAC, and an initialize string. The MAC addresses are ordered, with the low-order MAC preceding the high-order MAC. This process ensures that the client and AP order the MACs in the same manner.

5 The combined value is run through a pseudo random function (PRF) to generate a 512-bit PTK.

6 The client sends the SNonce it generated in Step 3 to the AP via an 802.1X EAPoL-Key message, protected with the EAPoL-Key MIC key.

7 The AP uses the SNonce to calculate the PTK in the same manner as the client.

8 The AP uses the derived EAPoL-Key MIC key to validate the integrity of the client's message.

9 The AP sends an EAPoL-Key message indicating that the client should install the PTK and its ANonce, protected with the EAPoL-Key MIC Key. This step allows the client to validate that the ANonce it received in Step 2 is valid.

10 The client sends an EAPoL-Key message protected with the EAPoL-Key MIC key, indicating the keys have been installed.

The PMK and PTK derive keys are unicast in nature. They only encrypt and decrypt unicast frames, and they are assigned to a single user. Broadcast frames require a separate key hierarchy because using the unicast keys would dramatically increase network traffic. The AP (the only entity in a BSS that can send broadcast or multicast traffic) would have to send the same broadcast or multicast frame to each user encrypted with the appropriate per-frame keys.

Broadcast and multicast frames use the group key hierarchy. The group master key (GMK) is at the top of the hierarchy and is derived on the AP. GMK derivation is based on a PRF that outputs a 256-bit GMK. The inputs into the PRF-256 are a cryptographically secure random number (or nonce), a text string, the MAC address of the AP, and the time in network time protocol (NTP) format. Figure 4-28 illustrates the group key hierarchy.

Figure 4-28 *The Group Key Hierarchy*

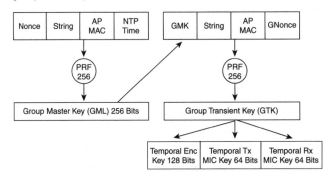

The GMK, a text string, the AP MAC address, and the GNonce (a value taken from the AP key counter) are concatenated and processed via a PRF, which outputs a 256-bit group transient key (GTK). The GTK is divided into a 128-bit broadcast/multicast encryption key, a 64-bit transmit MIC key, and a 64-bit MIC receive key. The keys encrypt and decrypt broadcast and multicast frames in exactly the same manner as unicast keys derived from the PMK.

The client is updated with the group encryption keys via an EAPoL-Key message. The AP sends the client the EAPoL message encrypted with the client's unicast encryption key. The group keys are purged and regenerated every time a station disassociates or deauthenticates the BSS. Also, if a MIC failure occurs, one of the countermeasures is to purge all the keys for the impacted receiver, and this purge includes the group keys.

AES Encryption

WEP encryption and 802.11 authentication are known to be weak. The IEEE and WPA are enhancing WEP with TKIP and providing robust authentication options with 802.1X to make 802.11-based WLANs secure. At the same time, the IEEE is also looking to stronger encryption mechanisms. The IEEE has adopted the AES to the data-privacy section of the proposed 802.11i standard. WPA does not include support for AES encryption. Later versions of WPA are likely to be released to align with 802.11i for interoperable AES encryption support.

The AES is the next generation encryption function approved by the National Institute of Standards and Technology (NIST). NIST solicited the cryptography community for new encryption algorithms. The algorithms had to be fully disclosed and available royalty free. Candidates were judged on cryptographic strength as well as practical implementation. The finalist, and the adopted method, is also known as the Rijndael algorithm. Like most ciphers, AES requires a feedback mode to avoid the risks associated with ECB mode. The IEEE has designed a mode for AES tailored to the needs of WLANs. The mode is known as Cipher Block Chaining Counter Mode (CBC-CTR) with Cipher Block Chaining

Message Authenticity Check (CBC-MAC), collectively known as AES-CCM. CCM mode is the combination of CBC-CTR encryption mode and the CBC-MAC message authenticity algorithm. The functions are combined to provide encryption and message integrity in one solution.

CBC-CTR encryption operates by using a counter to augment the key stream. The counter increments by 1 after encrypting each block. This process provides a unique key stream for each block. The plaintext frame is fragmented into 16-byte blocks. As each block is encrypted, the counter increments by 1, until all blocks are encrypted. The counter resets for each new frame.

CBC-MAC operates by using the result of CBC encryption over frame length, destination address, source address, and data. The resulting 128-bit output is truncated to 64 bits for use in the transmitted frame.

AES-CCM uses cryptographically known functions but has the overhead of requiring two operations for encryption and message integrity. This process is computationally expensive and adds a significant amount of overhead to the encryption process.

Summary

802.11 authentication and encryption as defined in the 1997 standard is deeply flawed. The authentication can be broken, as can the WEP encryption, in little time. TKIP promises to fix WEP and authentication in the short term, and 802.1X and AES promise to be a long-term answer to wireless security.

This chapter gave you insight into how to secure a WLAN and remove the obscurity surrounding wireless security in general. The key to deploying WLANs is deploy them as securely as possible while providing the best possible user experience.

This chapter covers the following topics:

- Characteristics of roaming
- Layer 2 roaming
- Layer 3 roaming and an introduction to Mobile IP

CHAPTER 5

Mobility

This book covers the major components of 802.11 wireless LANs (WLANs). Fundamental concepts such as medium access mechanisms, frame formats, security, and the physical interfaces build the foundation for understanding more advanced and practical concepts.

In keeping with this theme, this chapter covers mobility. *Mobility* is the quality of being capable of movement or moving readily from place to place. 802.11 WLAN devices provide this kind of untethered freedom. But there's more to mobility than the lack of a network cable. Understanding how mobility is implemented in 802.11 arms you with the knowledge you need to support or facilitate mobile applications. Many terms describe mobility, but this chapter uses the terms *mobility* and *roaming* to describe the act of moving between access points (APs).

Characteristics of Roaming

Defining or characterizing the behavior of roaming stations involves two forms:

- Seamless roaming
- Nomadic roaming

Seamless roaming is best analogized to a cellular phone call. For example, suppose you are using your cellular phone as you drive your car on the freeway. A typical global system for mobile (GSM) communications or time-division multiple access (TDMA) cell provides a few miles of coverage area, so it is safe to assume that you are roaming between cellular base stations as you drive. Yet as you roam, you do not hear any degradation to the voice call (that is what the cellular providers keep telling us). There is no noticeable period of network unavailability because of roaming. This type of roaming is deemed *seamless* because the network application requires constant network connectivity during the roaming process.

Nomadic roaming is different from seamless roaming. *Nomadic roaming* is best described as the use of an 802.11-enabled laptop in an office environment. As an example, suppose a user of this laptop has network connectivity while seated at his desk and maintains connectivity to a single AP. When the user decides to roam, he undocks his laptop and walks over to a conference room. Once in the conference room, he resumes his work. In the background, the 802.11 client has roamed from the AP near the user's desk to an AP near the conference room. This type of roaming is deemed *nomadic* because the user is not using network services when he roams, but only when he reach his destination.

What happens to application sessions during roaming? Many factors influence the answer to this question. Consider the following:

- The nature of roaming in 802.11.

- The operation of the application. Is the application connection-oriented or connectionless?

- The roaming domain. Does roaming occur with a single subnet or across multiple subnets?

- Roaming duration. How long does the roaming process take?

The Nature of Roaming in 802.11

802.11 roaming is known as "break before make," referring to the requirement that a station serves its association with one AP before creating an association with a new one. This process might seem unintuitive because it introduces the possibility for data loss during roaming, but it facilitates a simpler MAC protocol and radio.

If 802.11 were "make before break," meaning a station could associate to a new AP before disassociating from the old AP, you would need safeguards in the MAC to ensure a loop-free topology. A station connected to the same Layer 2 broadcast domain via simultaneous network connections has the potential to trigger broadcast storms. A "make before break" architecture would necessitate an algorithm such as 802.1D spanning tree to resolve any potential loops, adding overhead to the MAC protocol. In addition, the client radio would have to be capable of listening and communicating on more than one channel at a time, increasing the complexity of the radio (and adding to the overall cost of the devices).

Operation of the Application

The way the application operates directly correlates to its resilience during the roaming process. Connection-oriented applications, such as those that are TCP-based, are more tolerant to packet loss incurred during roams because TCP is a reliable and connection-oriented protocol. TCP requires positive acknowledgments, just as the 802.11 MAC does. This requirement allows any 802.11 data lost during the roaming process to be retransmitted by TCP, as the upper-layer protocol.

Although TCP provides a tidy solution for applications running on 802.11 WLANs, some applications rely on User Datagram Protocol (UDP) as the Layer 4 transport protocol of choice. UDP is a low-overhead, connectionless protocol. Applications such as Voice over IP (VoIP) and video use UDP packets. The retransmission capability that TCP offers does little to enhance packet loss for VoIP applications. Retransmitting VoIP packets proves more annoying to the user than useful. As a result, the data-loss roaming might cause a noticeable impact to UDP-based applications.

Roaming Domain

Chapter 1, "Ethernet Technologies," defines a *broadcast domain* as a network that connects devices that are capable of sending and receiving broadcast frames to and from one another. This domain is also referred to as a *Layer 2 network*. The concept holds true for 802.11 as well. APs that are in the same broadcast domain and configured with the same service set identifier (SSID) are said to be in the same roaming domain. Recall from Chapter 2, "802.11 Wireless LANs," that extended service set (ESS) is similarly defined as multiple basic service sets (BSSs) that communicate via the distribution service (wired network). Therefore, a roaming domain can also be referred to as an ESS. Why are 802.11 devices limited to a Layer 2 network for roaming? What about roaming between Layer 3 subnets? Remember that 802.11 is a Layer 1 physical interface and Layer 2 data link layer technology. The 802.11 MAC protocol is Layer 3 unaware. That is not to say that Layer 3 roaming is impossible because it is not. It means that Layer 2 roaming is natively supported in 802.11 devices, and some upper-layer solution is required for Layer 3 roaming.

The distinction between whether a device roams within a roaming domain or between roaming domains has a large impact on application sessions. Figure 5-1 depicts a Layer 2 roaming domain. The roaming user can maintain application connectivity within the roaming domain and as long as its Layer 3 network address is maintained (does not change).

Figure 5-1   *Roaming in a Layer 2 Roaming Domain*

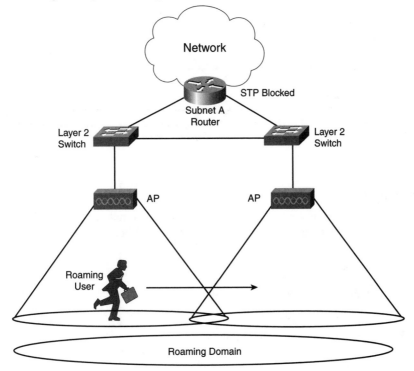

Figure 5-2 illustrates roaming across roaming domains. The roaming user is roaming from an AP on Subnet A to an AP on Subnet B. As a result, the Layer 3 network address must change to maintain Layer 3 connectivity on Subnet B. As the Layer 3 address changes, the station drops all application sessions. This scenario is described later in this chapter in the section, "Mobile IP Overview."

Figure 5-2   *Roaming Across Roaming Domains*

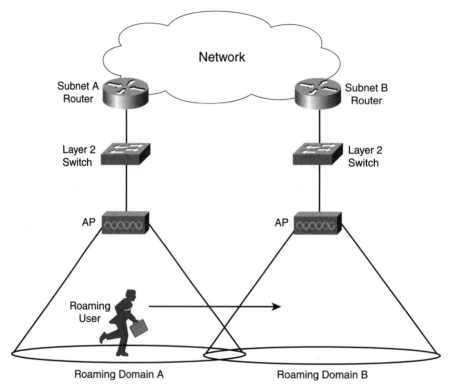

Roaming Duration

Roaming duration is the time it takes for roaming to complete. Roaming is essentially the association process that is described in Chapter 2; it depends on the duration of the following:

- The probing process
- The 802.11 authentication process
- The 802.11 association process
- The 802.1X authentication process

The cumulative duration of these processes equates to the roaming duration. Some applications, such as VoIP, are extremely delay-sensitive and cannot tolerate large roaming durations.

Layer 2 Roaming

Now that you understand some of the characteristics of roaming, the technical discussion of how Layer 2 roaming operates can begin. To place some perspective on roaming, a sequence of events must transpire:

- **The client must decide to roam**—Roaming algorithms are vendor-specific (and proprietary) and rely on factors such as signal strength, frame acknowledgment, missed beacons, and so on.

- **The client must decide where to roam**—The client must figure out which AP to roam to. It can do so by scanning the medium for APs either before the decision to roam, which is a process called *preemptive AP discovery*, or after the decision to roam, which is a process called *roam-time AP discovery*.

- **The client initiates a roam**—The client uses 802.11 reassociation frames to associate to a new AP.

- **The client can resume existing application sessions.**

Roaming Algorithms

The mechanism to determine when to roam is not defined by the IEEE 802.11 specification and is, therefore, left to vendors to implement. Although this issue posed an interoperability challenge early on with the first 802.11 products, vendors work together today to ensure basic interoperability. The fact that the algorithms are left to vendor implementation provide vendors an opportunity to differentiate themselves by creating new and better performing algorithms than their competitors. Roaming algorithms become a vendor's "secret sauce," and as a result are kept confidential.

It is safe to assume that issues such as signal strength, retry counters, missed beacons, and other MAC layer concepts discussed in Chapter 2 are included in the algorithms. For example, recall from Chapter 2 the discussion about distributed coordination function (DCF) operation. The binary exponential backoff algorithm for medium access incremented the frame-retry counter if the frame could not be transmitted after a number of attempts. This process alerts the client that it has moved out of range of the AP. In this case, the roaming algorithm monitors the frame-retry counter to help with decision making.

Also, roaming algorithms must balance between fast roam time and client stability. For example, an extremely sensitive roaming algorithm might not tolerate a missed beacon or missed acknowledgment frame. The algorithm might view these occurrences as degradation in signal and initiate a roam. But it is normal for such occurrences in a BSS, and as a result, a stationary station might roam, even though it is stationary. Although roaming would be expeditious, the result is degraded network throughput for the user.

Determining Where to Roam

Finding an AP to roam to is another mechanism that is vendor-specific. In general, there are two mechanisms for finding APs:

- Preemptive AP discovery
- Roam-time AP discovery

Each mechanism can employ one or both of the following mechanisms:

- **Active scanning**—The client actively searches for an AP. This process usually involves the client sending probe requests on each channel it is configured to use (channels 1 to 11 in North America) and waiting for probe responses from APs. The client then determines which AP is the ideal one to roam to.

- **Passive scanning**—The client does not transmit any frames but rather listens for beacon frames on each channel. The client continues to change channels at a set interval, just as with active scanning, but the client does not send probe requests.

Active scanning is the most thorough mechanism used to find APs because it actively sends out 802.11 probes across all channels to find an AP. It requires the client to dwell on a particular channel for a set length of time, roughly 10 to 20 milliseconds (ms) depending on the vendor, waiting for the probe response.

With passive scanning, the client iterates through the channels slower than active scanning because it is listening for beacons that are sent out by APs at a set rate (usually 10 beacons per second). The client must dwell on each channel for a longer time duration to make sure it receives beacons from as many APs as possible for the given channel. The client looks for different information elements such as SSID, supported rates, and vendor proprietary elements to find an AP. Although it can be a faster mechanism to scan the medium, some elements are not transmitted, depending on AP configuration. For example, an administrator might block the SSID name in the SSID IE from being transmitted in beacons, so the passive scanning client is unable to determine whether the AP is in the same roaming domain.

There is no ideal technique for scanning. Passive scanning has the benefit of not requiring the client to transmit probe requests but runs the risk of potentially missing an AP because it might not receive a beacon during the scanning duration. Active scanning has the benefit of actively seeking out APs to associate to but requires the client to actively transmit probes. Depending on the implementation for the 802.11 client, one might be better suited than the other. For example, many embedded systems use passive scanning as the preferred method, whereas 802.11 Voice over IP (VoIP) phones and PC client cards rely on active scanning.

Preemptive AP Discovery

Preemptive roaming is the function that provides the client the ability to roam to a predetermined AP after the client has made the decision to roam. This process allows for minimal total roaming time, which reduces application impact from roaming. Preemptive roaming does not come without a penalty, however.

For the client to predetermine which AP to roam to, the client must scan for APs during normal nonroaming periods. When the client is scanning, the client must change channels to either listen for other APs or to actively probe. This change creates two potential problems for the client that can impact the application, listed in the following and illustrated in Figure 5-3:

- **The client cannot receive data from the currently associated AP while it is channel scanning (active or passive)**—If the AP sends data to the client while the client is channel scanning (meaning the client is on a different channel from the AP), the client will miss the data, requiring retransmission by the AP.

- **The client application might experience throughput degradation**—The client is unable to transmit data while channel scanning (active or passive), so any applications running on the client can experience throughput degradation.

A unique opportunity exists for power-save clients that allow them to use preemptive roaming without the two problems. Consider this scenario: A client is a power-save client. The client is capable of transitioning into low-power mode as needed. The client can signal to the AP that it is going into power-save mode, but instead of immediately transitioning to low-power mode, the client can channel scan (either actively or passively) all or a select number of channels and look for new APs. The current AP queues frames destined for the client until the client "wakes up," so the client does not experience data loss due to channel scanning. The client can also queue frames targeted for transmission until channel scanning is complete, eliminating data loss in that respect as well.

This solution does reduce the effectiveness of a power-save operation, because the client radio is active during channel scanning instead of in low-power mode, and client applications might experience some delay because frames are queued in a transmit queue.

Preemptive AP discovery can be undermined by a fast-moving client. A client might move at a rate where the predetermined AP is no longer the ideal AP to roam to, causing an increase in the frequency of roaming decisions and an overall degradation in application throughput.

Roam-Time AP Discovery

The other option for AP discovery is to look for an AP after the decision to roam has been made. This process is similar to the process a client goes through on initiation power up, except that the association message the client sends to the new AP is actually a reassociation frame.

Figure 5-3 *Preemptive AP Discovery*

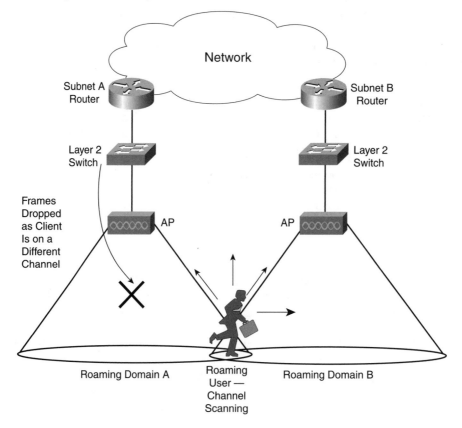

Roam-time AP discovery does not have the overhead of preemptive roaming during non-roaming times, but because the client does not know which AP to reassociate to, there can be a larger time penalty during the roaming process. Figure 5-4 shows roam-time AP discovery.

Figure 5-4   *Roam-Time AP Discovery*

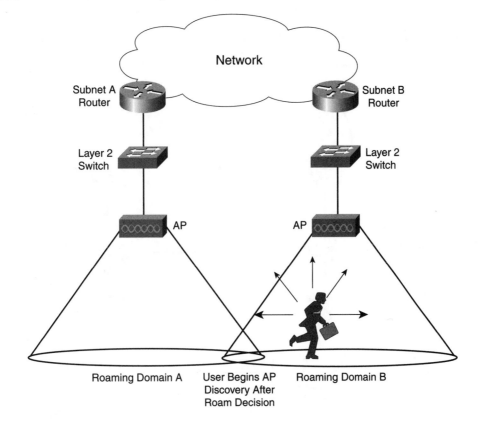

Layer 2 Roaming Process

The act of roaming includes more processes than just finding a new AP to communicate with. The following list includes some of the tasks for Layer 2 roaming:

1 The previous AP must determine that the client has roamed away from it.

2 The previous AP should buffer data destined for the roaming client.*

3 The new AP should indicate to the previous AP that the client has successfully roamed. This step usually happens via a unicast or multicast packet from the old AP to the new AP with the source MAC address set to the MAC of the roaming client.*

4 The previous AP should send the buffered data to the new AP.

5 The previous AP must determine that the client has roamed away from it.

6 The AP must update MAC address tables on infrastructure switches to prevent the loss of data to the roaming client.

* Tasks are not mandatory because they are not specified in the 802.11 standard.

Figure 5-5 and Figure 5-6 depict a client roaming between two APs in the same roaming domain. The APs are connected to different Layer 2 switches.

Figure 5-5   *An Application Sending Data to a Roaming Station*

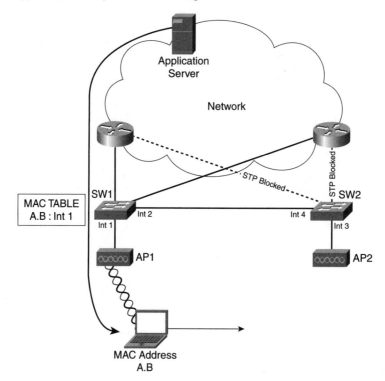

In Figure 5-5, the application server is sending data to the client with a MAC address of A.B. The Layer 3 switch (L3) forwards the frame with a destination MAC address A.B to SW1 via its interface 1 (Int 1). SW1 checks its forwarding table and forwards the frame to AP1.

In Figure 5-6, the client has roamed to AP2 from AP1, but AP1 does not know that the client has roamed away. The application server continues to send frames to L3, and L3 in turn forwards the frames via its Int 1 to SW1 and AP1. AP1 attempts to send the frames to the client but ends up dropping the frame because the client does not respond. AP2 resolves this situation by sending a packet to AP1 with the source MAC address set to the MAC address of the roaming client station, in this case, A.B. Figure 5-7 illustrates how the AP updates the switches' forwarding tables.

Figure 5-6   *Data Loss After a Layer 2 Roam*

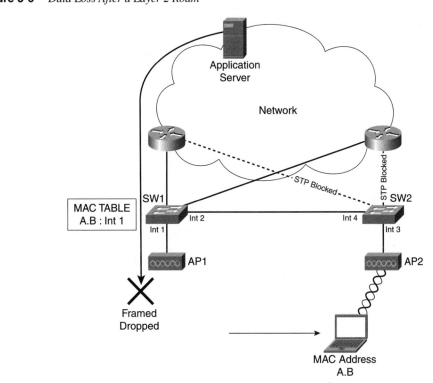

AP2 sends a frame with the source MAC address of the client to AP1. SW2 updates its forwarding table because it has received a new MAC address on an ingress port. The source address of the frame (the MAC address of the client) is added to the forwarding table and mapped to the ingress interface (i.e., MAC address A.B is mapped to Int 3). The L3 switch (L3) updates its forwarding table to indicate the destination is now accessible via interface 0 (Int 0). The frame is forwarded to SW1, and SW1 updates its forwarding table in the same manner. Note that SW1 purges the client's MAC entry in the forwarding table. Any inbound frames for the client are now correctly forwarded via SW2 and AP2.

Because the IEEE and the 802.11 standard do not address AP-to-AP communications via the distribution system (the wired interfaces in this case), AP vendors are left to implement such mechanisms on their own. Depending on the vendor, the mechanism can send a unicast or multicast frame with the source MAC of the client and the destination MAC of the previous AP, informing the previous AP the client has roamed and updating the switch MAC address tables in the process.

Figure 5-7 *Updating the MAC Address Tables After a Roam*

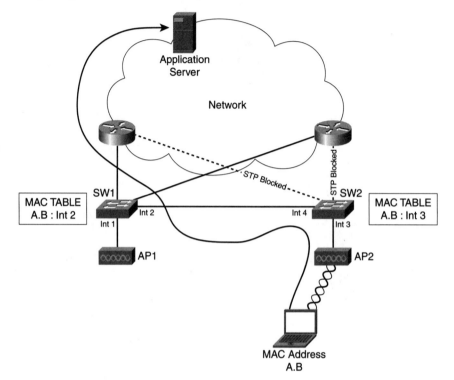

Layer 3 Roaming

Layer 3 mobility is a superset of Layer 2 mobility. An 802.11 client must perform a Layer 2 roam, including AP discovery, before it can begin a Layer 3 roam. This section focuses on issues surrounding Layer 3 roaming, specifically with the IP Protocol and Mobile IP extensions (RFC 2002). It covers the following topics:

- Roaming between roaming domains
- A Mobile IP overview

Roaming Between Roaming Domains

As previously discussed, a roaming domain is defined as APs that are in the same broadcast domain and configured with the same SSID. Stated another way, a client can only roam between APs in the same VLAN and with the same SSID. As WLAN deployments expand within an organization, roaming domains might need to scale beyond a single Layer 2 VLAN.

Consider the following scenario: Company A has a four-story building in which it has deployed a WLAN. The initial deployment was small, and the WLAN was a single Class C subnet for the entire building. This setup created a roaming domain across all four floors of the building. As time progressed, the number of users increased to the point that the subnet is full, and performance is degrading because of increased broadcast traffic.

Company A decides to follow its desktop subnet model and use a single subnet per floor for the WLAN. This setup introduces complications because now the roaming domains are restricted to a floor, not the entire building as before. With the new subnet model in place, application persistence when roaming across floors is lost. The application most impacted is Company A's wireless VoIP devices. As users move between the floors (and subnets) on their wireless phones, they drop their calls when they roam. Figure 5-8 illustrates this scenario. In this figure, an 802.11 VoIP phone is connected to a wired VoIP phone. As the user roams from AP1 on Subnet 10 to AP2 on Subnet 20, the session drops because the roaming user is now on a different subnet.

Figure 5-8   *Roaming Between Subnets*

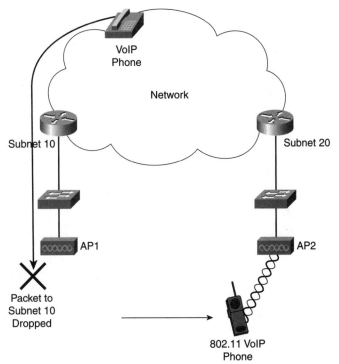

Mobile IP Overview

The scenario described for Company A is common. Many applications require persistent connections and drop their sessions as a result of inter-VLAN roaming. To provide session persistence, you need a mechanism to allow a station to maintain the same Layer 3 address while roaming throughout a multi-VLAN network. Mobile IP provides such a mechanism, and it is the standards-based, vendor-interoperable solution to Layer 3 roaming for WLANs.

A Mobile IP–enabled network has these key components:

- **Mobile node (MN)**—The MN is the roaming station.
- **Home agent (HA)**—The HA exists on routers or Layer 3 switches and ensures that a roaming MN receives its IP packets.
- **Foreign agent (FA)**—The FA exists on router or Layer 3 switches and aids the MN notifying the HA of the new MN location by receiving packets from the HA destined for the MN.
- **Care-of address (CoA)**—The CoA is a locally attached router that receives packets sent by the HA, destined for the MN.
- **Co-located care-of address (CCoA)**—A CoA that exists on the mobile node itself.

Roaming in a Mobile IP–aware network involves the following steps:

1 A station is on its home subnet if the station's IP address belongs to the subnet of the HA.

2 As the MN roams to a foreign subnet, the MN detects the presence of the FA and registers with the FA or with the MN CCoA.

3 The FA or MN CCoA communicates with the HA and establishes a tunnel between the HA and a CoA for the MN.

4 Packets destined to the MN are sent to the HA (via normal IP routing), as shown in Figure 5-9.

5 The HA forwards the packets via the tunnel to the MN.

6 Any packets the MN transmits are sent via the FA as if the MN were local on the subnet, as shown in Figure 5-10. (A "reverse tunnel" mode is available when the edge routers use ingress packet filtering.)

This summary provides a brief overview of the three main phases of Mobile IP:

- Agent discovery
- Registration
- Tunneling

The following sections highlight each phase.

Figure 5-9   *Packet Transmission to a Roaming MN*

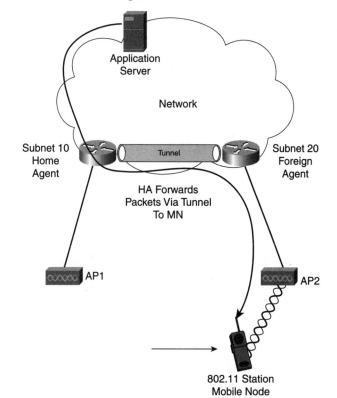

Agent Discovery

A roaming MN must determine that it is on a foreign subnet in a timely manner to minimize delay to running applications. HAs and FAs advertise their services by using the Internet Control Message Protocol (ICMP) Router Discovery Protocol (collectively known as IRDP) messages to send agent advertisements. As the MN establishes connectivity to the subnet it roams to, it listens for the periodic IRDP packets. The packets are sent to either the all-host multicast address (224.0.0.1) or the limited broadcast address (255.255.255.255). The IRDP packets are not sent to the subnet-specific broadcast address because the MN might not be aware of the subnet it has roamed to. In addition to periodic agent advertisements, an MN can solicit for advertisements after it detects that its interface has changed.

Figure 5-10 *Packet Transmission from a Roaming MN*

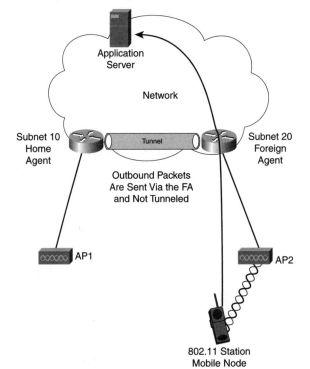

The agent advertisement contains two fields that allow the MN to determine whether it has roamed to a new subnet:

- The lifetime field from the agent advertisement
- The prefix-length extension

The lifetime field provides a time value that an agent advertisement is valid for. If no new advertisement has been received before the lifetime reaches zero, the MN should attempt to discover a new agent.

The prefix-length extension indicates the network address value of the advertising agent. A change in prefix length (indicating a change in network address or subnet) shows the MN it should attempt to discover a new agent.

Upon determining it is on a foreign subnet, the MN gleans the CoA from the agent advertisement. The CoA can take two forms:

- The address of the FA.
- CCoA (Note that the CCoA is not advertised by the FA, but it is probably acquired by the MN as a Dynamic Host Configuration Protocol [DHCP] option.)

A CoA pointing to the FA forces the FA (usually the subnet router) to handle Mobile IP administration for all foreign MNs on the subnet in addition to handling packet-forwarding duties. The benefit to this situation is that only a single tunnel is required from the HA to each unique FA.

A CoA that is temporarily assigned to the MN places the Mobile IP administrative burden on the MN and forces the HA to establish a unique tunnel to each roaming MN. Figure 5-11 contrasts these two methods.

Figure 5-11 *Contrast Between MN and CoA*

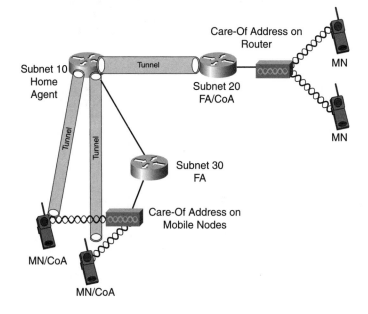

MN Registration

After the MN establishes a CoA and local mobility agent (either HA or FA), the registration process begins. The registration process securely creates a mobility binding on the FA and HA to facilitate the forwarding of packets to the MN. The registration process is as follows and is illustrated in Figure 5-11:

1 The MN sends a registration request to the FA. If the MN has a CCoA, this step is skipped.

2 The FA processes the registration request and forwards the request to the HA.

3 The HA accepts or declines the registration and sends a registration reply to the FA.

4 The FA processes the registration reply and relays it to the MN.

Figure 5-12 *The Mobile IP Registration Process*

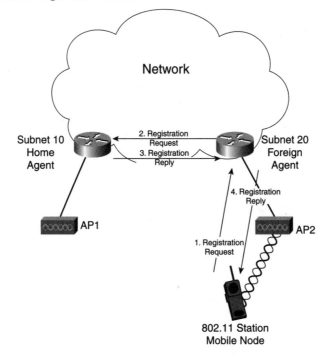

The registration request contains the following fields:

- **Simultaneous bindings**—The MN can request that the HA retain bindings to prior CoAs.

- **Broadcast packets**—The MN can request that the HA forward any broadcast packets which it receives on the home subnet.

- **Decapsulation by MN**—The MN may request to decapsulate tunneled packets itself. This option is only selected when the MN has a CCoA.

- **Minimal encapsulation**—The MN can request that the HA use minimal encapsulation to tunnel packets (RFC 2004).

- **Generic Routing Encapsulation (GRE)**—The MN can request that the HA use GRE encapsulation to tunnel packets.

- **Reverse tunneling**—The MN can request that its egress packets be tunneled back to the HA to forward to the destination.

- **Lifetime**—This field indicates the remaining time before the registration expires.

- **Home address**—This field indicates the IP address of the MN.

- **HA**—This field is the IP address of the MN's HA.
- **CoA**—This field is the IP address of the CoA and the termination point of the tunnel.
- **Identification**—This field is a 64-bit nonce used for sequencing registration requests and replies and preventing replay attacks on the registration packets.
- **Extensions**—A number of extensions are available yet not required for registration.

The registration reply contains the following fields:

- **Code**—This field is the result of the registration request. Table 5-1 contains the result values for this field.
- **Lifetime**—This field is the number of seconds remaining before the registration expires.
- **Home address**—This field is the IP address of the MN.
- **HA**—This field is the IP address of the HA.
- **Identification**—The contents of the field vary depending on the message-authentication mechanism used to process the registration request.
- **Extensions**—A number of extensions are available but not required for registration.

Table 5-1   *Registration Code Field Values*

Code Value	Source	Explanation
0	HA	Registration accepted
1	HA	Registration accepted, but simultaneous bindings not accepted
64	FA	Reason unspecified
65	FA	Administratively prohibited
66	FA	Insufficient resources
67	FA	MN failed authentication
68	FA	HA failed authentication
69	FA	Requested lifetime too long
70	FA	Poorly formed request
71	FA	Poorly formed reply
72	FA	Requested encapsulation unavailable
73	FA	Reserved and unavailable
77	FA	Invalid CoA
78	FA	Registration timeout
80	FA	Home network unreachable (ICMP error received)
81	FA	HA host unreachable (ICMP error received)

continues

Table 5-1 *Registration Code Field Values (Continued)*

Code Value	Source	Explanation
82	FA	HA port unreachable (ICMP error received)
88	FA	HA unreachable (other ICMP error received)
128	HA	Reason unspecified
129	HA	Administratively prohibited
130	HA	Insufficient resources
131	HA	MN failed authentication
132	HA	FA failed authentication
133	HA	Registration identification mismatch
134	HA	Poorly formed request
135	HA	Too many simultaneous mobility bindings
136	HA	Unknown HA address

The Mobile IP standard requires that some keyed message-authentication mechanism protect the registration messages between the MN and the HA (messages between the FA and HA can be authenticated but usually are not) and optionally allows messages between the MN and FA to also be protected. By default, the Hashed Message Authentication Codes with Message Digest version 5 (HMAC-MD5) is enabled. The HA must share a secret value with the MN, either statically configured or centrally stored on an authentication, authorization, and accounting (AAA) server. Figure 5-13 illustrates how the message authentication process is calculated.

Figure 5-13 *Securing Registration Messages*

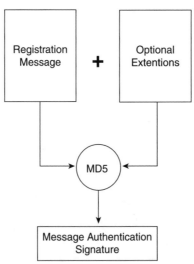

Other security issues might impact how you deploy Mobile IP in your network. If source address filtering checks (RFC 2827) are enabled on FA routers, the forwarding of packets from the MN via the FA cannot occur. The FA ingress interface can filter for only valid source IP addresses to prevent unauthorized devices from penetrating the network. This filtering poses an issue for MNs because they transmit packets with their home-network IP address, and as a result, all transmitted frames are dropped at the FA router.

To circumvent this issue, you must enable reverse tunneling. Reverse tunneling adds slightly to the administrative overhead for the CoA and HA but allows Mobile IP operation in a secured network.

Tunneling

Tunneling is synonymous with encapsulation. Tunneling allows two disparate networks to connect directly to one another when they normally would not or when they are physically disjointed. This capability is key for Mobile IP because tunneling is what allows the HA to bypass normal routing rules and forward packets to the MN.

A tunnel requires two endpoints: an entry point and an exit point. The entry point encapsulates the tunneled packets within another IP header. The new IP header might include some other parameters, but the basic function of the encapsulation header is to direct the packet to the tunnel endpoint. A packet received by the tunnel endpoint is stripped of the encapsulation header and forwarded to the MN. Figure 5-14 illustrates the packet-tunneling process.

Figure 5-14 *IP Packet Encapsulation*

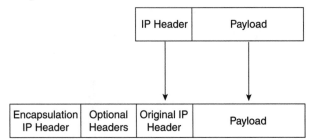

Mobile IP supports a few tunneling mechanisms:

- IP in IP encapsulation
- Minimal encapsulation
- GRE

IP in IP encapsulation is the only mandatory tunneling type in the Mobile IP specification, but the use of GRE and minimal encapsulation is common because each has slightly different impacts on the network that you can use to determine which best suits your requirements.

Some networks implement RFC 2827 filtering on their distribution router interfaces that only allow packets from a valid source network through. For example, a router interface has network 10.0.0.0/24 (IPs 10.0.0.1 through 10.0.0.254). An MN with a home address on 192.168.10.1 would not be able to send packets across the router because 192.168.10.1 is not in the 10.0.0.0/24 subnet. For the MN to send packets in this case, the FA must forward the packets back to the home subnet via the HA. Figure 5-15 illustrates this scenario. Reverse tunneling does incur additional packet overhead and application latency, but it facilitates the use of RFC 2827 filtering to maintain network security.

Figure 5-15 *Reverse Tunneling*

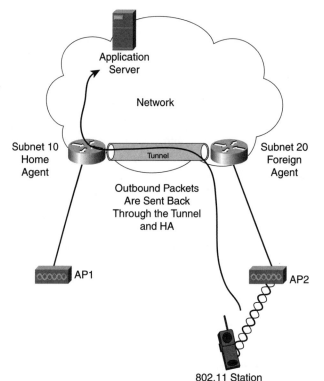

Summary

802.11 WLANs facilitate untethered network mobility, but to properly deploy a mobility-enabled WLAN, you must understand the nature of your applications that leverage your WLAN. Many WLAN deployments begin as coverage-oriented (usually a high user to AP ratio), where just providing network connectivity is the primary goal. As new applications emerge and are implemented, such as VoIP over 802.11, changes to the WLAN deployment are required. Coverage-oriented deployments must move to capacity-oriented deployments (low user to AP ratio, but more APs in the coverage area). The move to capacity-oriented WLANs requires most enterprise deployments to at least consider roaming across roaming domains and the impact to client stations that is imposed.

CHAPTER 6

QoS for 802.11 Wireless LANs—802.11e

The IEEE 802.11 working group chartered the 802.11e task group with the responsibility of enhancing the 802.11 MAC to include bidirectional quality of service (QoS) to support latency-sensitive applications such as voice and video. Also, new breeds of consumer electronics are looking to 802.11 as a wire replacement. Products such as cable and satellite receivers might one day send high-definition TV (HDTV) signals via 802.11 to TVs. DVDs and digital-video recorders might do the same. Imagine this scenario in a home environment where 802.11 is used for home networking as well as for wire replacement from the DVD player and satellite receiver to the TV. The new applications for 802.11 require an effective QoS mechanism to ensure that their latency-sensitive audio/visual data has priority over data such as Internet e-mail and web browsing. It would be irritating to have the movie you are watching interrupted because of e-mail or web traffic!

This chapter addresses how the IEEE 802.11 working group is addressing the requirement for QoS by reviewing the challenges for effective QoS in 802.11 networks, examining the QoS mechanisms in the draft text of the 802.11e draft standard, and discussing admission control.

Challenges for QoS in 802.11 Networks

802.11 networks work well for low-bandwidth, latency-*insensitive* data applications. Barcode scanners, personal digital assistants (PDAs), or laptops accessing files, web, or e-mail services can do so without the physical constraint of network cables or a significant loss of performance. But as enterprises start to embrace wireless LAN (WLAN) deployments, and as vertical market deployments such as healthcare and retail mature, the need for support of Voice over IP (VoIP) over wireless and video over wireless is mandatory.

If you think about it, it makes a lot of sense. Using VoIP over wireless can reduce the usage of cell phones in the work environment (where the company pays an airtime fee). This reduced use of cell phones gives network administrators a tangible dollar value to develop a return on investment (ROI) for a WLAN deployment.

QoS is a relatively mature technology for wired networks and is generally available on routers, switches, and end devices such as wired IP phones. For 802.11 WLANs, the contrary is true. It is an emerging technology that is hotly debated with the IEEE and the

WLAN industry as a whole. The key challenges for a QoS mechanism in 802.11 networks include the following:

- **A half-duplex medium**—802.11 is a shared, half-duplex medium, whereas most wired Ethernet deployments that leverage QoS are full duplex.

- **Same channel BSS overlap (also referred to as cochannel overlap)**—In cases where two adjacent 802.11 BSSs are on the same channel, interference and degradation to performance can occur.

- **Hidden node**—Nodes in range of the AP yet out of range with one another will collide and cause extensive contention in the BSS.

The following sections detail each of these challenges to 802.11 QoS.

QoS Impact of a Half-Duplex Medium

Chapter 2, "802.11 Wireless LANs," described the basic access mechanisms for 802.11 as defined in 1997 with dispersion compensating fiber (DCF) and PCF. Both mechanisms allow for only one station to transmit on the medium at a given time, whether it's the access point (AP) or a client station. Wired Ethernet, and in particular 802.3x full-duplex operation, creates a point-to-point link between Ethernet stations, allowing simultaneous transmit and receive of data frames. This setup allows the Ethernet medium to theoretically operate at two times its normal bandwidth. (A Fast Ethernet link can handle a transmit of 100 Mbps and a receive of 100 Mbps simultaneously, for a total of 200 Mbps). Stated another way, a station that needs to transmit does not contend with the station on the other side of the link, who might also need to transmit.

Contrast that scenario to one with 802.11 networks. Not only does the AP contend for the medium as the clients do, but the clients also contend for the medium among themselves. PCF operation did introduce the notion of polled access, where the AP can act as the point coordinator and poll each client to see whether it has traffic to send. Although in very low client count BSSs this setup is reasonable, it was found to cause more degradation in overall throughput than the normal contention-based access in DCF. With no mechanism to coordinate client transmissions and prioritize one client over another, vendors must overcome a major challenge to support latency-sensitive applications such as VoIP.

Cochannel Overlap

Cochannel overlap is a common occurrence in 2.4 GHz WLAN deployments with more than three APs. Because of the restriction of three nonoverlapping channels, some APs end up adjacent to APs on the same channel. What does this mean for the clients in those BSSs? Figure 6-1 shows a client in a cochannel overlap area. If both APs begin to transmit at the same time, the frames collide and both stations must back off and retransmit.

Figure 6-1   *Cochannel Overlap*

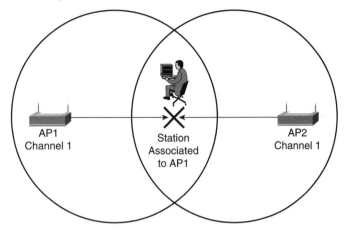

You can encounter another scenario, known as a *broadcast black hole*. When a BSS has a power-save station, all broadcasts and multicasts are sent after a DTIM beacon. In most cases, all the APs in an electronic switching system (ESS) have the same beacon interval and same DTIM interval. If the internal timers are somewhat close together on cochannel adjacent APs, both APs can send the broadcast or multicast traffic simultaneously, causing the frames to collide in the overlap area and the client in the overlap area to miss the frames. Unlike unicast frames, broadcast and multicast frames are not acknowledged and therefore are not retransmitted. Cochannel overlap can subvert QoS mechanisms by increasing contention in 802.11 networks, and coupled with the black hole situation, it can cause a client to not receive potentially critical traffic.

Hidden Node Impact on QoS

The hidden-node problem described in Chapter 2 poses an issue for providing QoS in 802.11 as well. Using request to send/clear to send (RTS/CTS) messages to reserve the medium addresses the hidden node problem, but again, RTS/CTS is typically employed after the detection of a collision and after the appropriate backoff. The increased latency can and often does impact latency-sensitive applications. Devices using RTS/CTS for each frame also incur a performance penalty, with a large amount of overhead traffic for each data frame.

QoS Mechanism Overview

The 802.11e task group has debated many issues, including those discussed in the previous section. It has devised two proposed solutions for the future of 802.11 MAC. Bear in mind that the proposed specifications are not yet ratified, and changes might occur after this book is printed. The current two proposed solutions are

- **Hybrid coordination function (HCF) with contention operation**—More commonly known as Enhanced DCF (EDCF)
- **HCF with polled access operation**

HCF in Contention Mode—The EDCF Access Mechanism

The draft 802.11e specification attempts to provide classification for up to eight classes of data. EDCF and HCF polled access leverages these eight classes, known as traffic classes (TC), which map to the eight classes defined in the 802.1D standard, as shown in Table 6-1. Traffic from QoS-enabled clients is categorized into four broader categories known as access categories (AC). ACs 0 to 3 map to the 802.1D priority classes.

Table 6-1   *802.11e TC-to-AC Mapping*

802.1D Value/TC	Common Usage	AC and Transmit Queue
1	Low priority	0
2	Low priority	0
0	Best effort	0
3	Signaling/control	1
4	Video probe	2
5	Video	2
6	Voice	3
7	Network control	3

Any system that supports QoS needs three key components for the system to work:

- A mechanism to classify the traffic
- A mechanism to mark the traffic with the appropriate QoS value
- A mechanism to differentiate and prioritize the traffic, based on the QoS value

The mechanism for classifying and marking data frames is outside the scope of the draft 802.11e document, but it is safe to assume that the application (such as a voice application on an 802.11 handset) can at least mark the IP precedence bits or differentiate services code point (DSCP) values. It is also safe to assume that a client device will map those Layer 3 values to the 802.11e traffic classes. With the traffic classified and marked, 802.11e provides the mechanism to differentiate and prioritize the traffic for transmission.

Channel Access for Differentiated Traffic

After the traffic is classified and placed in the appropriate queue, the next step is to transmit the frames. The challenge is how to provide priority to frames among client devices that are not directly communicating. EDCF addresses this challenge by introducing some new concepts and functionality:

- **Transmit opportunity (TXOP)**—A TXOP is the moment in time when a station can begin transmitting frames, for a given duration. Unlike basic medium access for DCF described in Chapter 2, where each frame and accompanying acknowledgment contends for the medium, a TXOP can facilitate multiple frames/acknowledgments as long as they fit within the duration of the TXOP (see Table 6-2).

- **Arbitration interframe space (AIFS)**—The AIFS is similar to the IFSs discussed in Chapter 2, but the size of the IFS varies based on AC. This process gives higher-priority stations a shorter AIFS and lower-priority stations a longer AIFS. The shorter the AIFS, the higher the chances of accessing the channel first.

Some existing concepts are used in new ways. In Chapter 2, the CW values CW_{min} and CW_{max} are set for every DCF station, and the values change only during backoff and channel access retries. In EDCF, different ACs can have different CW values to enhance the chance for higher-priority traffic to access the medium first.

Table 6-2 illustrates the default parameters for the CW values, AIFS, and TXOP for each AC.

Table 6-2 *Access Category Medium Access Parameters*

AC	CW_{min}	CW_{max}	AIFS	TXOP Limit (802.11b)	TXOP Limit (802.11a/g)
0	Standard 802.11 CW_{min}	Standard 802.11 CW_{max}	2	0	0
1	Standard 802.11 CW_{min}	Standard 802.11 CW_{max}	1	3.0 milliseconds (ms)	1.5 ms
2	$((CW_{min} + 1)/2) - 1$	Standard 802.11 CW_{min}	1	6.0 ms	3.0 ms
3	$((CW_{min} + 1)/4) - 1$	$((CW_{min} + 1)/2) - 1$	1	3.0 ms	1.5 ms

Some points worth mentioning about Table 6-2 follow:

- AC(0) is classified as best effort traffic, so the parameters nearly match standard DCF values with the exception of the AIFS, which has a value of DIFS + 1 slot time. Also, note that a TXOP duration limit of 0 allows for only a single frame to be transmitted.

- AC(1), with slightly higher priority, has the same channel-access parameters as an 802.11 DCF station, with the exception of a TXOP duration that allows for multiple frames to be transmitted and acknowledged.

- AC(2) has a smaller contention window than the lower-priority ACs and a longer TXOP. To illustrate the impact of the smaller contention window, consider the following:

  — The default initial CW_{min} value is typically 7 slot times. A DCF station randomly selects a backoff value between 0 and the CW_{min} (in this case, 7) and uses that as the counter value to decrement. With AC(2), the CW_{min} value of 7 changes to 3. The station now only has to select a backoff value ranging from 0 to 3, a much shorter time window. The CW_{max} value is also different, now using the CW_{min} value of 7. In this case, after the station has backed off and reached the CW_{max} value, it increments the retry counter much faster.

- AC(3) has the shortest contention window of the ACs but also has a shorter TXOP duration limit as well. AC(3) frames are typically network control or voice frames, which are small and don't require much "air" time to transmit successfully.

Each of the ACs exists within a QoS-enabled station or AP. It is possible for two or more ACs to collide internally. A lower-priority AC can still randomly select a short backoff and collide with a higher AC. In this case, the higher AC frame takes precedence and the lower AC is forced to back off and increase its CW.

Admission Control with EDCF

The purpose of QoS is to protect high-priority application traffic from low-priority application traffic. For example, QoS protects VoIP frames from Post Office Protocol 3 (POP3) frames. In cases where network resources are limited, such as 802.11 WLANs, it might be necessary to protect high-priority application traffic from other high-priority application traffic. It might sound odd, but consider this example. Suppose a BSS can accommodate a maximum of six simultaneous VoIP calls. Any data traffic that attempts to use the medium is prioritized below the VoIP traffic so that the call participants have a jitter-free, useful VoIP call experience.

Now a seventh call is initiated in the BSS. The BSS can only accommodate six calls, and the prioritization mechanism should allow the call to initiate as it matches the requirements to be classified as high-priority traffic. Yet if it is allowed to initiate, it will negatively impact the existing six VoIP calls, so all seven calls are performing poorly.

Admission control addresses this issue. In the same way that QoS protects high-priority traffic from low-priority traffic, admission control protects high-priority traffic from high-priority traffic. Admission control monitors the available resources of a network and intelligently allows or disallows new application sessions.

EDCF uses an admission control scheme known as distributed admission control (DAC). DAC functions at a high level by monitoring and measuring the percentage of utilization of the medium for each AC. The unused percentage of the medium is referred to as the *available budget* for the AC. This available budget is advertised to stations in the QoS parameter information element (IE) in the AP beacons. When the budget starts to approach 0, stations attempting to initiate new application streams avoid doing so, and existing nodes are not able to increase or extend their existing TXOPs that they are already using. This process protects the existing application streams from being impacted by new streams.

HCF in Controlled Access Mode

HCF operation is similar to the operation of PCF described in Chapter 2. The AP contains a logical entity known as the hybrid coordinator (HC) that keeps tracks of HCF client stations and schedules the polling intervals. Polled access as implemented in HCF allows a station to request a TXOP, instead of just determining that one is available, as with EDCF. HCF operation, combined with HCF admission control, allows the HC to intelligently determine what resources are available on the wireless medium and accept or reject application traffic streams. HCF can operate in two modes, one coexisting with EDCF and the other using a contention-free period (CFP), similar to PCF.

Contention-Free HCF Operation

Contention-free HCF operation operates as follows:

1 The AP beacon is sent, including the PCF compensating fiber (CF) parameter set IE that specifies the start time and duration of a CFP.

2 The HC offers a TXOP to HCF-capable stations by sending QoS CF-Polls to them.

3 The stations must reply back within a SIFS time interval with data frames or with a QoS null frame, indicating the station has no traffic or the frame it desires to send is too large to do so in the time allotted in the TXOP.

4 The CFP ends when the HC sends a CF-End frame, or the CFP duration expires.

Figure 6-2 illustrates this operation.

Interoperation of EDCF and HCF

Unlike PCF operation, HCF polled access can occur during the contention period and coexist with EDCF operation as well as DCF operation. Polled TXOPs are "delivered" to the HCF pollable stations and facilitate the transmission or reception of QoS data frames. The HC gains access to the medium before EDCF stations by having to wait only a PIFS interval before accessing the medium. Figure 6-3 illustrates the coexistence.

Figure 6-2 *Contention-Free HCF Operation*

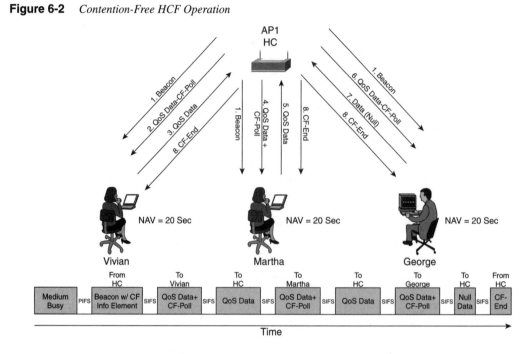

Figure 6-3 *Contention Period HCF Operation (Coexistence with EDCF)*

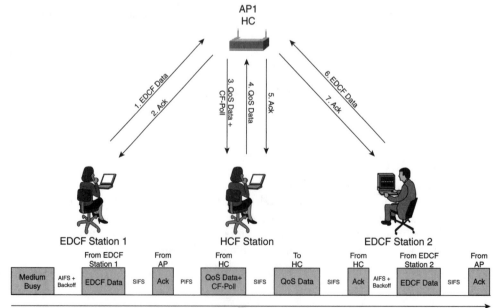

Admission Control with HCF

What truly differentiates HCF-controlled access operation from EDCF is HCF's admission-control mechanism. EDCF's use of DAC relies on the stations to interpret and respect the transmit budget advertised in the QoS parameter set IE. HCF requires that the station request particular reservation parameters for the application traffic stream, such as VoIP, from the HC. The HC can evaluate and determine whether there is enough budget available on the wireless medium to facilitate the requested traffic stream. The HC can then accept, reject, or even offer an alternative set of parameters to the station. As you can see, this mechanism is far more robust and effective than DAC. This robustness does not come without a penalty, however. The HC must keep a strict schedule of traffic streams, and depending on the implementation of the HC (which is not standardized but is left to vendor implementation), some implementations of HCF can be far more inefficient than others.

HCF admission control centers on the Transmission Specification IE, also known as the TSPEC. The TSPEC allows the client station to specify parameters such as

- Frame/stream 802.1D priority
- Frame size
- Frame rate (e.g., packets per second)
- Data rate (e.g., bits per second)
- Delay

Figure 6-4 depicts a TSPEC information element as defined in 802.11e draft 4.0.

Figure 6-4   *TSPEC IE Format*

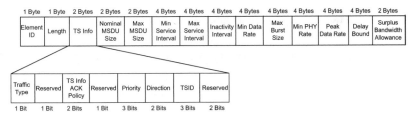

This data is sufficient for the HC to determine whether the wireless medium can sustain existing traffic streams and this newly requested stream without degrading any of the existing streams. The TSPEC also indicates to the HC how often the station is expecting to get polled. The station must generate a unique TSPEC for each traffic stream it wants to transmit and receive with priority and for each direction of the stream (i.e., a bidirectional VoIP call requires two traffic streams).

The HC can do one of three actions after receiving the TSPEC:

- Accept the TSPEC and grant the new traffic stream into the wireless medium
- Suggest an alternative set of TSPEC parameters to the client station
- Reject the TSPEC

To illustrate a scenario where a station sends a TSPEC that is accepted, assume a VoIP call is to be placed on an AP that has three existing calls in place and some sporadic data traffic. The sporadic data traffic is classified as "best effort" traffic, whereas the VoIP traffic is classified as "high priority."

The VoIP traffic is protected from the data traffic via HCF polling order and frequency. The traffic is also protected from EDCF traffic because it uses a HC and need only wait a PIFS interval before accessing the medium. EDCF stations must wait at least a DIFS interval and, in some cases, a DIFS plus one slot time (assuming the use of the default parameter set in Table 6-2).

The process for the new station to join the BSS and begin transmitting its traffic stream is as follows (and illustrated in Figure 6-5):

1 The station must authenticate and associate to the BSS.

2 The station sends an admission request using the management action (MA) request for QoS, containing its requested TSPEC for the VoIP call.

Note	A TSPEC is required for each direction, both from the client to the HC and from the HC to the client. The client must request both TSPECs.

3 The HC accepts the TSPEC and responds with a MA response for QoS to the station.

4 The HC sends a TXOP via a QoS data CF-Poll frame.

5 The station responds with a QoS data frame or burst of frames, depending on the duration of the TXOP.

In some cases, the HC might not be able to accommodate a new TSPEC without impacting existing traffic streams. The HC has the option to suggest an alterative TSPEC to the client or reject the TSPEC altogether. In the former scenario, the following process occurs (and illustrated in Figure 6-5):

1 The station joins the BSS via authentication and association.

2 The station sends an admission request using the MA request for QoS with its desired TSPEC.

3 The HC sends a MA response containing the alternative TSPEC to the client station.

4 If the alterative TSPEC is acceptable to the client, the process continues as with Step 3 from the previous list.

5 If the alterative TSPEC is not acceptable to the client, the client sends an MA to delete the TSPEC.

Figure 6-5   *HCF Admission Control Message Overview*

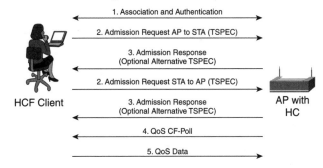

When the HC cannot accommodate the traffic stream, it sends a MA response rejecting the TSPEC, and the client station may then try again using a modified TSPEC.

Traffic streams can be removed in two ways:

- The TSPEC timeout elapses.
- The station or AP explicitly deletes the TSPEC.

With a TSPEC timeout, after the defined timeout period for the stream elapses, the HC sends the client station an MA for QoS to delete the TSPEC. The timeout is determined when the client station is polled and it responds with QoS-Null frames after several polls within a set window defined by the timeout value in the TSPEC. In the case where a QoS station or the HC desires to tear down a stream, a MA frame to delete the TSPEC is transmitted to the HC or client station, respectively.

Summary: The Challenges Facing EDCF and HCF

At the time of this writing, there are two major obstacles perplexing the IEEE with respect to 802.11e: an effective yet simple admission control for EDCF and the operation performance of HCF. These issues are hotly debated among the various vendors in the working group who endeavor to solve application issues.

DAC still presents performance problems because it does not strictly enforce admissions control. Stations may potentially transmit and negatively impact existing traffic streams. Resolution seems to surround the adoption of parameterized admissions control for EDCF as well (the use of TSPECs to admit or deny EDCF traffic). HCF has its share of issues. Proponents extol the virtues of polled access as the panacea for effectively using the medium and also providing the ability to nearly guarantee service. Detractors believe that practical implementations of HCF will fail, as did early PCF implementations, because of the cochannel overlap issues that plague the 2.4 GHz band. The effectiveness of HCF diminishes quickly with cochannel overlap.

Although the working group has not finalized the 802.11e standard, it continues to strive toward a practical and effective set of tools to extend and expand the implementations of 802.11 WLANs.

CHAPTER 7

Radio Frequency Essentials

Although it is one thing to understand the basic components of the 802.11 physical layers (PHYs), it is an entirely different task to understand when and where you can deploy wireless LANs (WLANs) and what limitations and regulations govern their deployment. As mentioned in Chapter 3, "802.11 Physical Layer Technologies," the use of unlicensed frequencies is one of the major enabling factors that has allowed WLANs in nearly every business segment. This chapter examines the rules that you need to know when planning your wireless deployment. It is also important to know the challenges that the radio designer faces, and although this chapter will not help you design an 802.11 radio, it will help you understand and evaluate the physical layer data that is presented by most equipment vendors. Every radio has a transmitter and a receiver; this chapter explains the basic performance parameters of these components. Armed with this knowledge, you can make intelligent and measured evaluations of the radios and antennas on the market.

Radio Basics

The term *radio* refers to electromagnetic transmission through free space at millimeter wave frequencies and below. It encompasses a wide range of applications, from AM and FM car radios to cellular phone radios and terrestrial digital microwave radios. Some, like AM and FM radios, are one-way or broadcast radios. The electromagnetic transmission occurs in only one direction, and it is often in a one-to-many type configuration. Alternatively, two-way radios allow transmission and reception by all parties; they can either be a point-to-point configuration, which is common in telecommunications backhaul applications, or a point-to-multipoint configuration, such as WLAN and cellular networks.

An important architectural distinction with two-way radio communication is the difference between frequency division duplex (FDD) and time division duplex (TDD). In FDD, you use a different frequency to carry information in each direction, and the two frequencies are separated enough in frequency that they don't interfere. Provided adequate separation is maintained, FDD can significantly simplify the radio and system designer's task, and it allows full-duplex type operation where simultaneous transmission and reception can occur. However, it also suffers the problem that you must allocate spectrum in two bands, and it can be spectrally inefficient because it locks up bandwidth in each direction. The alternative, TDD, does all radio communication on the same channel but with alternating periods of transmitting and listening. Although TDD does create a half-duplex situation at the physical layer and does require the radio to be able to very quickly switch from transmitting to receiving, it can be more spectrally efficient. It allows for easier channelization, and it can provide for time-varying allocation of bandwidth in each direction.

One of the most important characteristics of a radio is power. Specifically, the output power of the radio is presented to the transmission line, cable, or antenna and is usually measured in watts or milliwatts (mW). Comparisons of power values use a logarithmic scale to express the ratio in decibels (dB). The radio manufacturer provides the output power in dBm, which is decibels per 1 mW, or in dBW, which is decibels per 1 W. Table 7-1 provides some sample conversions between powers in watts and decibels.

Table 7-1   *Sample Watt and Decibel Values*

mW	W	dBm	dBW
1	.001	0	-30
2	.002	3	-27
5	.005	7	-23
10	.01	10	-20
20	.02	13	-17
50	.05	17	-13
100	.1	20	-10
1000	1	30	0
2000	2	33	3
4000	4	36	6

Antenna Basics

What is an antenna? The IEEE defines an *antenna* as "that part of a transmitting or receiving system that is designed to radiate or receive electromagnetic waves" (IEEE Standard 145-1993). In other words, it is the antenna that takes the radio frequency (RF) signal that the radio generates and radiates it into the air or that receives or captures electromagnetic waves for the radio. Usually, the transmit and receive properties are reciprocal, meaning that the parameters such as gain or radiation pattern or frequency are the same.

The next question you might ask is, "How does an antenna work?" According to the textbook that most antenna designers learned with—Stutzman and Thiele's *Antenna Theory and Design*—the key is radiation, a "disturbance in the electromagnetic field that propagates away from the source of the disturbance...disturbance is created by a time-varying current source." So the radio creates a time-varying voltage source at a particular frequency, which induces a time-varying current on the antenna that creates the aforementioned electromagnetic field.

Considerations of antenna performance make a distinction between the *near field*, close to the antenna, and the *far field*. In the far field, the distance from the antenna is much larger than the wavelength at which you are operating or much larger than the dimension of the antenna, in contrast to the near field. It is under far-field assumptions that antenna vendors specify the characteristics of the antenna. Keep this point in mind if you ever find yourself operating in the near field of antennas because the characteristics are different.

An important concept to understand is that of an *isotropic* radiator or antenna. It is a mathematical construct for an idealized lossless antenna that radiates equally in all directions. If you define a sphere with an isotropic radiator in its center, the electromagnetic field will be equal at all points on the surface of the sphere. The isotropic antenna is a useful reference point when we consider different antennas.

Antenna Properties

For you to make a judicious antenna decision, it is important to understand some of the properties that describe an antenna. They include, but are not limited to, an antenna's radiation pattern, directivity, gain, input impedance, polarization, and bandwidth.

The *radiation pattern* of an antenna describes the "angular variation of radiation at a fixed distance from an antenna." It is often expressed in terms of directivity or gain. The *directivity* of an antenna describes the intensity of the radiation in a given direction, relative to the average radiation intensity, or put another way, it indicates the radiated power density relative to a uniformly distributed radiated power. *Gain* expresses the same concepts as directivity, but it also includes losses on the antenna itself. You can define radiation efficiency that is used to scale the directivity to determine the gain; a perfect radiator has a radiation efficiency of 1. As all real antennas have losses, gain is the more frequently quoted parameter for an antenna. The units used to describe the gain are either dBi, gain in dB relative to an isotropic antenna, or dBd, gain in dB relative to a half-wave dipole antenna. To convert between dBd and dBi, merely add 2.2 to the gain expressed in dBd to get the gain in dBi. This conversion is important for you to remember because although most vendors express gain in dBi, some express it in dBd. Figure 7-1 shows a sample radiation pattern for a directional antenna.

NOTE	You can construct a dipole antenna by taking a transmission line and bending the ends outward to create oppositely charged poles that induce a time-varying current between them.

Figure 7-1   *Sample Radiation Pattern*

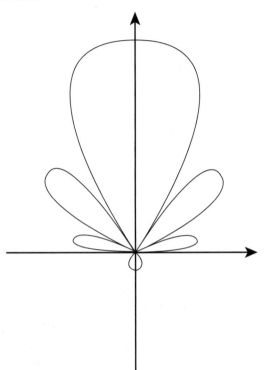

Remembering that this radiation exists in three-dimensional space, you often find that an antenna has a *main lobe* or beam, which is the direction of maximum gain, and that it is also characterized by *minor lobes*, often referred to as side and backlobes, depending upon the direction of the minor lobe relative to the main lobe. Vendors often describe antennas by the gain of the main lobe. When doing so, they also specify the *beamwidth* of the antenna. It is usually the principle half-power beamwidth, which is defined by the IEEE as follows: "In a radiation pattern cut containing the direction of the maximum of a lobe, the angle between the two directions in which the radiation intensity is one-half the maximum value." Take the previous antenna pattern and go to the points on either side of the main lobe where the gain is 3 dB lower than the maximum point of the lobe; this point is the half-power point, and it is where the angle between them gives the half-power beamwidth. Figure 7-2 illustrates this description.

Figure 7-2   *Half-Power Beamwidth*

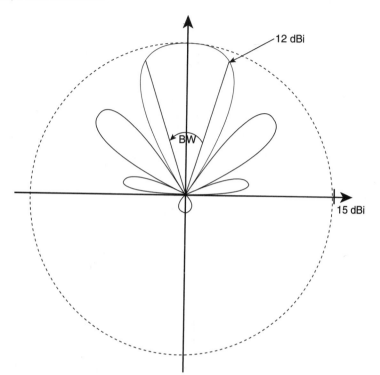

Related to an antenna's radiation pattern, the front-to-back ratio of an antenna compares the maximum gain of an antenna on its main lobe to the gain on a rearward facing lobe. In the sample radiation pattern, the front-to-back ratio is 20 dB, as shown in Figure 7-3. The main lobe gain is 15 dBi, and the back lobe is -5 dBi. The difference, 15 dBi...(-5 dBi) = 20 dB, is the front-to-back ratio.

Now that you understand the gain of an antenna, it is time to examine the actual power that is transmitted by a radio connected to an antenna. The effective radiated power (ERP) takes the gain of an antenna in units of dBd, relative to a half-wave dipole, and multiplies it by the net power offered by the transmitter to the antenna. However, you most often perform this operation in the log, or dB, domain, which means you add the gain of the antenna to the transmitter power. Because it is more common to express the gain of an antenna in dBi units, the more commonly used term for radiated power is effective isotropic radiated power (EIRP), which is the same as ERP but with the antenna gain expressed relative to an isotropic radiator.

Figure 7-3   *Front-to-Back Ratio*

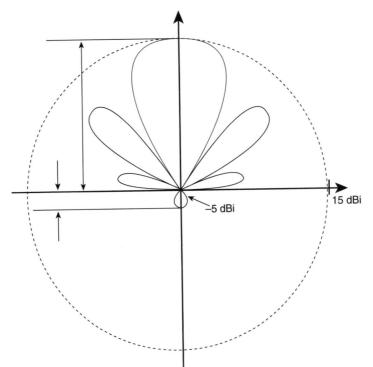

The electromagnetic waves emitted by an antenna can trace different patterns that affect propagation. The pattern depends upon the polarization of the antenna, which could be linearly or circularly polarized.

Most antennas that you find for WLANs are *linearly* polarized, either horizontal or vertical. In the former case, the electric field vector lives in the vertical plane, and in the latter the plane is horizontal. Vertical polarization is more common, although you might find scenarios where horizontal polarization works better. Although it isn't likely that you will use circularly polarized antennas indoors, using wireless bridging technology you might find applications for them. As with linearly polarized antennas, there are two cases: left-hand polarized and right-hand polarized. If the vector rotates clockwise as the wave is traveling toward you, then it is left-hand polarized.

Similarly, if it rotates counter-clockwise, it is right-hand polarized. Shooting a link over a body of water, where the polarization can rotate with each reflection, is an example of where circular polarization would be useful because it is invariant with respect to rotation. A linearly polarized antenna could switch from vertical to horizontal as it rotates.

In general, for a line-of-sight link, you should use the same polarization on both sides. A 21 dBi vertically polarized antenna might have only 1 to -4 dBi of gain in the horizontal plane; that is, the cross-polarization discrimination is typically 20 to 25 dB.

The radiation efficiency of an antenna is "the ratio of the total power radiated by an antenna to the net power accepted by the antenna from the connected transmitter." The antenna radiates some power as electromagnetic energy. All RF devices—radios, transmission lines, or antennas—have a characteristic *impedance*, which is the ratio of the voltage to the current at their terminal. With an antenna connected to a cable, if the antenna input impedance matches the radio and transmission-line impedance, then the maximum amount of power is transferred from the radio to the antenna. However, if there is an impedance mismatch, some of the energy is reflected back in the direction of the source, and the remainder is transferred to the antenna. The voltage standing wave ratio (VSWR) characterizes these reflections. If no reflections exist, the VSWR equals 1. As the VSWR increases, there are more reflections of greater magnitude. A VSWR of 2 means that 11 percent of the power is reflected.

A high VSWR and a lossy transmission line loses or wastes significant energy. Even more unsettling: With a high VSWR and high powers, a dangerous situation can develop as high voltages build up on the transmission line and, in extreme cases, cause arcing. However, this situation should never be an issue for you at the low power levels of your WLAN deployments.

The *bandwidth* of an antenna defines the range of frequencies over which the antenna provides acceptable performance, usually defined by the upper or maximum frequency and the lower or minimum frequency. Acceptable performance in this case means that characteristics of the antenna, such as the antenna pattern and the input impedance, do not change over the operating range of frequencies. Some antennas are considered *broadband*, which is loosely defined as those antennas for which the ratio of the maximum frequency to the minimum frequency is greater than 2. However, because broadband antennas often have poor gain performance and because the currently allocated 802.11 WLAN frequencies do not require a broadband antenna, the only instance in which you might be offered a broadband antenna is if you want to cover the entire 2.4 GHz Industrial, Scientific, and Medical (ISM) band along with the 5 GHz Unlicensed National Information Infrastructure (U-NII) band with a single antenna.

Remember when you make your antenna choices that many of the antenna properties are interrelated, so that although it might seem optimal to maximize or minimize all the antenna's characteristics, this task is often not possible. For example, if you select a very wide beamwidth, you sacrifice gain; if you select a broadband antenna, you might find that the antenna pattern is not uniform. So it is important to determine what characteristics are important for your particular deployment and optimize your choice accordingly.

Types of Antennas

You will come across many types of antennas in your lifetime. Rather than list all of them, this section describes the types of antennas that you are most likely to find in WLAN applications. Figure 7-4 shows several different types of antennas. As previously mentioned, an isotropic radiator is an idealized nonrealizeable antenna that has a uniform radiation pattern in all directions.

Figure 7-4   *WLAN Antennas*

Dipole Antenna

Patch Antenna

Yagi Antenna

Omnidirectional Antenna

Dish Antenna

With a half-wave dipole, the length from end to end is equal to half the wavelength at that frequency. An omnidirectional antenna provides uniform gain in all directions on a plane, often the horizontal plane. Dipole antennas are usually omnidirectional. Omnidirectional antennas are typically used in general WLAN deployments because they provide coverage in all directions. A Yagi-Uda antenna is constructed by forming an linear array of parallel dipoles.

Yagi antennas are some of the more common directional antennas because they are so easy to build. Directional antennas, such as Yagis, typically provide coverage in hard-to-reach areas or where more range is needed than an omnidirectional antenna can provide.

Patch antennas, another type of directional antenna, are formed by placing two parallel conductors with a substrate between them. The upper conductor is a patch that can be simply printed on a circuit board. It is relatively simple to form an array of patches, the antenna patterns of which combine to form various directed beam shapes. Patch antennas are often useful because of their rather slim profile, in contrast to that of a Yagi antenna. In the broad category of directional antennas are broadside antennas, in which the main beam is perpendicular to the plane of the antennas; end fire antennas, in which the main beam is in the plane of the antenna; and pencil beams, which provide a single, very narrow and often high-gain lobe to the antenna.

Chapter 10, "WLAN Design Considerations," discusses the circumstances under which you might use each type of antenna.

Receiver Performance Basics

Radio receivers are characterized by their receiver sensitivity, which is the minimum signal level for the receiver to be able to acceptably decode the information. The acceptability threshold is governed by a particular bit error rate (BER), packet error rate (PER), or frame error ratio (FER). For example, the 802.11a standard specifies that the minimum compliant receiver performance at a 54 Mbps data rate is –65 dBm at a 10 percent PER. Note that the receiver sensitivity is also at a specific data rate because each modulation scheme has its own signal-to-noise ratio (SNR) requirement. In general, the higher the data rate, the higher the SNR required and hence the higher the receiver sensitivity level. The receiver sensitivity of the radio is also governed by the receiver noise figure. All receivers have some base underlying noise level, either from the precision of the digital processing or from the performance of the analog components. This noise level is the noise floor. As the noise floor rises, so too does the receiver sensitivity because the minimum signal level over the noise, SNR, is fixed for the modulation scheme. This concept is depicted in Figure 7-5. To evaluate the performance of a radio, receiver sensitivity is one of the important inputs to your link-budget calculation that ultimately determines the achievable data rates and ranges. In general, you want the lowest receiver sensitivity that is economically feasible.

Figure 7-5 *Receiver Sensitivity Calculation*

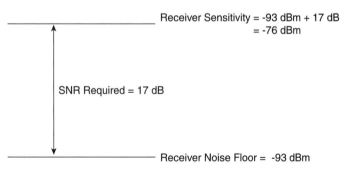

Receiver Sensitivity = -93 dBm + 17 dB
= -76 dBm

SNR Required = 17 dB

Receiver Noise Floor = -93 dBm

802.11b Minimum Radio Performance

To ensure satisfactory system performance between equipment manufactured by different vendors, the 802.11b PHY standard defines minimum radio performance levels that all equipment must satisfy for compliance. At an FER less than .08 with a Physical Layer

Convergence Procedure service data unit (PSDU) length of 1024 octets at an 11 Mbps data rate, the minimum receiver sensitivity is –76 dBm at the antenna connector. Under the same conditions, the receiver maximum input level is –10 dBm at the antenna connector, and the adjacent channel rejection of another compliant 802.11b transmitter is 35 dB at the antenna connector. For adjacent channel rejection, the receiver must be able to adequately filter or operate in the presence of an adjacent signal to maintain the 0.08 FER. To test adjacent channel rejection, the desired signal is placed 6 dB over the minimum receiver sensitivity level, and the adjacent channel signal is placed 41 dB over that same level. In the discussion of the 802.11b spectral mask, you will see what the likely resultant channel signal contribution is from the interferer.

802.11a Minimum Radio Performance

Similar to 802.11b, 802.11a also defines minimum radio performance parameters. Table 7-2 provides the minimum receiver sensitivity, adjacent channel rejection, and alternate adjacent channel rejection at the antenna connector for the 802.11a data rates at a PER less than 10 percent with a 1000-byte PSDU length. In the rejection performance, the desired signal is placed 3 dB over the minimum sensitivity level and the interferer at the level given by the ratio indicated.

Table 7-2   *Minimum 802.11a Minimum Radio Performance*

Data Rate (Mbps)	Minimum Sensitivity (dBm)	Adjacent Channel Rejection (dB)	Alternate Adjacent Channel Rejection (dB)
6	-82	16	32
9	-81	15	31
12	-79	13	29
18	-77	11	27
24	-74	8	24
36	-70	4	20
48	-66	0	16
54	-65	-1	15

The receiver maximum input level under the same conditions is –30 dBm. 802.11a also specifies the clear channel assessment (CCA) sensitivity, which states that a compliant radio must indicate busy with 90 percent probability within 4 microseconds if the received level is greater than or equal to –82 dBm during the preamble. If the preamble is missed, then the level is –62 dBm.

System Performance

Ultimately, what concerns you and the users of your WLAN network from a radio performance perspective is coverage and throughput. They are directly related to the range at each data rate. To determine the range, you must know how to translate from the system gain that you can provide to the corresponding range in your environment. Under free space, line-of-sight conditions, this process is relatively straightforward because the path loss is proportional to the square of the distance or range. The range is that distance at which the path loss equals the system gain. In other words, you require 6 more dB each time you double your distance. However, the typical indoor WLAN environment is cluttered with walls, desks, people, and other objects, all of which degrade the signal and increase the loss. As Chapter 8, "Deploying Wireless LANs," discusses, the only way to get an accurate understanding of the path loss in your environment is to conduct a site survey. However, it is still useful to understand the mechanisms that affect system performance and how to determine your system gain for comparison with other systems.

A *link budget* is the tool that you can use to determine the overall system gain. You need to know the following pieces of information for you system:

- Radio transmit power
- Transmit cable loss, if any
- Transmit antenna gain
- Receiver antenna gain
- Receiver cable loss, if any
- Receiver sensitivity at the desired data rate

The *cable loss* is a function of the frequency and should be provided in the cable specification by the vendor. In general, as frequencies increase, so too does cable loss, so you want to be more careful with remote antennas and long RF cable runs in the U-NII bands than in the 2.4 GHz ISM band. For example, a 100-foot cable run of LMR-400, a fairly common low-loss RF cable, has a cable loss of 10.5 dB at 5.3 GHz but only 6.5 dB at 2.4 GHz.

If you multiply the transmit power and the antenna gains and then divide by the cable losses and receiver sensitivity, you get the overall system gain:

$$System\ Gain = \frac{p_{Tx} * g_{Tx} * g_{Rx}}{l_{Tx} * l_{Rx} * l_{Rx}}$$

Alternatively, if you perform the operations in the log or dB domain, it is merely a matter of addition and subtraction:

$$System\ Gain_{dB} = P_{Tx} + G_{Tx} + G_{Rx} - (L_{Tx} + L_{Rx} + S_{Rx})$$

Table 7-3 provides two sample link budgets using hypothetical radios at 2.4 GHz with a 50-foot cable run at the access point (AP) in both cases. The table provides both the downstream, AP to client, and upstream, client to AP, link budgets for both systems. System B uses a lower-performing AP with lower transmit power and higher receive sensitivity. You can see that in the downstream, system B is 3 dB worse than system A, but in the upstream, it is 11 dB worse. For system A, the downstream limits the overall range and data rate, but for system B is limited by the upstream. In a free-space environment, system A would have a 5 dB link-budget advantage, resulting in nearly twice the range at the same data rate. Each 6 dB increase in link budget doubles the range in free space. In this way, you can see that you must consider the overall system gain when evaluating the coverage and throughput that two wireless systems can provide.

Table 7-3 *Sample Link Budget*

	System A Downstream	System A Upstream	System B Downstream	System B Upstream
Transmit Power (dBm)	20	15	17	15
Transmit Cable Loss (dB)	3.3	0	3.3	0
Transmit Antenna Gain (dB)	6	2	6	2
EIRP (dBm)	22.7	17	19.7	17
Receiver Antenna Gain (dB)	2	6	2	6
Receiver Cable Loss (dB)	0	3.3	0	3.3
Receiver Sensitivity (dBm)	-76	-87	-76	-76
System Gain (dB)	100.7	106.7	97.7	95.7

As previously mentioned, other mechanisms also influence the performance of your system. They include, but are not limited to, the following:

- Interference
- Multipath
- Fading

Interference occurs when some other signal source is producing energy on the channel in which you are trying to operate. It could be another WLAN radio operating on the same channel or some other device that produces energy in the same band. The stronger this source of interference, the stronger your receive signal level must be to decode the desired signal. You can think of it as raising the receiver sensitivity much the same way that raising the noise floor does, and if the undesired signal is too strong, you might not be able to operate at all. This effect is shown in Figure 7-6.

Figure 7-6   *Receiver Sensitivity in Presence of Interference*

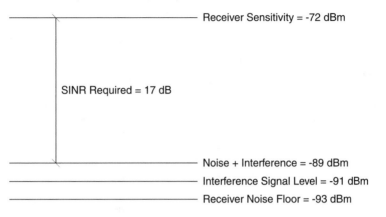

Receiver Sensitivity = -72 dBm

SINR Required = 17 dB

Noise + Interference = -89 dBm

Interference Signal Level = -91 dBm

Receiver Noise Floor = -93 dBm

Multipath occurs when the desired signal reaches the receiving antenna via multiple paths, each of which has a different propagation delay and path loss. These different paths are usually caused by reflections off objects in the environment or off inhomogeneous atmospheric conditions. Each of these received paths are summed at the antenna, and depending upon the delays and the attenuation of each path, multipath fading can occur. Figure 7-7 shows an example of summing the different multipath rays.

Figure 7-7   *Summing Multipath Rays*

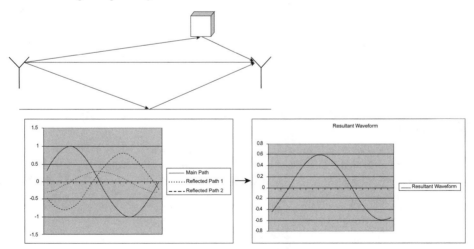

Fading is a time-varying change in the path loss of a link with the time variance governed by the movement of objects in the environment, including the transmitter and receiver themselves. For example, you might be sitting in a conference room with a wireless laptop and be connected to an AP in the hallway. If someone closes the door to the conference room, the path loss drops, resulting in a lower received signal level. This scenario is a fade.

Flat fading occurs when the entire signal across the whole channel fades. With broadband signals like 802.11, frequency-selective fading can also occur. The signal might be significantly attenuated at certain frequencies but not at others. If you think back to orthogonal frequency-division multiplexing (OFDM), you will recall that it independently energizes individual frequencies and then codes and interleaves across them. This process provides OFDM with a distinctive advantage over other modulation schemes like Complementary Code Keying (CCK) in that if a frequency selective fade occurs, it might only attenuate a few tones of an OFDM signal, thereby allowing the coding and interleaving to restore the original bit stream. With CCK, the entire bit stream might be lost.

Depending upon the multipath characteristics, it can change the path-loss model from that of free space, which is proportional to the square of the distance, to a path loss that is proportional to the fourth power of the distance. Under these circumstances, the path loss would increase by 12 dB ($10*\log(2^44)=12$) instead of 6 dB ($10*\log(2^22)=6$) every time the distance is doubled. In other words, if you are communicating in an environment with full line of sight between the transmitter and receiver and no clutter to reflect or absorb energy, you need to add 6 dB to your link budget to double the range. However, for a large number of multipath reflectors, you might need to add 12 dB to your link budget to double the range.

The multipath profile is not only time varying, but it is also a function of location. Points in space that are very close to each other can experience very different fades (i.e., multipath spatial variation). You have experience with this phenomenon in your everyday life when sitting at a traffic light listening to your car radio, you roll forward or backward a few inches only to discover drastically different reception. This spatial variation in multipath is one of the main reason why WLANs employ multiple or diversity receive and transmit antennas. If these antennas are separated by at least a wavelength, then the signals they receive become uncorrelated, so when one is experiencing a fade, the other might not. Most WLAN devices use selection diversity in which the radio determines which antenna is receiving the better signal, and then uses that signal.

Unlicensed Wireless

The Federal Communications Commission (FCC) has regulatory control over the wireless spectrum in the United States. Although many countries have similar spectrum regulations, unlicensed wireless can vary by country and continent. This section highlights the major spectrum regulations.

Standards Bodies

The three main standards bodies that influence the development of WLANs are Wi-Fi Alliance, IEEE, and ETSI.

The Institute of Electrical and Electronics Engineers (IEEE) is a non-profit technical professional association that, among other things, forms internationally accepted standards, such as the 802.11 WLAN standards. The standards workgroups meet on a regular basis to update, amend, and draft new standards.

While the IEEE drafts the standards that govern WLANs, it is the Wi-Fi Alliance that certifies the interoperability of WLAN products, based upon the IEEE specification. By using Wi-Fi certified products, you are assured of a level of interoperability that goes beyond what is provided by the IEEE 802.11 standard. Similar to the IEEE, the Wi-Fi Alliance is a non-profit international trade organization made up of vendors and manufacturers.

The European Telecommunications Standards Institute (ETSI) is another non-profit organization that was formed in 1988 to generate telecommunications standards for Europe. With respect to 802.11 WLANs, ETSI has helped unify the European countries around a common set of transmission regulations. ETSI also drafted a competing set of standards for operation in the 5 GHz bands, but 802.11 appears to have more momentum at the time of this writing.

In the United States, the ISM band includes the 2.4 GHz to 2.4835 GHz band. The FCC has determined that nonradiating equipment could radiate RF in these bands. As an example, a microwave oven radiates RF in the 2.4 GHz band because that is the frequency band used by the oven to cook food. The FCC allows for secondary spectrum users to take advantage of this band by using spread spectrum technology. A secondary user is a user who does not own the primary license for a given set of frequencies.

In the United States, the Code of Federal Regulations 47 (CFR47) codifies the telecommunications rules put forth by the FCC. Part 15 of CFR47 governs the use of unlicensed radiators, whether they are intentional, unintentional, or incidental. The part 15 rules strictly regulate power output to make sure the secondary user does not interfere with the primary user. In general, a secondary user uses a frequency (or set of frequencies) at power levels far lower than what the primary user, such as a ham radio operator, has a license for. With microwave ovens, the primary user of the 2.4 GHz frequency set radiates RF anywhere from 600 to 1000 watts. An 802.11 radio typically radiates RF anywhere from 30 to 100 milliwatts. This setup allows a primary user to overpower a secondary user if their RF paths cross.

ISM Band Frequencies

The ISM band has individual channels for use by unlicensed devices. The channels and their allocations are governed by regulatory bodies and can vary slightly from country to country.

Table 7-4 summarizes the WLAN channels in the ISM band and their allocation in different regulatory domains, including the FCC in the United States, the European Telecommunications Standard Institute (ETSI), Japan, and Israel.

Table 7-4   *ISM Band WLAN Channel Allocations*

Channel	Center Frequency	FCC	ETSI	Japan	Israel
1	2.412	X	X	X	
2	2.417	X	X	X	
3	2.422	X	X	X	X
4	2.427	X	X	X	X
5	2.432	X	X	X	X
6	2.437	X	X	X	X
7	2.442	X	X	X	X
8	2.447	X	X	X	X
9	2.452	X	X	X	X
10	2.457	X	X	X	
11	2.462	X	X	X	
12	2.467		X	X	
13	2.472		X	X	
14	2.483			X	

The 802.11b standard defines a spectral mask that is depicted in Figure 7-8. Relative to the carrier-frequency peak, all spectral emissions must be less than –30 dBr at +/- 11 MHz from the carrier frequency and less than –50 dBr at +/- 22 MHz from the center frequency.

Figure 7-8   *802.11b Spectral Mask*

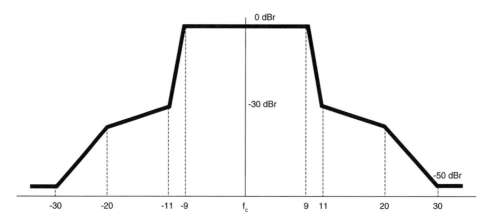

In Figure 7-9, the spectral emissions mask has been superimposed on the 11 U.S. channels. You can tell that despite having 11 channels allocated, there are actually only 3 nonoverlapping channels: 1, 6, and 11.

Figure 7-9   *Nonoverlapping 802.11b Channels*

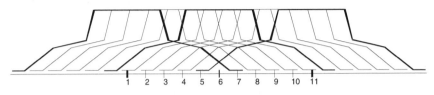

2.4 GHz ISM Band Transmit Power Levels

In the United States, CFR47 part 15.247 specifies the transmit power levels that might be used in the 2.4 GHz band. For spread spectrum systems, a 1 W peak output power with up to a 6 dBi antenna might be utilized. This combination results in a 36 dBm EIRP. For fixed-location, point-to-point links, such as what you might set up with wireless bridges, you can increase the antenna gain as long as the transmitter power is reduced by 1 dB for every 3 dB increase in antenna gain over 6 dBi. If the radio is not being used in a fixed, point-to-point application, then the transmit power must be reduced by 1 dB for every 1 dB increase in antenna gain over 6 dBi, thereby maintaining a 36 dBm EIRP limit.

For countries adopting ETSI rules, the European Telecommunications Standard (ETS) 300 328 regulation specifies the transmit power levels that may be used. It allows for a 100 mW, or 30 dBm, EIRP. In Japan, the MPT ordinance for regulating radio equipment, article 49-20 governs transmission in this band. For direct sequence spread spectrum (DSSS) signals, a 10 mW/MHz output power can be used. For frequency hopping spread spectrum (FHSS) signals, that same 10 mW/MHz can be used at frequencies from 2.471 to 2.497, but from 2.400 to 2.471 only 3 mW/MHz can be used. Israel currently follows ETSI rules for output power levels.

U-NII Band WLAN Frequencies

At press time, the U-NII band frequencies are primarily available for use in the United States and in countries that have adopted FCC-type spectrum rules. As previously stated, the U-NII 1 band extends from 5.15 to 5.25 GHz, the U-NII 2 band is immediately adjacent to it at 5.25 to 5.35 GHz, and the U-NII 3 band resides at 5.725 to 5.825 GHz. The channel numbering begins at 5.000 GHz and extends upwards from there in 5 MHz increments. This numbering provides for a channel-numbering scheme that covers the entire 5 GHz band should those frequencies ever become available for use by WLANs. Figure 7-10 shows the 8 nonoverlapping channels in the U-NII 1 and 2 bands. Note that the center frequencies for the edge channels are 30 MHz from the band edge.

Figure 7-10 *U-NII 1, 2, and 3 Channels*

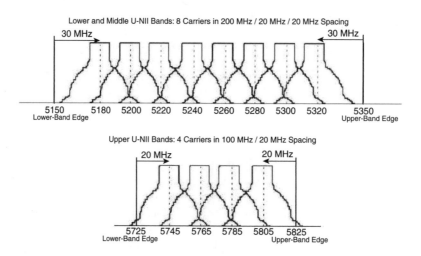

Figure 7-8 also shows the U-NII 3 channels. In contrast to the lower 5 GHz bands, the center frequencies in the U-NII 3 band are only 20 MHz from the band edge. This fact is important for you to remember when considering the spurious emissions and spectral mask requirements for this band because it proves to be more challenging for radio designers who design for the lower bands.

U-NII Band Spurious Emissions and Spectral Masks

CFR47 part 15.407 specifies spurious emissions requirements for the three U-NII bands. For the U-NII 1 band, all emissions outside the 5.15 to 5.35 GHz band must be less than an EIRP of –27 dBm/MHz, transmissions are for indoor use only, and an integral antenna must be in use. For the U-NII 2 band, you have the option of following these same rules, although you may use the band for indoor and outdoor use with nonintegral antennas if all emissions outside of 5.25 to 5.35 are less than an EIRP of –27 dBm/MHz. For U-NII 3 band transmission, all emissions outside the band edges, 5.725 and 5.825, must be less than an EIRP of –17 dBm/MHz; furthermore, as you move to 10 MHz from the band edges, all spurious emissions must be less than or equal to an EIRP of –27 dBm/MHz.

The 802.11a standard also defines a spectral mask for transmission in the U-NII bands. The transmitted spectrum must be 0 dBr, relative to the maximum spectral density of the signal, out to a maximum bandwidth of 18 MHz, and then it must be less than –20 dBr at 11 MHz from the center frequency, -28 dBr at 20 MHz, and –40 dBr at 30 MHz. Figure 7-11 shows this spectral mask.

Figure 7-11 *802.11a Spectral Mask*

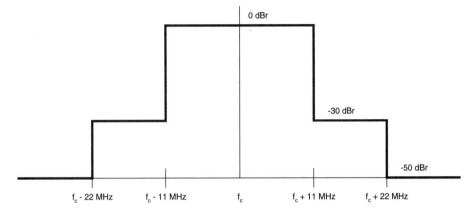

Taking your knowledge of the spectral mask and the adjacent channel rejection specified in Table 7-2, you can determine that the interfering energy contribution of an adjacent 802.11a signal while you are operating at a 6 Mbps data rate could be as high as –14 dBr, relative to your signal level, at the center frequency, as shown in Figure 7-12.

Figure 7-12 *Adjacent Channel Interference*

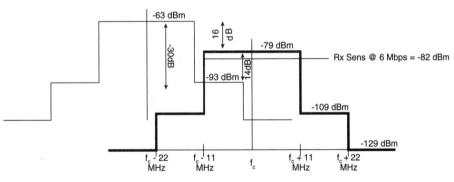

You should keep this in mind as you plan your channel allocations because contributions from multiple adjacent channels can start to accumulate.

It is also important for you to be aware of the spectral mask and spurious emissions requirements when you employ remote antennas. When vendors certify their radios and antennas with the FCC, they specifically set power levels based not only upon EIRP limits, but also upon these spectral mask constraints. It might appear that they have set antenna gains and power levels that fall below the EIRP limits, but in many cases, this setting might be necessary to meet the spectral mask requirements. For this reason, you should not exceed the vendor-suggested EIRP limits for each type of antenna and radio.

U-NII Band Transmit Power Limitations

The three U-NII bands have different transmit power limitations. The U-NII 1 band is intended for indoor use only at the lowest levels. The U-NII 3 band has the highest levels because it is intended for outdoor, longer-range applications.

The following transmit power limitations are set by 802.11a for operation in the U-NII bands:

- In the U-NII 1 band, you can use up to a 40 mW, 16 dBm, transmitter with up to a 6 dBi gain antenna for a 22 dBm maximum EIRP. In addition, for each dB of antenna gain over 6 dBi, you must reduce the transmitter power by 1 dB.

- In the U-NII 2 band, you can use up to a 200 mW, 23 dBm, transmitter with up to a 6 dBi gain antenna for a 29 dBm maximum EIRP. In addition, for each dB of antenna gain over 6 dBi, you must reduce the transmitter power by 1 dB.

- In the U-NII 3 band, you can use up to a 800 mW, 29 dBm, transmitter with up to a 6 dBi gain antenna for a 35 dBm maximum EIRP. In addition, for each dB of antenna gain over 6 dBi, you must reduce the transmitter power must be reduced by 1 dB. U-NII 3 operation allows for the use of a 23 dBi antenna without a transmitter power reduction for fixed-location, point-to-point links. This setup results in a 52 dBm maximum EIRP under these conditions.

Summary

This chapter discussed the essential physical-layer evaluation points for a radio system along with the specific rules that govern their operation. Key items to remember are that it is not enough to evaluate a radio based upon its transmit power. You must consider the entire link budget with receiver and transmitter performance characteristics. Armed with this tool, you should be able to make an informed evaluation of radios from different vendors.

CHAPTER 8

Deploying Wireless LANs

Understanding how the 802.11 protocol operates, the behavior of mobile nodes, MAC layer security, and quality of service (QoS) is necessary for making wireless LAN (WLAN) deployment decisions. There is far more to deploying access points (APs) than running cable and ceiling-mounting the devices. The physical aspect of performing a site survey gives an administrator visibility into what coverage area each AP provides, the number of APs required to cover the given area, and channel and transmit power settings. You, as an administrator, must also incorporate

- Roaming patterns of wireless clients
- Applications used by wireless clients

These two primary areas shape the decisions you make when determining how many APs to use, the amount of coverage overlap, and the locations of upper-layer devices, such as authentication servers.

WLAN Deployment and Application Impact

WLAN deployments impact application use differently. It is important for you to understand these impacts as you plan your WLAN deployment. The keys are the following:

- Effective per-client throughput
- Streaming versus bursty application types
- Medium contention and application latency

Effective per-client throughput is decreased as each new client joins the base station subsystem (BSS). Although each user is not explicitly guaranteed a specific amount of bandwidth, the distributed coordination function (DCF) medium-access mechanism provides fair access to the wireless medium, suggesting that each client has equal access to (and a portion of) the wireless medium. In a world where switched 10 Mbps and 100 Mbps Ethernet are commonplace, sharing 11 Mbps or even 54 Mbps (802.11b and 802.11a, respectively) among 10 to 25 other clients can be perceived as a step backward.

Given an 11 Mbps data rate for 802.11b networks and a shared, half-duplex medium, it is reasonable to expect no more than 6 Mbps of actual throughput. The total available throughput among 25 clients yields roughly 245 Kbps per client. Extending the same ratio to 802.11a

BSSs with a 54 Mbps data rate, a reasonable throughput rate is roughly 22 Mbps, yielding an average throughput rate in the range of 880 Kbps per client. Note that this number is just a reference, assuming all clients are transmitting and receiving equal amounts of data.

Application types significantly impact these numbers. A streaming application type, such as voice, has much different characteristics from those of a bursty application type, such as HTTP or Post Office Protocol 3 (POP3). A typical G.711 bidirectional voice call has a average throughput requirement of 240 Kbps at the MAC layer. Given this figure, you might mistakenly assume that 25 voice calls can operate per BSS (240 Kbps $\cong$ 5.86 Mbps).

But each bidirectional call also requires a forwarding rate of 200 frames per second (50 frames per second and 50 802.11 acknowledgments per second for each direction of the call, yielding 200 frames per second). Assuming the 802.11b MAC only supports 1200 packets per second, you can sustain only six voice calls per BSS, a marked difference from the throughput-only metric. Note: That number does not factor any data on the AP, just the voice calls. Any data traffic on the AP degrades the voice calls without some sort of admission-control mechanism or QoS/prioritization mechanism.

You can see how AP density—that is, the number of APs in a coverage area—plays an important role in application support. A coverage-only deployment would not scale to provide each client Voice over IP (VoIP) over 802.11, whereas a capacity-oriented deployment can have the necessary client-to-AP density.

Bursty application types have erratic and unpredictable behavior, making scaling determinations a guessing game for AP density calculations. Although there is no widely accepted heuristic rule to estimate future client traffic for accessing the web, downloading e-mail, or accessing client/server applications, a good rule of thumb is to set a limit of 25 users per AP.

Medium contention in 802.11 is similar to medium contention in 802.3 half-duplex wired networks. All stations have equal access to the medium, and the greater the number of stations, the greater the chance for frame collision, backoff, and retransmission. As detailed in Chapter 2, "802.11 Wireless LANs," the same issues exist for 802.11 DCF stations.

The logical result of contention is induced latency in the BSS. Stations are spending more time trying to access the medium instead of transmitting and receiving frames. This process leads to upper-layer protocol timeouts and has the potential for dropped application sessions.

When these scenarios exist, it is advisable to opt for high-density deployments to avoid or mitigate these situations. There are costs associated with denser AP deployments, but given the low cost of APs, and the costly impact to productivity, it makes sense to correctly deploy WLANs initially rather than perform a second site survey and augment an existing deployment.

You can make many tweaks to client stations to account for high-contention BSSs:

- **Adjusting the fragmentation threshold**—The fragmentation threshold specifies the largest size a frame can be before being fragmented. As detailed in Chapter 2, the smaller frames have a better chance of successfully being received by either client or AP.

- **Adjusting the Ready to Send (RTS) threshold**—The RTS threshold specifies the largest size a frame can be before the transmitter sends an RTS. An RTS allows the transmitter (either AP or client) to effectively reserve the medium for a given amount of time to send a frame and receive the expected acknowledgment.

WLAN setups generally do not employ either of these mechanisms because they are manually set on the clients and not signaled by the AP. Either the user or the network administrator must configure each client station during times of congestion, which is not practical or scalable in large WLAN deployments. Also, you must set the values for fragmentation and RTS thresholds with care. The performance improvements they provide come with a cost (namely, increased contention and frame overhead).

WLAN Deployment Planning

There are two general methodologies in deploying WLANs:

- Coverage oriented
- Capacity oriented

This section discusses both types using a typical office floor plan, as shown in Figure 8-1.

Figure 8-1   *Typical Office Floor Plan*

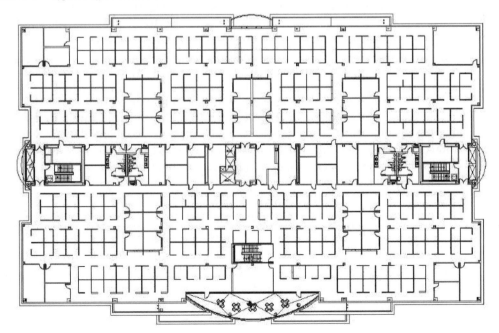

Coverage-Oriented WLANs

A coverage-oriented WLAN is designed to provide maximum WLAN coverage with the least amount of APs. (A typical coverage-oriented network provides a user to AP ratio of 25 to 1.) Some characteristics of a coverage-oriented deployment include the following:

- Bursty, low packet rate application types, such as barcode scanning and database queries

- Low bandwidth requirements, allowing data rate scaling down to lower data rates such as 1 or 2 Mbps

- Ease of maintenance because of little or no support staff local to the WLAN

In coverage-oriented deployments, the typical applications have low packet rates and low bandwidth requirements. Because of these meager demands on the WLAN, the users can expect effective throughput in these deployments to be quite high.

This setup allows more users to leverage the WLAN while still maintaining adequate performance.

These types of deployments might be common in warehouse environments or retail environments where WLANs are mission critical for inventory control and just-in-time purchasing and where the IT staff is in a central site, with no local support staff to troubleshoot coverage issues.

Also, it might be common for small or medium branch offices to opt for such a deployment as an alternative to installing wired Ethernet. In these cases, the branch offices experience a significant amount of relocation and Category 5 cabling expenses are minimized. A simple-to-deploy WLAN provides basic network connectivity such as file and printer sharing.

Figure 8-2 illustrates the example floor plan from Figure 8-1 with a coverage-oriented WLAN deployment.

Figure 8-2 provides WLAN coverage with roughly 25 to 30 users per AP. To provide complete coverage for the floor, the plan uses 14 APs. Note that the deployment provides coverage to all areas, including storage closets, restrooms, and stairwells where coverage might not be normally required. It is reasonable to assume that other possible deployment configurations use fewer APs, but the configuration in Figure 8-2 is used for the sake of simplicity and illustration.

Figure 8-2   *Typical Office Floor Plan with a Coverage-Oriented WLAN*

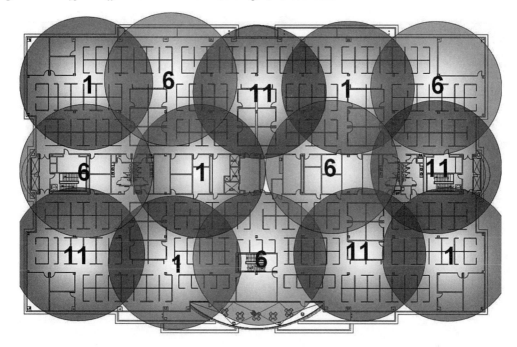

Capacity-Oriented WLANs

A capacity-oriented WLAN is designed to provide maximum throughput and packet rate for each client in a BSS. Capacity-oriented cell sizes are smaller than coverage-oriented cells, requiring a higher AP density. Capacity-oriented deployments are required for areas that have the following characteristics:

- High packet rate applications
- Latency-sensitive applications
- Smaller-sized subnet deployments (or multiple subnets per coverage area)
- Dense client population

Figure 8-3 illustrates the same floor plan with a capacity-oriented deployment. Note that there are more than twice as many APs in the capacity-oriented deployment (30 APs versus 14 APs).

The coverage area each AP provides is much smaller than in Figure 8-2; in fact, the cells are nearly half as small. Each AP provides coverage for roughly 12 users, and the entire deployment requires 30 APs as opposed to 14 APs in the coverage-oriented deployment.

Figure 8-3   *Typical Office Floor Plan with a Capacity-Oriented WLAN*

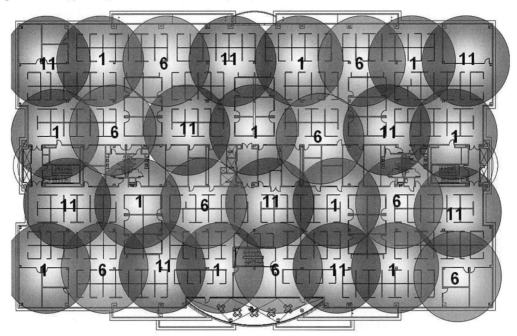

Phased AP Deployment—Migrating from Coverage-Oriented Deployments to Capacity-Oriented Deployments

A large number of deployments begin by providing coverage in common areas, such as conference rooms. The usual result from such a deployment is that users near the conference room leverage the WLAN while those who are farther away do without. These deployments are the seed to full-coverage deployments after the WLAN has been in place for some time. The user demand for WLANs usually forces the IT department to fully deploy at some point, so it might be useful to prepare for full deployments even when starting with a partial deployment.

It makes sense to perform an initial site survey for a complete coverage deployment. Figure 8-4 shows a partial deployment given the same coverage-oriented site survey from Figure 8-2. The deployed APs provide coverage to the common areas and conference rooms in the floor plan. The black dots represent the locations of APs for future deployment that will not interfere with the existing APs. Note that the deployed APs are in the same places as in Figure 8-2. This setup allows future deployments to occur without the need for additional costly site surveys.

Figure 8-4   *Partial AP Deployment*

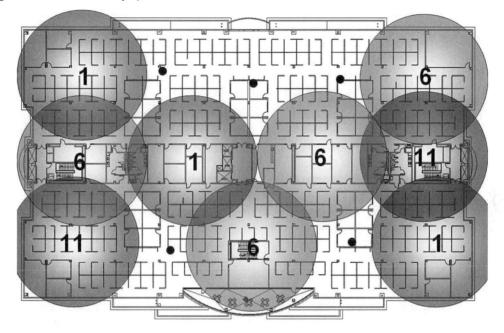

Site Survey

Ultimately, what you as a system administrator or site surveyor need to know is the number, location, and configuration of APs in your facility. To understand how best to discover this information, as explained earlier, it is important to determine whether the end goal is a capacity-, coverage-, or hybrid-driven design that emphasizes both aspects. The physical aspect of performing a site survey gives an administrator insight into what coverage area each AP provides, the number of APs required to cover the given area, the channel and transmit power settings and style or gain of antennas required. With this information, an administrator can determine the user-to-AP ratio and estimate throughput and forwarding rate per user in a coverage-oriented deployment. For a capacity-oriented deployment, you might start from the desired throughput and forwarding rate per user and the user density to determine the user-to-AP ratio. In addition, you need to weigh other factors, such as the limitations of the wired infrastructure and its ability to service your APs. In the end, you will place and configure your APs to maximize the performance in the basic service area.

Site Survey Challenges

As the site survey engineer, you face many challenges, and you need to understand and evaluate them up front before you even start performing the physical site survey. For example, if you don't understand the wired infrastructure in a warehouse, you might find that you are placing APs in locations that exceed the 100 meter (m) Category 5 100BASE-T cable lengths. The result might be that you spend hours performing measurements, only to discover that you need to start over at the beginning. Many of the obstacles that you face can be specific to your industry, as in the previous warehousing example, where the vastness of the facility can require unique solutions. Although this section discusses the types of challenges you face and how to look for them, Chapter 10, "WLAN Design Considerations," places those challenges into specific industries.

In addition to considering the size of the facility, you also need to be aware of how the wireless propagation environment can change over time. Working off the previous warehousing example, the environment provides different propagation characteristics with fully stocked shelves rather than empty shelves. You also need to pay attention to objects that tend to reflect microwave energy, causing multipath, as introduced in Chapter 7, "Radio Frequency Essentials," or objects that absorb the radio waves, making propagation itself challenging. Shelves stocked with energy-absorbing paper products, for example, tend to limit the overall propagation of radio signals, while also providing obstructions that can create coverage shadows in much the same way that they can shadow light. In the opposite extreme, with fully exposed empty metal shelves, free propagation occurs along with potentially harmful multipath. Your survey needs to consider both extremes and the specific needs of the network under these conditions. To cover a deployment that will vary from empty shelves to fully stocked over time, you likely want to employ smaller or more directional coverage areas that put the RF energy right where it is needed from locations that will never be obstructed. At the same time, you want to minimize the amount of energy that bleeds into other areas when shelves are empty, either by lowering the transmit power settings or by utilizing directional antennas. In all cases, you need to take careful signal-strength measurements during the site survey to ensure a robust design.

In a retail environment, the demands on the network can change from light usage to heavy usage as store managers use a small number of 802.11 phones during business hours, and then large numbers of employees flood the wireless network during nightly inventory sessions using barcode scanners. These scanners might require the transmission of many small transaction packets that need to arrive at their destination within a certain amount of time. In contrast, a streaming video display of specials might just require very high throughput. In the former case, it is critical that you achieve 100 percent coverage wherever the scanners might be operating. Because there is little data to share, it is satisfactory to only provide lower data rate coverage in some areas. The video case will likely require high data rate coverage, but it will only be at a fixed location or at a subset of the locations where scanner coverage is required.

You might not be able to control some sources of interference, such as some cordless phones, microwave ovens, and even other WLAN networks. Non-802.11–based cordless phones represent the most common source of harmful interference to WLAN networks. These phones are often designed to operate in either of the 2.4 GHz or 5.8 GHz ISM bands, utilizing either frequency-hopping or direct-sequence technology. The degree of degradation, if any at all, depends upon the numbers and types of phones in use. Some consumer-grade 2.4 GHz phones might clutter the entire band, whereas others are more spectrum friendly. If only a single phone is in use, as in the home, the best guidance is to place the base station away from APs or locations where client activity is anticipated. An office environment with many phones might raise the overall noise floor, thereby inhibiting WLAN transmissions. The best guidance is to either use an 802.11-compliant phone system or keep your data and phone networks in different frequency bands.

The other interference concern, which often appears in healthcare applications, is mission-critical equipment to which your network could be a harmful source of interference. Because the 2.4 GHz ISM band was allocated for medical devices, some hospitals might have units operating in this band. In general, WLANs operate at much lower transmit power levels than medical devices, and you might be able to place them upon channels where medical devices are not located or at power levels where they will not interfere. First and foremost, you need to understand where your medical devices are located and what their characteristics are. WLAN equipment that is compliant with the requirements of the International Electrotechnical Commission (IEC) 601-1.2 meets the industry limits. This compliance does not ensure that interference will not occur, although it might reduce the chances. For complete assurance, if your facility does use mission-critical equipment in the 2.4 GHz band, you might find that the easiest design choice is to use 802.11a in a non-ISM band such as the U-NII-1 band.

The physical environment itself might provide other challenges if it requires your equipment to operate under extreme temperature, high or low humidity, or wet conditions. You might find that you need to provide coverage inside a refrigerated room in a warehouse, for example. In this case, it might be necessary to place the AP inside a heated enclosure if the required operating temperature falls outside the range specified by the manufacturer. Similarly, if you are creating outdoor hotspots and do not want to run a long RF cable from an indoor location for the AP to the outdoor antenna location, you might place the AP in a properly rated NEMA enclosure to protect it from the rain and elements.

If you need to provide coverage on multiple floors of a facility such as an apartment building, you also need to remember that your first-floor network might interfere with your second-floor network and vice versa, depending upon the design and construction of your building. This potential will lengthen the site survey process because it will be necessary not only to measure the signal strength on the desired floor, but also to measure it on the floor above and the floor below.

In retail or education environments, you might have special aesthetic requirements to hide the network infrastructure, either to protect it from vandalism or to meet specific corporate requirements. Under these circumstances, it is common to place plenum-rated APs above ceiling panels, if that space is available, and then place the antenna in the ceiling or wall itself. Because they are small and flat, patch antennas often work well in these circumstances.

In addition to these challenges, you need to consider the characteristics of the end-user clients. This consideration includes such factors as the types of client devices that your network will need to support, the nature of the workforce using the clients, and the type of applications they are running over the WLAN. With stationary PCs in an office environment, there will be very little roaming, so coverage can be more focused with less overlap. Even if laptops are in use, it might not be necessary to provide high data rate coverage away from desks and conference rooms. If your firm is an engineering firm that runs applications with high-bandwidth applications, such as CAD tools, you need to maximize capacity with much smaller cells and fewer users per cell. In contrast, if your end users are running session-based applications on barcode scanners, they might have minimal bandwidth requirements but require coverage that allows for seamless roaming with support for connectivity at all locations. With voice, your network will be filled with many small data packets, so you must understand the capacity of your WLAN infrastructure devices with respect to voice. In these examples, there can be no holes in your coverage. Some specialized client devices might not even support higher data rates. You must also take into account this possibility. From all these questions, your most basic need is to understand the throughput and packet-forwarding requirements on your network, on a global scale and in localized special requirements.

Wi-Fi CERTIFIED

 The Wi-Fi CERTIFIED on your client devices ensures a base level of interoperability between devices from different vendors. It is imperative that both your access points and client devices have this logo. The Wi-Fi Alliance, as discussed in Chapter 7, "Radio Frequency Essentials," performs interoperability testing so you can safely deploy without fear of interoperability concerns.

As indicated earlier, it is not enough to understand these wireless-driven requirements, but you must also have a thorough understanding of the LAN infrastructure to which you are interfacing. One of the most important questions is, "What is the topology of your network?" You need to understand the networking equipment, hubs, switches, and routers that you are connecting to and where it is located. You must also understand what types of media interfaces your LAN can provide. It is most likely unshielded twisted-pair (UTP), but it might also be fiber. Remember that 100BASE-T Ethernet can only run 100 m over Category 5 UTP. If Dynamic Host Configuration Protocol (DHCP) is in use, where is the server and what lease times are in use? A WLAN network of clients might have very different LAN client network requirements.

You need to know whether cabling is routed through plenum spaces and whether your infrastructure equipment needs to be capable of being deployed there. Most buildings have firewalls, and the National Electric Code specifies procedures for penetrating them. You should measure cable lengths with straight segments and 90 degree turns; provide for service loops for the cabling contractor to deal with unforeseen issues; and, if antenna cables are in use, minimize their length and be aware of the losses they introduce at your operating frequency.

Site Survey Tools

With your WLAN challenges, requirements, and goals, it is time to gather the tools you need to conduct your site survey:

- The client device, radio, and antenna that you expect to service with your network.
- APs with battery packs to run the APs for at least 8 hours.
- Two of each type of antenna you anticipate using.
- Mounting tools for the AP, battery pack, and antenna. They can include brackets, duct tape, and zip ties.
- Markers to indicate the locations of APs.
- Measuring wheel for horizontal and vertical distances.
- RF cable or attenuator, if you anticipate using remote antennas.
- A SW tool that provides the receive signal level, signal quality, noise and interference level, and packet transfer performance.

Conducting the Survey

After you gather all the necessary tools, it is time to conduct the survey. Remember, as indicated at the beginning of this section, the questions you need to answer during your site survey are

- Where are the APs located?
- How are they mounted?
- How do they connect to the LAN?
- Where do you need to install cables and power?
- What antennas are used, and where are they located and mounted?
- How should you set configuration parameters that result in coverage factors such as power and data rate?
- What channel settings should be used?

The answers should be detailed enough that someone else could perform the install.

Considering the two extremes of a coverage-oriented approach and a capacity-oriented approach, your physical survey follows slightly different steps. With both, you should set channel assignments to avoid overlap and do each survey on the channel that will be used. You should also survey at the minimum desired data rate. In the multifloor case, remember that the floors above and below are part of the extremities, and you need to make measurements there as well. Do all measurements on the channel you intend to use—or you might get bitten by unknown interference. If cells seem smaller than expected, try changing channels because there might be interference issues.

With the coverage-oriented approach, choose one of the edges of your desired coverage area and place an AP there. Now, walk toward the center of the desired coverage area, until you locate the boundary of desired coverage. Move the AP to that location and survey the coverage. At this point, you have two options:

- Take the same approach with the other extremities and then fill in the holes in the middle.

- Place the next AP at the edge of the current one, find its coverage edge, and move the AP to that location. Work your way around the facility in a similar fashion.

With either of these approaches, you need to define your edges to allow for the appropriate level of overlap. Figure 8-5 shows an example of the extremity approach, and Figure 8-6 shows the AP-to-AP approach. In each figure, the channel in use is indicated in the center of each range circle. The lighter-shade APs indicate the initial locations used to determine the center point for the AP. The arrows show how the positioning of one AP determines the next AP's location.

Figure 8-5   *Coverage-Oriented Extremity Plus Hole-Filling Survey*

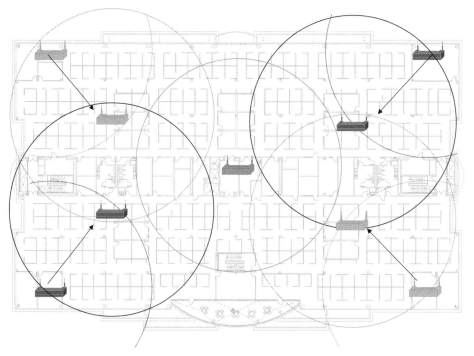

With a capacity-oriented approach, determine the number of users you want to attach to each AP and the user density, and from that, determine the desired cell radius. Use the same techniques as before, but adjust the power until you achieve the desired size cell. You should most likely use the extremity approach when you have isolated pockets of users, but you might use the other approach when the user density is fixed throughout the environment.

Depending upon the complexity of the site and the requirements, you might experience a lot of trial and error. You need to be creative at times because there might be many solutions to the puzzle.

Figure 8-6   *Coverage-Oriented AP-to-AP Survey*

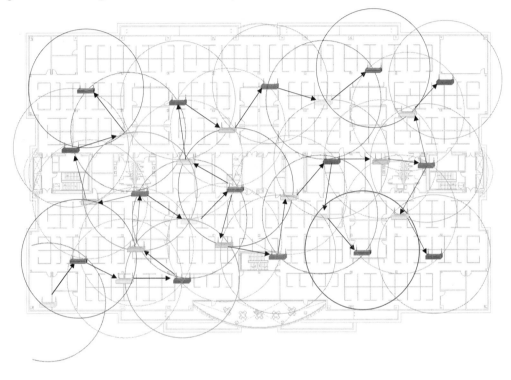

NOTE   For example, you can use directional antennas such as Yagis to cover the aisles of a warehouse, if only one end has Ethernet connectivity at, or you could run fiber out to the APs located at the far end.

Upper-Layer Considerations

After you finish a site survey and physical deployment mapping, the second phase of WLAN deployment can begin. A secure WLAN requires an authentication, authorization, and accounting (AAA) server such as RADIUS to allow for user-based authentication. In addition, you should also deploy a mechanism to manage the WLAN, either by extending an existing management platform, such as CiscoWorks, or by introducing a domain-specific platform just to manage the WLAN.

802.1X Deployment Considerations

Chapter 4, "802.11 Wireless LAN Security," covers security in depth and delves into how 802.1x is ingrained in the WiFi Protected Access (WPA) specification and the forthcoming 802.11i standard for WLAN security. The solution requires a AAA server to provide user-based authentication. The AAA server is probably located in a secured data center, several router hops away for the network edge. With the advent of Layer 3, wire rate switching, you can measure the network latency between the network edge and the data center in single digit milliseconds, if not microseconds.

802.1x-based deployments become more complicated when distributed across a WAN link. WAN links are generally lower bandwidth than LAN connections, and as a result, congestion can occur on these links. Congestion can have a significant impact on 802.1x-based authentication in that dropped RADIUS packets can cause client-station authentications to time out and fail, as well as potentially impact roaming, as depicted in Figure 8-7.

Figure 8-7   *WAN Link Congestion Impacting 802.1x Authentication in Remote Sites*

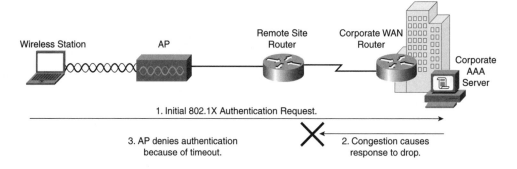

You can alleviate the problem in a couple of ways:

* Use QoS to prioritize 802.1x RADIUS packets across the WAN.
* Install a local AAA server at the remote site.

Prioritizing 802.1X RADIUS Packets Using IP QoS

Using QoS to prioritize RADIUS packets is easy. It provides priority for 802.1x packets during WAN congestion. For those who already have QoS deployed to support VoIP applications, the process to augment Cisco router and switch configurations in nominal.

VoIP typically has an IP precedence value of 5 and a differentiated services code point (DSCP) value of expedited forwarding (EF). Video usually has an IP precedence of value of 4 and DSCP value of AF41 through AF43. VoIP call control (MGCP or H.323) usually has an IP precedence value of 3 and DSCP value of AF31 to AF33. 802.1X RADIUS packets can be viewed as control traffic that is network critical, so it is reasonable to classify it along with VoIP call control with an IP precedence of 3 or DSCP of AF31 to AF33. These values are summarized in Table 8-1.

Table 8-1   *IP QoS Summary*

Function	IP Precedence Value	DSCP Value
Voice (VoIP)	5	EF
Video	4	AF41–AF43
Signaling (VoIP call control, 802.1x)	3	AF31–AF33
Normal data	0	0

Using QoS to prioritize 802.1x RADIUS traffic does not solve every issue associated with remote site authentication. The following issues persist:

- WAN outage
- WAN latency

If the WAN link were to become unavailable, the client station would be unable to access the WLAN, barring the user from accessing local resources. WAN links with very high latency (such as VSAT) can also negatively impact authentication because the AP or client might simply time out the authentication attempt. This scenario leads to poor station performance.

Local Authentication at Remote Sites

Local authentication at remote sites might seem like the obvious answer to the problem, but by no means is it a panacea. Deploying AAA servers at remote sites has issues:

- **Expense**—Large remote-site deployments require at least one server per site.
- **Manageability**
  - Authentication servers could number into the thousands, depending on the deployment.
  - The replication of user databases to large numbers of remote sites can be problematic.
  - Administrator access can be an issue if remote-site administrators need to constantly access the central server.

Some vendors, such as Cisco Systems, incorporate WAN survivability into their APs to let customers avoid the expense and to manage the headaches associated with local AAA servers, as shown in Figure 8-8.

Although the solution is not perfect, it enables administrators to confidently deploy WLANs in remote sites while maintaining a single authentication database to manage.

Figure 8-8   *Local Authentication Service on the AP*

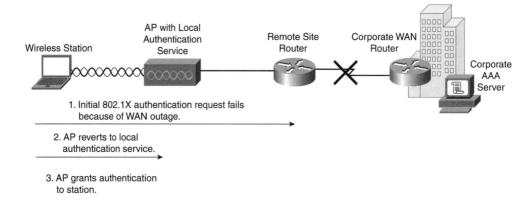

Managing WLANs

Network management, and in particular WLAN management, is a topic that requires a book unto itself. This section highlights some key concepts to consider during deployment.

In any type of network,

> *You cannot manage what you cannot measure.*

Many large networks can have as many as a thousand managed devices. In a typical large enterprise WLAN deployment, it is not uncommon to see nearly three times that many APs. WLANs can have a major impact on how you manage your network and also challenge the existing tools you use. To have a WLAN that performs as reliably as a wired LAN and minimize the management complexity, you need a management solution that includes WLAN management.

Many early adopters of WLANs have been plagued by the management burden of WLANs. Most cost-effective management packages hardly scale to several thousand devices without requiring multiple management stations, and none offer RF-specific management functionality. This absence left these deployments with poor-performing WLAN deployments and forced administrators to develop their own toolkits for effectively managing WLANs. Today, however, most laptops ship with 802.11 network interface cards (NICs) as standard equipment, and users are starting to rely on WLANs and demand the same level of availability as wired networks.

Many WLAN management solutions provide wired-like management services: Simple Network Management Protocol (SNMP) polling, fault monitoring, trap collection, configuration distribution, firmware distribution, and so on. No available solutions give the administrator insight into the radio network itself. WLAN performance varies widely with each implementation. Materials in the walls and the location of external interferers such as microwave ovens can impact the performance of WLANs, and the introduction of Bluetooth devices, ad-hoc clients, and neighbors using WLANs can degrade the performance of a WLAN to the point of making it useless.

Radio management gives the administrator clear visibility into all these issues and, depending on the solution implementation, can automate the control of radio parameters such as frequency/channel selection and client/AP transmit power to adapt to harsh RF environments.

Seek solutions that provide this functionality because it will make your job as an administrator much easier. RF networking is such a drastic departure from wired networking that without years of experience, finding a management tool that performs complex site survey calculations, path loss, interference detection, and possible location services certainly makes sense.

Summary

The decisions you make when deploying a WLAN are crucial to optimal WLAN performance:

- What kinds of users will use the WLAN (highly mobile versus nomadic)?
- What kinds of applications will these users use on the WLAN?

Although these two questions are basic and almost self-explanatory, they are typically overlooked at deployment time. They are the foundation for saving costs during the life of the deployment, namely in selecting a deployment scenario, whether it is coverage oriented or capacity oriented.

Once you understand how you want to deploy, knowing what tools to use to perform site surveys and the best practices for a site survey can save you time and money for a tedious and time-consuming task. Today, site surveying is a manual task, meaning that the person doing the survey performs all the measurements and calculations. With the growth of WLANs and management tools that automate some of these processes, it is reasonable to expect the same performance and reliability from a WLAN as you do from a wired network.

CHAPTER 9

The Future of Wireless LANs

Predicting the future of any technology is always challenging, but in this chapter, you learn about some current and upcoming technologies that might change the face of WLANs. Several of these technologies are not actually suitable for wireless LANs (WLANs) but might well provide complementary solutions.

The first technology we consider is Bluetooth, which is actually a current technology designed for short-range wireless, essentially as a cable replacement over distances typically limited to less than 10 feet. Bluetooth is often referred to as a personal-area network (PAN). Then, we discuss ultra wide band (UWB), an extension of Bluetooth with much higher data rates that uses short duration and low power pulses. On the other end of the spectrum, free space optics (FSO) have long been studied as a point-to-point wireless technology that leverages fiber-optic transponders to transmit gigabits of data without using optical fiber. Finally, 100 Mbps WLANs are in the early development stages to extend 802.11 and will most likely be the next-generation technology adopted for the applications described in this text.

As indicated earlier, some of these technologies might serve complementary markets and solutions to WLANs, some might supplant 802.11 WLANs, and some might die out.

Bluetooth

Of all the technologies considered in this chapter, Bluetooth is likely the most advanced technology from the development perspective. Additionally, acceptance of Bluetooth devices and solutions creating PANs has grown since the technology was made available to consumers several years ago. As stated earlier, the design intent of Bluetooth is to replace cables that would connect devices that are within close proximity, less than 10 meters (m), such as a computer and keyboard or possibly even on a person with a cell phone and microphone. Figure 9-1 shows an example that uses Bluetooth wireless links instead of messy and tangling cables to connect peripherals to the desktop PC.

Figure 9-1   *Cable Replacement by Bluetooth*

Bluetooth devices operate in the same 2.4 GHz Industrial, Scientific, and Medical (ISM) band as 802.11 and 802.11b WLAN devices, and many of the same Federal Communications Commission (FCC) part 15 rules govern their use and emissions. These rules require that they don't cause harmful interference to licensed users and state that they have no protection from interference from other users, licensed or unlicensed. This point is important, because in the future, they will likely be a common source of interference to WLANs and vice versa as laptop manufacturers begin to embed both devices into their product offerings. Similar to WLANs, they are also subject to interference from microwave ovens and cordless telephones.

Each device on a Bluetooth network (or *piconetwork*, a small, self-contained network) is either a master or a slave. The master initiates the wireless links, and the slaves respond to the master. In general, any Bluetooth device can be a master or a slave and can change roles or even assume both roles in different networks. A Bluetooth multipoint network can have up to seven active slaves per master. All the slaves communicate only to the master, so any communication between slaves must pass through the master. Scatternets are created when a device is a slave in more than one piconet or when it is a master in one or a slave in the other.

Most Bluetooth devices provide an effective isotropic radiated power (EIRP) of 0 decibels per milliwatt (dBm), although the specification does define three classes of Bluetooth devices:

- Class 1 transmitters can provide up to 20 dBm (100 milliwatts [mW]) but must employ transmit power control so that they only employ the minimum power necessary for reliable communication.
- Class 2 transmitters have a maximum transmit power of 4 dBm (2.5 mW).
- Class 3 transmitters provide 0 dBm (1 mW).

Because Bluetooth was designed as a cable replacement, often for battery-powered devices, Class 1 Bluetooth transmitters are not common. The Bluetooth modulation scheme employed is Gaussian frequency shift keying (GFSK), just like frequency hopped spread spectrum (FHSS) WLANs, with a symbol rate of 1 Msps resulting in a base data rate of 1 Mbps.

Similar to older 802.11 WLANs, Bluetooth is a time division duplex (TDD) access mechanism using FHSS. The 2.4 GHz ISM band is divided into 79 1 MHz channels by one Bluetooth scheme, and each piconet hops through the channels in a pseudo-random manner. Bluetooth devices transmit each packet on a new hop channel. For a point-to-point or single slave piconet, 625 microsecond slots, each on a new channel, are created and numbered, with the master transmitting in even slots and the slave in odd slots. Each slot allows the transmission of 366 bits. With multipoint piconetworks, once again the master transmits in the even slots, but any given slave can only transmit if the packet in the previous slot was addressed to it. All slaves receive broadcast packets, but none can transmit in the timeslot following a broadcast packet. Because it breaks up the data to be sent into 366-bit packets, the protocol overhead can be quite high, so the Bluetooth specification allows the transmission of three-slot or five-slot multislot packets. They are transmitted on the same channel, and when the transmission finishes, the next transmission occurs on the channel that would have been used had the multislot packet not been present. In other words, some of the channels in the hop sequence are skipped. Either masters or slaves can use multislot transmission. Figure 9-2 shows a sample transmission sequence on a multipoint network with two slaves, with the master utilizing a multislot packet to one slave.

Figure 9-2   *Sample Bluetooth Transmission Sequence*

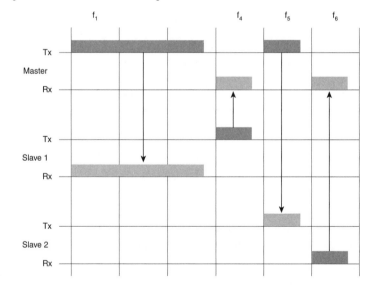

Bluetooth provides two different types of physical links:

- Asynchronous connectionless links (ACLs) are most often used for data communication where data integrity is often a much higher priority than latency. Packet retransmission corrects error packets.

- Synchronous connection-oriented (SCO) links create a circuit-switched, scheduled, low-latency point-to-point link between a master and a slave with no packet retransmission.

Each Bluetooth device has a unique 48-bit Bluetooth device address. Active slaves are provided with a 3-bit active member address by the master, whereas inactive or parked slaves are given an 8-bit parked member address. These parked slaves synchronize to the master's timing and hop sequence, and they listen for broadcast packets, where the master uses the parked member address to unpark them. The master also assigns them an access request address that specifies a special access window in which they can send an unpark request. As stated earlier, all Bluetooth devices can be either a master or a slave, and a master is nothing more than the device that initiates a piconet, whereas the slave is the device that enters the piconet at the request of the master. A master can initiate low power modes, sniff, hold, and park—to conserve energy, to allow more than seven slaves in a piconet, to provide the master with time to bring other slaves into the piconet, or to provide a means to be in multiple piconets, creating a scatternet.

Because scatternets are a bit different from anything that 802.11 WLANs provide, it is useful to examine them in more detail. The three most common uses for a scatternet are

- To provide a mechanism for a device to enter an existing piconet by forming a scatternet with the master
- To enable cross-piconet communication
- To create a limitless store-and-forward network

Although these tools might appear to be rather useful, Bluetooth faces some challenges. For the devices themselves, they must maintain synchronization with two independent piconets. From a throughput perspective, the timing offsets between the two piconets reduce performance, and higher-layer protocols face challenges with routing and error recovery. With ACL traffic, a scatternet member can use the sniff, hold, and park modes to manage the two piconets, but with SCO traffic, each scatternet member must alternate between its two piconets. All this work can create such significant challenges that in the end, you might be better off having your device disconnect from one piconet before connecting to another one or installing two Bluetooth devices with a single host.

The Bluetooth Special Interest Group (SIG) that created the Bluetooth specification, and that manages the ongoing technical working groups in addition to other activities, actually defined several usage models for specific applications using devices from different vendors. Usage models include, but are not limited to, the following:

- The three-in-one phone provides cellular and cordless phone operation in addition to walkie-talkie functionality.
- The ultimate headset provides an audio interface to other devices such as telephones, computers, and stereo systems.
- The Internet bridge allows a cellular phone to provide a bridge between Internet access via the cellular network and a computer with a Bluetooth interface.
- The object push and file transfer usage models permit the basic transfer of information between enabled devices.

Mapping the appropriate profiles, which are the basic Bluetooth building blocks, creates these usage models. These profiles

- Allow developers to reduce the many options that Bluetooth provides to only those that are required for the necessary function
- Provide procedures for a function to be taken from a base set of standards
- Provide a common user experience across devices from different manufacturers

In summary, Bluetooth by design solves a different problem than 802.11 addresses, that of cable replacement. As such, it is characterized by a lower transmission rate, a shorter range, lower power consumption, and lower cost in general. Because both Bluetooth and 802.11 WLANs operate in the same frequency band and are potential sources of interference to each other, it will be interesting to see how laptop manufacturers solve the problem of collocated Bluetooth and 802.11 devices.

UWB

UWB is a new technique for which the FCC has defined preliminary guidelines for using extremely wide relative bandwidth signals generated via short, low power pulses and that could allow high-bandwidth, interference-resilient communication. The FCC defines UWB as a signal that has a fractional bandwidth, the ratio of the signal bandwidth to the carrier frequency, of greater than 25 percent. The FCC guidelines allow you to transmit UWB signals across a wide breadth of spectrum that is already occupied by many other incumbent technologies which are relatively narrowband relative to a UWB signal. This arrangement is allowed under the principle that the emission limits are so low, even with the large numbers of transmitters, there is no perceptible impact upon existing technologies and systems. UWB systems use the very wide bandwidth to separate out the narrowband interference from existing systems. At press time, no standard exists for the pulses, their frequency, or the modulation technique, but nonetheless the technology holds great promise.

The FCC Report and Order that specifies new rulings creates several classes of UWB devices, each with its own set of emissions limits:

- Low-frequency imaging systems consisting of ground penetrating radars (GPR)
- High-frequency imaging systems consisting of GPRs, wall imaging, and medical imaging
- Mid-frequency imaging systems for through-wall imaging and surveillance systems
- Indoor communication and measurement systems
- Outdoor handheld communication and measurement systems
- Vehicular radar systems for collision avoidance, improved airbag activation, and suspension systems

The limits for the classifications, with the exception of vehicular radar systems, are summarized in Table 9-1.

Table 9-1   *UWB Emissions Limits*

Classification	Part 15 Frequency Band	Part 15 Emissions Limits (dBm/MHz)					
		< .960 GHz	.960–1.61 GHz	1.61–1.99 GHz	1.99–3.1 GHz	3.1–10.6 GHz	> 10.6 GHz
Low-frequency imaging	< 960 MHz	-41.25	-65.3	-53.3	-51.3	-51.3	-51.3
High-frequency imaging	3.1–10.6 GHz	-41.25	-65.3	-53.3	-51.3	-41.3	-51.3
Mid-frequency imaging	1.99–10.6 GHz	-41.3	-53.3	-51.3	-41.3	-41.3	-51.3
Indoor	3.1–10.6 GHz	-41.3	-75.3	-53.3	-51.3	-41.3	-51.3
Outdoor	3.1–10.6 GHz	-41.3	-75.3	-63.3	-61.3	-41.3	-61.3

Vehicular radar systems have a pass band that extends from 22 to 29 GHz. Table 9-2 summarizes the vehicular classification emissions limits.

Table 9-2   *UWB Emissions Limits for Vehicular Radar Systems*

Classification	Part 15 Frequency Band	Part 15 Emissions Limits (dBm/MHz)					
		< .960 GHz	.960–1.61 GHz	1.61–22 GHz	22–29 GHz	29–31 GHz	> 31 GHz
Vehicular	22–29 GHz	-41.3	-75.3	-61.3	-41.3	-51.3	-61.3

As you can see, these emissions levels are quite low. In fact, they are at or below the spurious emissions limits for all intentional radiators and at or below the unintentional emitter limits. The emissions limits for ISM devices are a good 40 dB higher than what is called out by the FCC for UWB, so UWB signals should just appear as random noise to most receivers. From the perspective of interference to UWB from other radios, the large processing gain that the very high fractional bandwidth enables should remove the narrower band interference. With regards to multipath, the high fractional bandwidth also allows for a large pulse-separation period, relative to the pulse duration, so RAKE receivers should be able to constructively use multipath energy.

| NOTE | In addition to producing emissions in the desired channel and band of operation, all radiators also generate unintentional or spurious emissions at other frequencies. In fact, many electronic devices that are not communication devices, such as microwaves, produce spurious emissions. The strength of these emissions is very tightly restricted by spurious emissions limits. |

| NOTE | A RAKE receiver takes the multiple copies of a transmitted signal that are generated by the unique propagation paths which create multipath and combines them to form a stronger composite signal than could be generated by any of the individual copies. When the duration of the pulses of a Bluetooth waveform are very short relative to the separation in time between pulses, the RAKE receiver is better able to separate out the copies. |

The major challenges that UWB faces follow:

- UWB calls for the design of RF devices of extremely wide RF bandwidth, devices that do not exist today. It is the nature of the technology that it will always be operating in the presence of interference at power levels much higher than the desired signal.

- The bandwidth of the signal requires faster processing than can be done digitally today.

- As with the RF challenge, there will be a similar challenge to design antennas with the desired bandwidth.

- UWB is only an FCC initiative, so a major global standardization effort is necessary.

UWB is obviously well in front of the bleeding edge of technology and it will need to overcome many challenges. Over time, however, if the fundamental principles are correct, it could provide a wireless revolution similar to what 802.11 is producing today.

FSO

FSO attempts to leverage optical and laser technology advances in the fiber-optical realm to create short-range, high-bandwidth, line-of-sight, physical-layer point-to-point links through the transmission of near-infrared signals through the air. It brings the promise of multigigabit wireless transmissions but with some severe limitations that so far have precluded it from widespread acceptance and deployment. However, depending upon your specific circumstance, it just might provide a solution that can work for you, as an alternative to an 802.11 wireless bridge.

The main technological challenges that FSO links face follow:

- Fog, which consists of tiny water droplets and can absorb, scatter, or reflect light, is the major challenge. Other forms of weather, such as rain and snow, have a lesser effect, although very heavy rain or blizzard conditions can also brink down a link.

- Absorption, which is a function of the wavelength of the light in use, can decrease the power of the light beam. Absorption most often comes from fog or aerosols such as dust, sea salt, or man-made pollutants.

- Scatter, especially when the scattering particle is similar to the wavelength, can significantly attenuate the beam intensity because it redirects energy in random directions. The scattering particles could be fog, haze, or pollutants. As the link range increases, so do the scattering losses.

- Physical objects, such as birds, can actually temporarily interrupt FSO links.

- Building sway can disturb the alignment of the transmitter and receiver and disrupt the link.

- Turbulence, which occurs when heated objects create moving air pockets of differing temperatures, causes time-varying changes in the index of refraction at the air-pocket interfaces. It can result in beam wander as it randomly reflects through the pockets, scintillation in the form of intensity fluctuations, and increased beam spread.

Fortunately for the FSO community, the two most common fiber-optic communication wavelengths, 850 and 1550 nanometer (nm), happen to align with two atmospheric absorption windows.

A simple FSO transmitter consists of an LED or laser light source connected to a telescope formed from lenses or mirrors and a receiver that has a similar optical assembly that focuses light energy on a photo detector. The use of LEDs, while providing a cheap solution, in general limits the bandwidth to the hundreds of Mbps over much shorter ranges than lasers can achieve. Because semiconductor lasers are fairly small and high power, and because they are in use by the fiber-optic community as well, most FSO vendors build their systems around these components. The optical subsystem of mirrors and lenses usually contributes the most to the size of FSO systems and requires a very precise and costly calibration and alignment procedure that must be maintained across temperature variations as the lenses and mirrors expand and contract.

To achieve any significant ranges, it is necessary to use a very narrow beam divergence, such as a milliradiant. As you move the receiver away from transmitter, the beam diverges to diameters that are larger than the receive telescope, and any transmitted energy that is not collected results in geometrical path loss. For example, as shown in Figure 9-3, with a 2-milliradiant beam divergence and a link range of 500 m, the beam diameter will be 1 m. However, if the receiving optics collects energy from a 10 centimeter (cm) diameter region, only 1 percent of the energy will be collected, for a 20 dB loss in the link budget. For every doubling of the distance, the geometric path loss is increased by 3 dB in clear air.

Figure 9-3   *Geometric Path Loss Example*

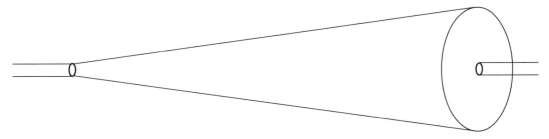

Decreasing the beam divergence makes the initial alignment of the link more challenging and also makes it more susceptible to building sway, which can result in a pointing loss. To combat this problem and enable the use of narrower beams, you use tracking and acquisition systems. They usually include an auto-tracking feature that can use a deflection-detection system, such as an array of detectors. With these systems, the output is processed in real time to drive a gimbal that adjusts in the vertical and horizontal plane.

The installation process for an FSO link can be somewhat more time-consuming than that for an 802.11 wireless bridging link, mainly because of the many previously discussed challenges. You must meticulously plan the site survey with a significant fade margin built in for environmental effects. During the installation, you must take care to keep the link far enough above sources of air turbulence, and the alignment itself must be pinpoint. Because of the potential harmful effects to your eyes, you must take care with the high-power lasers, especially with equipment operating with an 850 nm wavelength because that frequency can easily penetrate the eye.

Despite all these caveats, the promise of Gbps links at a fraction of the cost of fiber trenching might make this technology viable for your application. Similar to 802.11, FSO operates in an unlicensed manner, but unlike radios, they are not subject to interference. With the proper precautions and planning, you can end up with a solution that provides years of reliable service.

100 Mbps WLANs

Several companies offer 108 Mbps WLANs today, but because there is no standard, they don't interoperate. In general, they combine two of the available 802.11a channels, forming a single "new channel" that is twice as wide as a standard channel. In the near future, we might see the formation of a higher throughput task group in 802.11. It is anticipated that such a task group would not only focus on achieving a 100 Mbps data rate, but also strive for a 100 Mbps throughput experience for users—because it is what they have come to expect from their wired LANs. To achieve this experience, it will need to make modifications to the 802.11 physical layer (PHY) and the 802.11 MAC. The group must weigh questions of coexistence and backward compatibility in addition to those of basic viability regarding spectral efficiency, range, and power consumption.

From a usage-profile perspective, the two main drivers for 100 Mbps throughput WLANs will be throughput equivalence with wired 100BASE-T Ethernet and wireless multimedia for the home. The former will further the cause of the fully wireless office because wireless will provide the same throughput experience as wired. The latter will be driven by the desire to provide high-quality audio and video to all parts of the home without wiring and also support Internet surfing.

Summary

This chapter considered three complementary technologies. UWB will most likely be a replacement for Bluetooth because it is seeking to address the same wireless PAN space as Bluetooth but with much higher data rates. FSO has been deployed as a point-to-point technology when the right conditions exist, but because it still has not gained mainstream acceptance, it will likely be surpassed or integrated with point-to-point radio techniques. The real future of 802.11 lies with a 100 Mbps WLAN standard that will be the next quantum step forward after 802.11g and 802.11a.

CHAPTER 10

WLAN Design Considerations

A wireless LAN (WLAN) is typically viewed as access points (APs) that connect to the access layer of a LAN as a transparent bridge, allowing wireless clients to appear as though they are connected directly to the wired network while retaining the mobility that wireless networking provides.

The truth is that WLANs are complex and APs and clients must work in concert with one another to abstract the complexity of the 802.11 protocol. As such, a solid design and deployment plan is required to retain the easy-to-use interface to the clients.

This chapter introduces you to the specific design considerations for some of the most common WLAN deployment scenarios: retail, healthcare, branch office/telecommuter, education, public safety, and public access.

Considerations for Retail Stores

Luckily for most WLAN vendors, one market that relies on WLANs as a mission-critical application is the retail market. Next time you walk into your favorite home-improvement store, electronics store, or department store, look at the walls and ceiling. You're bound to find APs, or at the very least antennas mounted, to provide coverage for 802.11 client devices.

These types of business rely on client/server applications surrounding inventory control and supply-chain management. WLANs provide the employees the mobility they need in a store environment to quickly and efficiently check inventory with instantaneous updates to backend systems and databases, providing a huge cost savings in both timeliness and improved accuracy. The introduction of Voice over IP (VoIP)-enabled 802.11 clients has also been accepted by many companies as a replacement for proprietary narrowband, licensed, radio-frequency (RF) systems, 900 MHz systems, or two-way radios. These new VoIP handsets can provide functions over and above a typical voice handset by also providing two-way paging functionality and web-based application support. For example, an employee can clock in by simply logging into her VoIP handset and receive work assignments. Use of thin client interfaces on these data-capable VoIP handsets lets you deploy custom applications to streamline mundane or tedious operational tasks. One example includes interactive text-based messaging. For example, a store manager can sent a broadcast message to all active handsets to instruct one employee to do a particular task. All employees receive the message, and the one can acknowledge the message and proceed to complete the task.

Retail stores have taken advantage of WLAN technology far prior to the ratification of 802.11 in 1997. Many companies were producing proprietary 2.4 GHz and 900 MHz wireless system in the 1990s and licensed narrowband systems in the 1980s, along with client devices such as barcode scanners. As you can imagine, most barcode-scanning applications have meager bandwidth requirements because the data stream is small and bursty in nature. For that reason, many of these early deployments were coverage-oriented in nature. Site surveys focused on minimizing the total number of APs required and providing maximum coverage. In a typical home-improvement warehouse, it is uncommon to see three to five access points cover the entire facility.

Today, the use of VoIP and a more diverse client base (including laptops, personal digital assistants [PDAs], and wireless printers) demands more capacity from the infrastructure. Newer deployments now consist of 10 to 20 APs just to provide the capacity and coverage for the insurgence of these converged applications.

Retail networks have many characteristics that distinguish them from other types of networks. Retail stores typically have the following:

- Numerous stores (hundreds, sometimes thousands, of locations in different geographical locations)
- Nonredundant, low bandwidth WAN connections back to a hub site or central site
- Little or no information technology (IT) or networking staff on hand at the individual stores
- Minimal IT infrastructure at the local stores

Figure 10-1 depicts a typical nonconverged retail store network.

The capacity and coverage issue is overcome with a more dense AP deployment; however, the preceding issues add new twists to how the network administrator designs and deploys a store network. A retail store typically has the following characteristics that a network manager needs to consider when designing a WLAN:

- Primary client/server applications are housed locally in the store.
- Converged applications (VoIP and security) are centralized at the hub or central site.
- Management solutions can scale to support the large number of managed APs.

The store needs the ability to operate during outage conditions. Given that most WAN links are nonredundant, centralized backend databases would be useless to a store during a WAN outage. For this reason, the primary application servers are generally housed locally in the store.

Figure 10-1 *A Typical Retail Store Network*

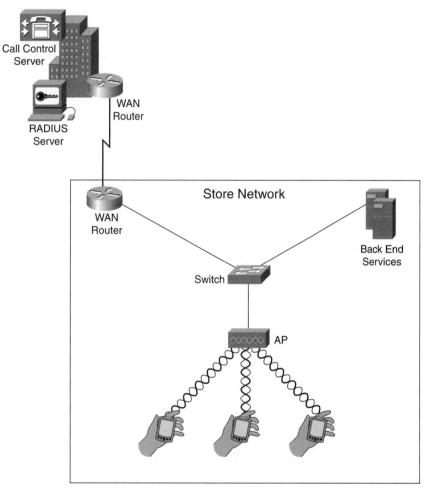

VoIP is generally a centrally managed application to make it cost effective. A WAN outage can impact VoIP signaling and operation. In response to this issue, many vendors offer survivability modes, where local-network infrastructure can detect the loss of central connectivity and assume a survivability mode. This mode allows an employee in a call to continue without noticing the outage (unless the call was across the WAN link). The same premise holds true for WLAN security. The emerging standards in the IEEE 802.11 task group I and Wi-Fi Protected Access (WPA) interoperability specification require the use of an authentication, authorization, and accounting (AAA) server for user-based authentication. RADIUS servers (the most common AAA server used for WLAN security) have limited management for decentralized deployments and face major challenges for administration and account synchronization. Most retail companies opt to centrally house this service to minimize these limitations. The downside to this approach is its vulnerability to WAN outages. If the WAN link or central AAA server becomes unavailable, wireless devices cannot authenticate and as a result are unable to access resources local to the store network. In such a situation, a wireless barcode scanner cannot access the inventory database located in the store because it cannot authenticate to the WLAN.

One solution for VoIP survivability in retail stores is Cisco Survivable Remote Site Telephony (SRST). SRST is typically implemented in branch-office routers, and the feature monitors VoIP signaling traffic back to the central call control server (the Cisco Call Manager). If the central server becomes unavailable due to WAN outage or server failure, the SRST device takes over call control so that in-store calls are possible.

Cisco also offers a similar solution for WLAN authentication survivability. Routers or switches running Cisco IOS Software with the IEEE 802.1X local authentication service can remain active and securely authenticate even when connectivity to the central AAA server is lost. These solutions provide maximum uptime for the WLAN and its applications while minimizing the impact and expense to the WAN. Figure 10-2 illustrates a retail store network with survivability functions incorporated.

Scaling network-management systems to adequately service large AP deployments is still a lingering issue for WLANs. Management tools that are widely available today are typically designed for wired networks. Large-scale retail deployments can range anywhere from hundreds to thousands of APs requiring the same element management of wired networks, including configuration and image management, reporting, and trending. These tools do not scale to meet the needs of most wireless deployments. As a result, network administrators are left to their own devices in designing creative and effective ways to manage their store networks. Many vendors are developing management platforms that rise to the occasion by providing the scalability and tools required to manage wireless networks. These tools have lacked the integration into wired management platforms necessary to allow a single point of management visibility into the ever-changing network. Retail customers have raised their voices and demanded that either tools be made available from their current vendors or they will switch vendors!

Figure 10-2 *A Retail Store Network with Survivability Features*

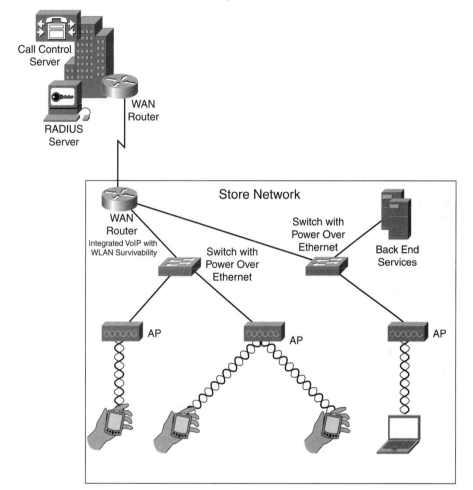

Healthcare Design Considerations

Wireless usage in healthcare has significantly increased with the proliferation of 802.11b devices and the erosion of price of 802.11b equipment. Healthcare environments see an immediate return on investment (ROI) with the use of WLANs, namely in the form of patient tracking, distribution of medication, claim collection for insurance companies, and increased doctor and nurse mobility (lending to faster patient response time and turn-around time).

Many companies are starting to deliver mobile applications on PDAs that allow doctors and nurses to process claims forms to insurance companies in a timely and, more importantly, accurate manner. This process reduces the number of rejected claims caused by human error and reduces the turn-around time for payment. Also, many healthcare information-systems vendors are starting to look at WLANs as an automation mechanism to deliver mobile applications.

Mobile healthcare applications exhibit the same characteristics as a retail store—from a packet perspective. That is, the traffic is low bandwidth and bursty. These deployments are usually coverage-oriented to reduce the number of APs, and it is common to see directional antennas to focus coverage of long hospital corridors, as opposed to use of the standard 2.2 dBi omnidirectional dipole antenna.

Many healthcare facilities with existing deployments are re-evaluating their coverage-oriented deployments to facilitate VoIP applications as well. Use of VoIP handsets allows healthcare staff to be reachable while they are mobile, again reducing patient response time and turn-around time. The coverage-oriented deployments that currently exist do not provide adequate capacity to facilitate VoIP over WLANs, so many deployments are being re-site–surveyed to facilitate VoIP as a primary application.

In the same vein as VoIP, location-based services are also gaining momentum in the healthcare market, although most of today's systems are non-802.11. Once these systems, which allow the pinpointing of a node to a 3 to 6 feet accuracy, can leverage 802.11 equipment, a new market of location aware applications will appear. These applications will track healthcare staff and patients, quickly locate equipment during an emergency, and display location-sensitive data when a staff member walks in proximity to a patient.

Enterprise Branch Office and Telecommuter Design Considerations

Many of the design considerations for enterprise campus deployments are covered in detail in Chapter 8, "Deploying Wireless LANs." This section focuses on two other enterprise deployment types for WLANs: the branch office and the home telecommuter. Both of these deployment types are increasing in number and popularity and have specific considerations that are not captured by campus or large deployment guidelines.

Design Considerations for Enterprise Branch Office Deployments

As stated earlier, the economic crunch that hit the United States economy in late 2000 placed a financial barrier on enterprise spending. Any expenditure required significantly more justification than it did in years past. As WLAN technology has matured, and many of the key barriers to deployment (namely security) are addressed, enterprises are starting to embrace WLANs not so much for campus or headquarter deployments, but rather as a wired network replacement in small branch offices.

A large number of enterprises experience a significant amount of turnover in their branch offices. A major cost associated with this turnover has been the cost of Category 5 cabling for the data network. IT planners see a tremendous cost savings by leveraging WLANs in branch offices as a replacement for wired networks. 802.11 client devices are available for every platform, including laptops, PDAs, printers, and servers, and at the same time, 802.11 VoIP handsets are becoming more prolific. This availability gives an IT planner a great deal of flexibility for branch-office deployments. The WLAN is a truly converged network, allowing file and print services, voice, and Internet access, all at relatively low cost.

Enterprise branch offices are similar to retail store deployments in that a large number of branches or remote sites can connect via WAN links to a central site. Branch offices tend to have meager infrastructure requirements, as with retail stores, but they differ in a number of ways:

- Redundant, high-bandwidth WAN connections back to hub site or central site
- Some form of IT/networking staff local to the office
- Some application back ends local to the site but a majority housed centrally
- No mission-critical application that requires WLANs

Figure 10-3 depicts a WLAN-enabled branch office. Note the key differences between the branch office network and the retail store network: A redundancy WAN minimizes the requirement for local services (both for AAA servers for WLAN security and VoIP survivability), and almost every device is WLAN enabled. This setup is necessary to maximize the ROI of the WLAN. Remember that most enterprises do not have a mission-critical application that requires WLANs. WLANs in these environments provide value based on their cost reduction for cabling and portability.

This is a tremendous boon for the WLAN industry. WLAN technology is viral in nature. Most users get "addicted" to its flexibility and freedom and demand that they cannot work effectively without it. Many vendors estimate that deployments in the branch offices will force enterprises to deploy wireless in the campus headquarter sites.

Interestingly enough, enterprise branch office deployments share many of the challenges that retail stores do with security services (location of the AAA server), WAN survivability, and WLAN management. Many of the solutions developed to cater to the retail markets are being leveraged by the enterprise branch offices. It is important to note that in many cases, however, WAN survivability is addressed by WAN redundancy—that is, redundant WAN hardware and circuits. Enterprise branch offices tend to rely on applications and data that resides in enterprise data centers at the central site. Loss of WAN connectivity can in some cases halt operations in remote sites, necessitating such an investment in the WAN.

Figure 10-3 *A WLAN-Enabled Branch Office*

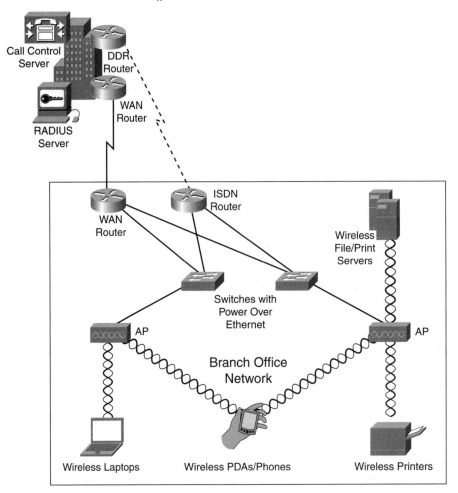

Design Considerations for Enterprise Telecommuters

Enterprise telecommuters have many cost-effective mechanisms to access corporate data resources. Where once only expensive, clear-channel WAN circuits, or switched data services such as ISDN, were viable high-bandwidth options over dialup services, today telecommuters can select from a number of high-speed broadband solutions. Such solutions includes high-speed digital subscriber line (DSL) services, broadband cable modems, and high-speed satellite services, all for under $100 per month (in the United States). Couple with this availability the introduction of cost-effective, secure, and manageable virtual private network (VPN) equipment, and enterprises can extend the reach of their data networks and applications to an employee's home. Figure 10-4 illustrates a telecommuter's network solution where VPN over high-speed broadband Internet access facilitates access to the corporate network.

Figure 10-4 *Telecommuter Network Using VPN and High-Speed Broadband Internet Access*

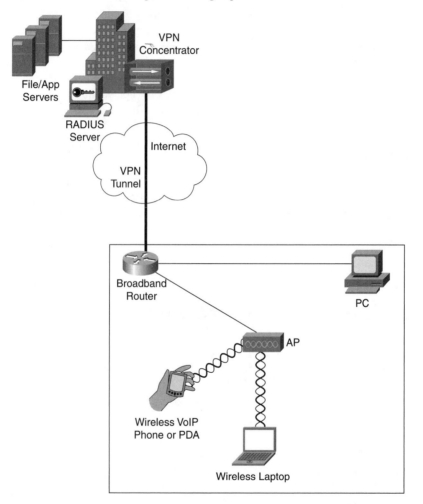

In some cases, the VPN client resides on the user's laptop or PC, establishing a secure tunnel from his machine to the VPN concentrator. This setup gives only a single device with the appropriate VPN client software access to the enterprise network. You would be unable to deploy devices such as IP phones in the employee's home. In Figure 10-4, the broadband router acts as a VPN client and all devices behind it are capable of accessing the corporate network. This setup enables network administrators to provide the telecommuting employee with a solution that leverages all corporate converged applications.

Although Figure 10-4 illustrates a network where the user has access to all converged applications, it also has the potential for many security holes. When the user has the VPN tunnel terminate on a specific endpoint, such as a laptop or PC, access to corporate resources are limited to that specific user and device. However, the scenario in Figure 10-4 allows any device behind the broadband router to access the corporate network via the VPN tunnel. With the proliferation of low-cost APs widely available and targeting the home market, the probability of an unsecured AP being connected to such a home network is extremely high. If the AP is not configured to operate securely, it is no different from having an unsecured AP operating in the corporate network. What is worse is that network administrators have next to no chance of detecting these APs. In a corporate campus, it is recommended that IT departments roll out rogue AP detection mechanisms and perform routine "walk-throughs" to manually detect rogue APs. This detection is just not possible with telecommuters.

The solution to this problem lies with the imminent 802.11i standard. Once 802.11i-compliant APs are widely available, IT departments can easily roll out hardware that is preconfigured and that leverages the central AAA servers for secured access. Although it does not prevent users from connecting unauthorized devices, using 802.1X on switch ports on the broadband router might also deter this behavior. Also, most employees that do connect rogue APs to networks do so not out of malice, but for the convenience the service provides. The IT department rolling out wireless in the home will have a huge impact on the reduction of rogue APs in the home.

Education Design Considerations

Like healthcare and retail, education at both the university level and the primary/secondary level has experienced widespread adoption of wireless technologies. Educational institutions often do not have the luxury to lock network access to a particular room, nor can they afford to constantly reconfigure and retool their networks. WLANs give them the opportunity to provide ubiquitous coverage so that they can bring the network to the student instead of bringing the student to the network. As computers have become a larger part of the learning process, the time and resource savings that wireless brings has proven to be rewarding.

More than just the convenience and the cost savings, you might find that many school buildings were designed before the computer revolution. It just might not be feasible to run wires to the student. WLANs don't have these sorts of boundaries, so you can now bring the network to places where it might not have been possible several years ago. The time and cost savings of not having to wire or rewire often pays for the expense of the wireless infrastructure.

The physical deployment of wireless in an educational environment faces the same challenges as an enterprise office with many individual offices in the form of classrooms. You often need wireless coverage in the open spaces of grass-covered quadrangles and congested student unions and cafeterias. The greatest challenge schools face today is ensuring that the infrastructure can support a multivendor client environment. Even with the model of specialized computer purchase plans at the university level, it is common for students to provide their own computers and, with the low cost of WLAN client hardware, supply their own wireless network interface cards (NICs). At the primary/secondary level, it is common for a group that is separate from the network-infrastructure group to make computer-purchase decisions. These scenarios create a situation that can include client devices with many different operating systems and with wireless NIC devices that need to communicate with a common infrastructure.

At the time of this writing, running a multivendor environment with 802.11b and 40-bit or 128-bit WEP does not present much of a challenge because wi-fi–certified 802.11b devices are readily available. In time, the same will hold for 802.11a and 802.11g. The biggest catch at this point involves security because you might want to restrict the access level for different user groups. For example, overall access to a university network might be limited to students, educators, and staff while nonaffiliates are directly routed to the Internet. Even within the network community, there are different classes with students not having the same level of access as faculty.

WPA, as introduced in Chapter 4, "802.11 Wireless LAN Security," provides a secure interoperable environment, but you might still be left with the task of supporting legacy, pre-WPA clients. If your AP infrastructure supports the use of VLANs, you can manage access by different user groups, students, and staff, according to VLANs. Similarly, you can provide different levels of security on different VLANs so that the individuals with computers that do not support 802.1x type authentication, for example, would still be allowed access to parts of the network. In this way, you can handle pre-WPA clients and operating systems that might not support your authentication mechanism.

You might also find temporary classrooms or remote educational sites need access to your network. Rather than trench or lease lines to these locations, the easiest and most rapidly deployable solution might be to employ wireless bridges to connect the remote network with the school network, as discussed in Chapter 2, "802.11 Wireless LANs."

Public Access Design Considerations

Public access refers to those deployments where the intent is to provide Internet access via the wireless medium to the general public in particular areas. The desire to provide this type of service has grown in hotels, cafes, airports, and any other locales where people congregate. As many of these businesses do not intend to provide free offerings, many of the developments in public access have been in the area of authentication that ties into billing systems. For deployments in Europe, integration of Subscriber Identity Module (SIM) smart-card authentication schemes has been key so that the solution can easily tie into existing Global System for Mobile Communication (GSM) billing systems. The authentication scheme can also determine what services a particular client is permitted to use.

The billing question raises the biggest user-experience issue for public access today, *roaming*. Roaming refers to the ability to use networks from multiple providers while maintaining a single customer-vendor relationship. At the time of this writing, for the most part, if you go to a different locale, you need to purchase airtime with the vendor providing the service, rather than have it billed to your home account. WECA has formed a wireless Internet service provider roaming (WISPr) committee. Because it is not a standards body, the output will be little more than best-practice suggestions. With the integration of SIM-based billing systems into 802.1x authentication schemes, the situation is improving, and with time, it is anticipated that roaming agreements between service providers will become a reality.

Figure 10-5 shows a sample architecture of a public access solution with multiple public access hot spots connected to a single point of presence (POP). An integrated service selection gateway (SSG) pops up the main user interface screen, handles the authentication process, and then directs and manages traffic based upon the profile and services purchased. The figure shows the SIM authentication interface to the signaling system 7 (SS7) network, along with the Internet connection.

Figure 10-5 *Sample Public Access Architecture*

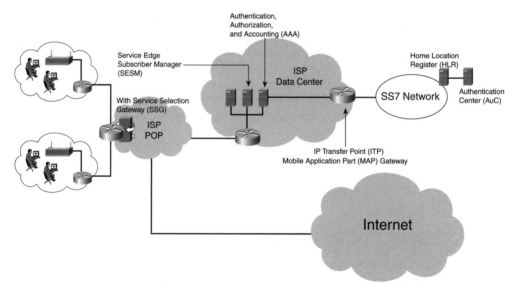

The actual physical deployment of a public access hot spot is the most straightforward part of the problem at hand, with many of the same design techniques of other markets applying equally well here. In addition, on a small scale in a captured public market, you can fairly easily handle the billing and authentication mechanisms. As previously indicated, the true challenge is in the billing and roaming areas, and this area is where much of the development in this field will focus.

The Wi-Fi ZONE designation, provided by the Wi-Fi Alliance, means that the service provider offering the public-access service is using Wi-Fi CERTIFIED gear for an easy user experience. Wi-Fi ZONE providers are required to provide quality customer service and a high level of service that supports VPNs back to corporate networks. Either as a client looking for access or as a service provide, the designator is a key component of public access.

Public Safety Design Considerations

Public safety departments have used mobile radio technology for more than 70 years. However, it has most often been nothing more than a low data-rate service suitable for carrying voice and/or a small amount of data. With the advent of 802.11, we are on the doorstep of a data revolution that could see the delivery of voice, video, and high-speed data directly to first responders. A pilot program in one community has police officers carrying PDAs with an 802.11 wireless feed from wireless cameras inside crime scenes while the crime is taking place, while still other programs facilitate the sharing of database information across city and county boundaries.

Given the unlicensed nature of the 802.11 frequencies, most public safety deployments employ the formation of zones of 802.11 coverage as an overlay to currently licensed lower data-rate solutions. Figure 10-6 illustrates a sample coverage scenario with 802.11 service in the central business district and lower-rate mobile radio coverage throughout the rest of the region. In more rural communities, via cooperative management of the spectrum, more ubiquitous shared public safety, business, and public access coverage might be possible with access segmented via VLANs. Depending on whether the desire is to bridge mobile networks or just to provide client access, you can use either wireless bridges or APs. Obviously, it is paramount that you the use adequate security in the form of authentication and encryption to secure public safety information, either in the form of the latest 802.11 security mechanisms or via VPNs.

Figure 10-7 illustrates a deployment using wireless bridges to connect public safety vehicles to the municipal network, with video feeds, while creating a hot spot coverage zone around the vehicle for handheld devices. (VPNs provide security.)

Figure 10-6 *802.11 Coverage for Public Safety*

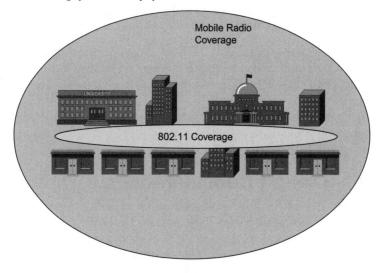

Figure 10-7 *Example Public Safety Network*

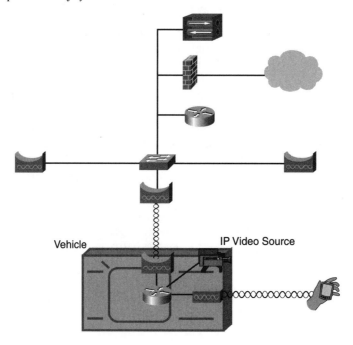

In short, 802.11 can provide a complement to existing public safety mobile radio technologies that facilitates information sharing in a way that was never before possible. Because of the lack of interference protection, it is not suitable for widespread ubiquitous coverage but rather is a secondary technology. When used appropriately, it can provide a compelling and easy-to-use and -install solution.

Summary

This chapter introduced a number of different applications of WLANs in such diverse areas as healthcare, education, and public safety. In each of these areas, WLANs have enabled either efficiencies or actual applications that were not previously available. This chapter introduced the challenges of each application area, such as interoperability in a multiclient environment, along with potential solutions, such as the use of VLANs to segment user classes.

Numerics

3DES (Triple Data Encryption Standard) The de-facto standard for IP Security (IPSec) and virtual private network (VPN) encryption.

10BASE2 Implementation of Ethernet that runs over thin, RG-58, or RG-59 coaxial cable. A 10BASE2 segment has a maximum distance of 185 meters (m).

10BASE5 Implementation of Ethernet that runs over thick coaxial cable, and each segment has a maximum distance of 485 m.

10BASE-FL Implementation of Ethernet that runs over multimode fiber cabling. Each 10BASE-FL link has a maximum distance of 2 kilometers (km).

10BASE-T Implementation of Ethernet that runs over Category 3 or 5 unshielded twisted-pair (UTP) cabling. Each 10BASE-T segment has a distance of 100 m.

100BASE-CX Implementation of Gigabit Ethernet that runs over shielded twisted-pair (STP) cabling. Each 1000BASE-CX segment has a maximum distance of 25 m.

100BASE-FX Implementation of Fast Ethernet that runs over multimode fiber cabling. A 100BASE-FX segment has a maximum distance of 400 m in half-duplex mode and 2 km in full-duplex mode.

100BASE-LX Implementation of Gigabit Ethernet that runs over single-mode fiber cabling. Each 1000BASE-LX segment has a maximum distance of 5 km.

100BASE-TX Implementation of Fast Ethernet that runs over Category 5 UTP cabling. A 100BASE-TX segment has a maximum distance of 100 m.

100BASE-X Collective term for both 100BASE-TX and 100BASE-FX Fast Ethernet topologies.

802.1X The IEEE standard for port-based, Layer 2 authentication in 802 networks.

802.3 The IEEE standard for wired Ethernet topologies. This specification encompasses Ethernet, Fast Ethernet, and Gigabit Ethernet today.

802.5 The IEEE standard for Token Ring topologies.

802.11 The IEEE standard for wireless, Ethernet-compatible wireless LANs (WLANs).

802.11i The IEEE standard for link layer security for 802.11 networks.

802.11e The IEEE standard for link layer quality of service (QoS) for 802.11 networks.

802.11 slot time A time value derived from the physical layer (PHY) based on radio frequency (RF) characteristics of the basic service set (BSS).

1000BASE-SX Implementation of Gigabit Ethernet that runs over multimode fiber cabling. Each 1000BASE-SX segment has a maximum distance of 220 m.

1000BASE-T Implementation of Gigabit Ethernet that runs over Category 5 UTP cabling. Each 1000BASE-T segment has a maximum distance of 100 m.

A

AAA server A server that provides authentication, authorization, and accounting functions.

AC (access category) Transmit queues for 802.11e QoS-enabled devices.

access layer A term used for design networks that indicates the edge of a network. In a LAN, the access layer provides end stations with connectivity to the network.

acknowledgment frame What a station receiving a frame sends back to the sending station to acknowledge the frame.

active scanning A client actively searching for an access point (AP). It usually involves the client sending probe requests on each channel it is configured to use and waiting for probe responses from APs.

AES (Advanced Encryption Standard) The latest standard encryption algorithm endorsed by the National Institute of Standards and Technology (NIST). AES is based on the Rijndael encryption algorithm.

AES-CCM The mode of AES used in 802.11i.

AID (association identifier) A logical port on the AP for the wireless station.

AIFS (arbitration interframe space) Varying interframe spaces based on an AC's priority.

antenna The part of the radio system designed to radiate or receive electromagnetic energy.

AP (access point) The central point of communications for all stations in a BSS.

auto negotiation Allows a station and Ethernet device (which can support one or more Ethernet variants such as 10BASE-T, 100BASE-TX, or 1000BASE-T) to automatically synchronize speed and duplex mode.

authentication server An AAA server for 802.1X or Extensible Authentication Protocol (EAP) authentication.

authenticator The entity to which a supplicant wants to secure connectivity.

B

beacon frame An 802.11 management frame used by the AP to update the BSS of the AP's presence and its parameters.

Bluetooth A short-range wireless technology designed to create personal area networks.

block cipher A cipher that generates a key stream of a fixed size. The plaintext must be fragmented into matching size blocks during the encryption operation.

bridge An Ethernet network device that physically separates two Ethernet collision domains.

broadcast domain An internetwork of devices that are capable of sending and receiving broadcast frames to and from one another.

broadcast frame A single frame destined to all stations in a broadcast domain.

BSS (basic service set) A group of 802.11 stations communicating with one another via an AP.

C

CCK (complementary code keying) A physical layer spreading technique used by the 802.11b standard to achieve 5.5 and 11 Mbps data rates.

CFP (contention-free period) A time period where access to the wireless medium requires polling via the point coordination function (PCF) or hybrid coordination function (HCF).

CoA (care of address) The device that receives packets sent by the home agent (HA) destined for the mobile node (MN). The CoA can exist on the MN itself or on the foreign agent (FA).

cochannel overlap Overlap of two BSSs that are on the same channel.

collision The result of two frames being transmitted in the same collision domain at the same time.

collision domain An internetwork of Ethernet devices that contend for a single medium.

contention period The time duration where distributed coordination function (DCF) stations contend with one another to access the medium.

core layer A term used for designing networks that indicates the center of a network. The core layer should forward frames or packets as fast as possible between routers or switches.

CSMA/CA (carrier sense multiple access with collision avoidance) The basic medium access method for 802.11 networks.

CSMA/CD (carrier sense multiple access with collision detection) The basic medium access method for Ethernet networks.

CW (contention window) The time period when the 802.11 medium is idle.

D

DAC (distributed admission control) Enhanced DCF (EDCF) admission-control mechanism where stations determine whether they should transmit based on budget advertisements from the AP.

data link layer The second layer of the Open System Interconnection (OSI) reference model. Consists of two sublayers: the data link sublayer and the logical link sublayer.

data link sublayer Also known as the MAC layer, this sublayer focuses on topology-specific implementations. For example, 802.5 Token Ring networks have a different MAC from that of 802.3 Ethernet networks.

dBi Unit for describing antenna gain relative to an isotropic antenna.

dBm Unit for power measured relative to 1 milliwatt.

DCF (distributed coordination function) CSMA/CA operation in 802.11 wireless LANs. DCF is the required basic access mechanism for all 802.11 devices.

DIFS (DCF interframe space) The amount of time after the medium becomes available that a station must wait before beginning DCF medium access. A DIFS is equal to a short interframe space (SIFS) plus two slot times.

directivity Describes the intensity of the radiation pattern emanating from an antenna.

distribution layer A term used for designing networks that indicates the layer of the network that segments the networks into distinct Layer 2 broadcast domains by using routers or Layer 3 switches. Network services, such as access control lists (ACLs), route filtering, and Network Address Translation (NAT), are applied at the distribution layer.

DQPSK (differential quadrature phase shift keying) The symbol-encoding mechanism used for 2 Mbps 802.11 operation.

DSSS (direct sequence spread spectrum) The modulation technique used for 802.11 WLAN networking.

duplex A term that describes whether a network topology allows simultaneous transit and receive by network devices (see *full duplex*) or not (see *half duplex*).

E

EAP (Extensible Authentication Protocol) A Point-to-Point Protocol (PPP) authentication framework.

EAP-MD5 (Message Digest 5) An EAP authentication type based on Challenge Handshake Authentication Protocol (CHAP) authentication.

EAP-TLS (Transport Layer Security) An EAP authentication type based on TLS authentication. Digital certificates are used for client- and server-side mutual authentication.

ECB (electronic code book) A mode of encryption where the same plaintext always produces the same ciphertext.

EDCF (Enhanced DCF) Mandatory 802.11e contention-based traffic prioritization and medium access method.

EIRP (effective isotropic radiated power) A measurement that indicates the actual power that is radiated from an antenna.

ESS (extended service set) A collection of BSSs that communicate with one another through the distribution system (usually the wired Ethernet port on an AP).

Ethernet The IEEE 802.3 standard for wired 10 Mbps network operation. Other higher-speed variants to Ethernet are Fast Ethernet and Gigabit Ethernet.

Ethernet slot time The time it takes for an Ethernet frame to traverse the network diameter.

Ethertype The data contained in the payload of a MAC frame.

F

FA (foreign agent) An agent on routers or Layer 3 switches that aids the MN in determining it has roamed and in receiving packets from the HA.

fading Occurs when the power level of the signal drops because of various environmental factors.

Fast Ethernet The IEEE 802.3u standard for 100 Mbps network operation.

FCS (frame check sequence) A field in MAC frames to determine whether an error has occurred during transmission. The FCS value is computed and inserted into the frame by the transmitting station. The receiving station recalculates the FCS value and compares it to the FCS value in the frame. If the values match, the frame has been received error free.

FDD (frequency division duplex) A duplex method that uses a different frequency to carry information in each direction.

FDDI (Fiber Distributed Data Interface) The ANSI X3T9.5 standard for 100 Mbps network operation. FDDI uses a Token Ring–like topology with a multimode fiber cable plant.

FHSS (frequency hopped spread spectrum) A modulation technique that hops from channel to channel.

FSK (frequency shift keying) A modulation technique that shifts between two frequencies to represent 0s and 1s.

full duplex A network topology where stations can transmit and receive data simultaneously.

G

Gigabit Ethernet The IEEE 802.3z and 802.3ab standard for 1000 Mbps network operation.

GMK (group master key) The master key for broadcast and multicast frame encryption operations, including encryption and message integrity.

GSM (global system mobile) A common cellular phone standard.

GTK (group transient key) The link layer key used to encrypt multicast and broadcast frames. The GTK is derived from the GMK.

H

HA (home agent) An agent on routers or Layer 3 switches which ensures that a roaming MN receives its IP packets.

half duplex A network topology where stations can either transmit or receive data at any moment.

HCF (hybrid coordination function) Optional 802.11e polled access medium mechanism.

hidden node When two stations are out of range of one another, but both are in range of the AP, the stations are said to be hidden from each other.

hub A half-duplex Ethernet device with multiple ports. A hub allows a single Ethernet signal to be repeated out many ports.

I

IAPP (Interaccess Point Protocol) Protocol used by APs to communicate with one another.

IBSS (independent basic service set) A group of 802.11 stations communicating directly with one another. An IBSS is also referred to as an ad hoc network because it is essentially a simple peer-to-peer WLAN.

ICV (integrity check value) A weak MIC function defined in 802.11. The ICV uses a CRC-32 to provide message integrity for 802.11 frames.

IRDP (Internet Router Discovery Protocol) Protocol used by FAs and HAs to send agent advertisements.

isotropic antenna An ideal lossless antenna that provides the same gain in all directions.

IV (initialization vector) A numeric value that is concatenated to the key before the key stream is generated to avoid the same key generating the same key stream.

L–M

LEAP A Cisco-developed EAP authentication type based on Microsoft CHAP (MS-CHAP) authentication.

logical link sublayer Standard across all 802-based networks, this sublayer contains a simple frame protocol that provides connectionless frame delivery.

MIC (message integrity check) Guarantees to the frame receiver that the frame is truly from the sender (as opposed to a man-in-the-middle) and that the frame has not been tampered with during transmission.

MN (mobile node) A mobile-IP–aware roaming station.

mobile IP A protocol that allows for a MN to retain a static IP address as it roams across VLANs.

multicast frame A single frame destined to many stations in a broadcast domain.

multipath Occurs when multiple versions of the transmitted signal arrive at the receiver via different paths.

mutual authentication Authentication where not only does the network authenticate the client, but the client also authenticates the network. This authentication is a requirement for 802.11i authentication.

N–O

NAV (network allocation vector) The virtual carrier-sense function for 802.11 stations. The NAV is a timer on every station that is updated by data frames transmitted on the medium. A station wanting to transmit must have a NAV that is equal to 0 before it can begin DCF operation.

network diameter The distance between Ethernet stations at the extreme ends of a broadcast domain.

nonce Number once. A number that is used only one time, primarily for cryptographic functions such as authentication or encryption.

OFDM (orthogonal frequency-division multiplexing) A modulation technique used to provide very high data rates for 802.11a and 802.11g.

Open authentication The 802.11 mandatory authentication type. Open authentication is a null authentication type, where any station is granted access.

P

passive scanning Scanning where the client does not transmit any frames but rather listens for beacon frames on each channel. The client continues to change channels at a set interval, just as with active scanning, but the client does not send probe requests.

PBCC (packet binary convolutional coding) An optional coding technique used in 802.11b.

PCF (point coordination function) Mode of medium access for 802.11 BSSs where the AP (or point coordinator) polls PCF-pollable stations for data to transmit.

PEAP (Protected EAP) An 802.1X authentication type where server-side authentication happens using digital certificates and client-side authentication happens via another 802.1X authentication type, such as EAP-MD5.

PIFS (PCF interframe space) The amount of time after the medium becomes available that a station must wait before beginning PCF medium access. A PIFS is equal to a SIFS plus one slot time.

PMK (pairwise master key) In 802.11i networks, PMK is the dynamic key generated by 802.1X authentication.

PTK (pairwise transient key) The key used for link layer encryption in 802.11i networks.

R

radio A communication device used for electromagnetic transmission through free space.

RADIUS server A specific implementation of an AAA server.

RC4 (Rivest Cipher 4) The cryptographic engine used for WEP encryption.

receiver sensitivity The minimum signal level for the receiver to be able to decode the received signal.

repeater A half-duplex Ethernet device. A repeater repeats an Ethernet signal to increase the network diameter of a given Ethernet topology. For example, you can use a repeater to extend the distance of a 10BASE-T network from 100 m to 200 m.

roaming domain APs that are in the same broadcast domain and configured with the same service set identifier (SSID).

S

Shared Key authentication A challenge/challenge-response authentication type included in the 802.11 standard where a WEP key is the shared secret.

SIFS (short interframe space) The shortest amount of time stations wait before attempting to access the medium. A SIFS is typically used to manage frames. For example, after a station receives a data frame, it waits for a SIFS and then sends an acknowledgment frame.

spectral efficiency A measure of the information bits that can be communicated or the amount of spectrum that is used to convey that information.

SSID (service set identifier) A logical grouping for 802.11 devices.

stream cipher A cipher that generates a key stream to match the size of the plaintext or unencrypted data frame.

supplicant The device that is attempting to access the LAN using 802.1X authentication.

switch A multiport Ethernet bridge that typically uses hardware acceleration to increase the performance of switching Ethernet frames between collision domains.

T

TC (traffic class) Eight distinct classifications for data as defined in 802.11e.

TDD (time division duplex) A modulation scheme that uses a different time slot to carry information in each direction.

TKIP (Temporal Key Integrity Protocol) An encryption and MIC algorithm included in the 802.11i standard that uses per-frame keys and lightweight message integrity to fix weaknesses in the WEP and ICV functions of in the 802.11 standard.

Token Ring A logical ring-based topology with deterministic, noncontention-based medium access. Typical data rates are 16 Mbps and 4 Mbps.

TXOP (transmission opportunity) A moment in time when a station can begin transmitting frames for a given duration. A TXOP can facilitate multiple frames/acknowledgments as long as they fit within the duration of the TXOP.

U–Z

ultra-wide band A new technology that provides very high data rates through the use of very short durations and very low power pulses.

unicast frame A single frame destined to a specific station in a broadcast domain.

VLAN (virtual LAN) A broadcast domain.

VSWR (voltage standing wave ratio) A measure of the reflections formed from impedance mismatches along transmission lines.

WEP (Wired Equivalent Privacy) A Layer 2 encryption algorithm based on the RC4 algorithm to provide data privacy for 802.11 networks.

INDEX

Numerics

D

F

N–O

P–Q

T

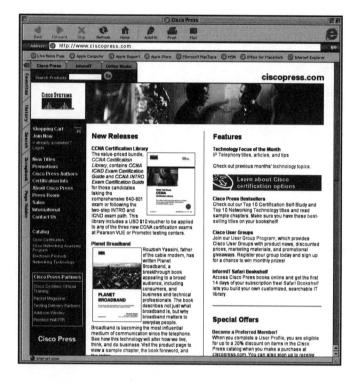

Wireless

Deploying License-Free Wireless Wide-Area Networks
Jack Unger
ISBN: 1587050692 • **Available Now**

Deploying License-Free Wireless Wide-Area Networks is the first book that provides complete, real-world "start-to-finish" design, installation, operation, and support information for wireless ISPs and other organizations deploying outdoor wireless WANs—including coverage of 802.11a, 802.11b, 802.11g, and proprietary-protocol networks. This vendor-neutral book covers all brands of broadband wireless equipment and explains the principles upon which all wireless equipment is based. Inside, you find step-by-step instructions and crystal-clear explanations that walk you through initial planning stages and onto full wireless network operation.

Whether you're an IT director, ISP engineer, network architect, or field technician, *Deploying License-Free Wireless Wide-Area Networks* is your essential reference. With practical, in-depth coverage of the real-world challenges of outdoor, license-free wireless WAN deployment, this book provides a comprehensive, vendor-neutral guide to successful wireless network design and operation.

Local-Area Networks

Cisco Catalyst QoS:
Quality of Service in Campus Networks
Richard Froom, Mike Flannagan, Kevin Turek
1-58705-120-6 • **Available Now**

Cisco Catalyst QoS is the first book to concentrate exclusively on the application of QoS in the campus environment. This practical guide provides you with insight into the operation of QoS on the most popular and widely deployed LAN devices: the Cisco Catalyst family of switches. Leveraging the authors' extensive expertise at Cisco in the support of Cisco Catalyst switches and QoS deployment, this book presents QoS from the campus LAN perspective. It explains why QoS is essential in this environment in order to achieve a more deterministic behavior for traffic when implementing voice, video, or other delay-sensitive applications. Through architectural overviews, configuration examples, real-world deployment case studies, and summaries of common pitfalls, you understand how QoS operates, the different components involved in making QoS possible, and how QoS can be implemented on the various Cisco Catalyst platforms to enable truly successful end-to-end QoS applications.

Cisco Field Manual: Catalyst Switch Configuration
David Hucaby, Stephen McQuerry
1-58705-043-9 • **Available Now**

This book presents concise implementation advice for families of Cisco Catalyst features, including configuration fundamentals, Layer 2 interface configuration, Layer 3 interface configuration, VLANs and trunking, Spanning Tree Protocol (STP), Layer 3 switching, multicast, server load balancing, access control, switch management, quality of service (QoS), and voice. Additional appendixes provide you with critical details on well-known ports and addresses, specialized switch modules, VLAN extension, and a cabling guide. The quick-reference format allows you to easily locate the information you need without searching through thousands of pages of documentation, saving you time and helping you get the devices up and running quickly and smoothly.

Cisco LAN Switching
Kennedy Clark, Kevin Hamilton
1-57870-094-9 • **Available Now**

Cisco LAN Switching provides the most comprehensive coverage of the best methods for designing, utilizing, and deploying LAN switching devices and technologies in a modern campus network. Divided into six parts, this book takes you beyond basic switching concepts by providing an array of proven design models, practical implementation solutions, and troubleshooting strategies. Part I discusses important foundation issues that provide a context for the rest of the book, including Fast and Gigabit Ethernet, routing versus switching, the types of Layer 2 switching, the Catalyst command-line environment, and VLANs. Part II presents the most detailed discussion of Spanning-Tree Protocol in print, including common problems, troubleshooting, and enhancements, such as PortFast, UplinkFast, BackboneFast, and PVST+. Part III examines the critical issue of trunk connections, the links used to carry multiple VLANs through campus networks. Entire chapters are dedicated to LANE and MPOA. Part IV addresses advanced features, such as Layer 3 switching, VTP, and CGMP and IGMP. Part V covers real-world campus design and implementation issues, allowing you to benefit from the collective advice of many LAN switching experts. Part VI discusses issues specific to the Catalyst 6000/6500 family of switches, including the powerful Native IOS Mode of Layer 3 switching.

Cisco Press

Learning is serious business.

Invest wisely.

Fundamentals

Data Center Fundamentals
Mauricio Arregoces, Maurizio Portolani
1-58705-023-4 • **Available Now**

Data Center Fundamentals helps you understand the basic concepts behind the design and scaling of server farms using Data Center and content switching technologies. It addresses the principles and concepts needed to take on the most common challenges encountered during planning, implementing, and managing Internet and intranet IP-based server farms. An in-depth analysis of the Data Center technology with real-life scenarios make *Data Center Fundamentals* an ideal reference for understanding, planning, and designing web-hosting and e-commerce environments.

IP Addressing Fundamentals
Mark Sportack
1-58705-067-6 • **Available Now**

IP Addressing Fundamentals explains simply and clearly how the IP address space works and how it is used. This is a reader-friendly book that details the fundamentals of the IP address space from the ground up. *IP Addressing Fundamentals* unravels the mysteries of subnetting, supernetting, and CIDR; thoroughly explains the binary mathematics of IPv4's addressing space; and demonstrates how an IP address becomes an active component in both networks and internetworks. Author Mark Sportack prepares you for real-world success by walking you through some of the issues and traps that lie in wait for anyone who needs to plan or manage the use of an IP address space. Most importantly, this book doesn't presume you already know what the entire IP addressing puzzle looks like.

IP Addressing Fundamentals imparts a profound command of IP addressing through a clear and concise writing style. Basics are reinforced with detailed information and numerous examples of how the concepts work. This book builds upon concepts presented in earlier chapters and concludes with fairly advanced topics that will become increasingly useful to midlevel network engineers.

Fundamentals

Cisco CallManager Fundamentals
Anne Smith, John Alexander,
Chris Pearce, Delon Whetten
1-58705-008-0 • **Available Now**

Cisco CallManager Fundamentals provides examples and
reference information about CallManager, the call processing
component of the Cisco AVVID (Architecture for Voice, Video,
and Integrated Data) IP Telephony solution. *Cisco CallManager
Fundamentals* uses examples and architectural descriptions to
explain how CallManager processes calls. This book details
the inner workings of CallManager so that those responsible
for designing and maintaining a Voice over IP (VoIP) solution
from Cisco Systems can understand the role each component
plays and how they interrelate. You'll learn detailed information
about hardware and software components, call routing, media
processing, system management and monitoring, and call detail
records. The authors, all members of the CallManager group at
Cisco Systems, also provide a list of features and Cisco solutions
that integrate with CallManager. This book is the perfect
resource to supplement your understanding of CallManager.

High Availability Network Fundamentals
Chris Oggerino
1-58713-017-3 • **Available Now**

High Availability Network Fundamentals discusses the need for
and the mathematics of availability, then moves on to cover
the issues affecting availability, including hardware, software,
design strategies, human error, and environmental considerations.
After setting up the range of common problems, it then delves
into the details of how to design networks for fault tolerance
and provides sample calculations for specific systems. Also
included is a complete, end-to-end example showing availability
calculations for a sample network.

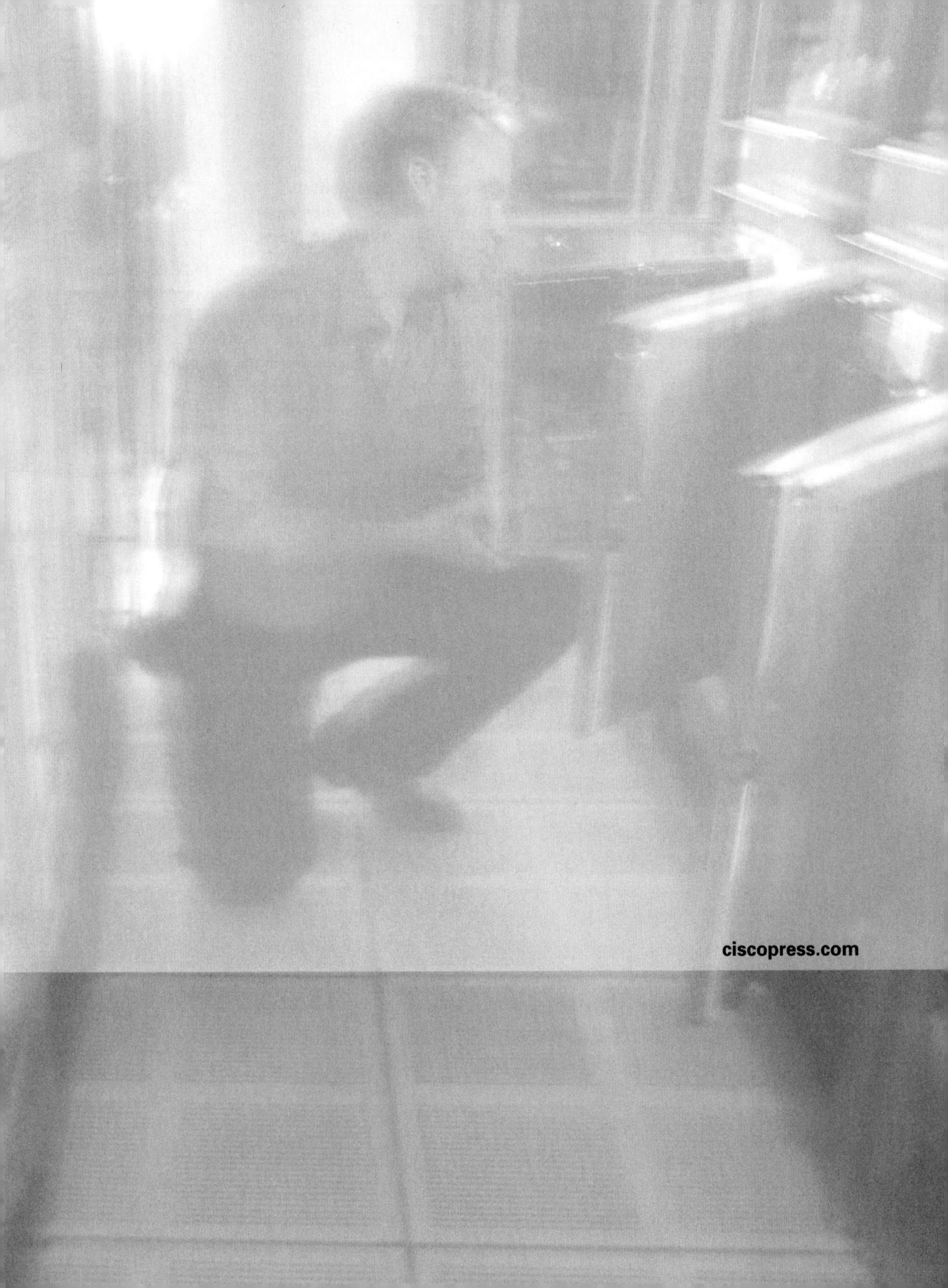
ciscopress.com

Fundamentals

Voice over IP Fundamentals
Jonathan Davidson, James Peters
1-57870-168-6 • **Available Now**

Voice over IP (VoIP), which integrates voice and data transmission, is quickly becoming an important factor in network communications. It promises lower operational costs, greater flexibility, and a variety of enhanced applications. *Voice over IP Fundamentals* provides a thorough introduction to this new technology to help experts in both the data and telephone industries plan for the new networks.

You learn how the telephony infrastructure was built and how it works today, the major concepts concerning voice and data networking, transmission of voice over data, and IP signaling protocols used to interwork with current telephony systems. The authors cover various benefits and applications of VoIP and how to ensure good voice quality in your network.

IP Routing Fundamentals
Mark Sportack
1-57870-071-X • Available Now

IP Routing Fundamentals is the definitive introduction to routing in IP networks. This comprehensive guide explores the mechanics of routers, routing protocols, network interfaces, and operating systems. Author Mark Sportack explains how routers can be used in today's networks, and suggests how they might be used in networks of the future.

This reference provides essential background information for network professionals who are deploying and maintaining LANs and WANs, as well as IT managers who are seeking information on how evolving internetworking technology will affect future networks. Part I discusses the many roles routers play in networks, Part II talks about the inner working of routers, Part III works with the operational issues of routing protocols, and Part IV addresses implementation issues that provide practical insight, in addition to a discussion of the future of routing.

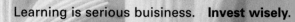

Learning is serious buisiness.   **Invest wisely.**

IF YOU'RE USING

CISCO PRODUCTS,

YOU'RE QUALIFIED

TO RECEIVE A

FREE SUBSCRIPTION

TO CISCO'S

PREMIER PUBLICATION,

PACKET™ MAGAZINE.

Packet delivers complete coverage of
cutting-edge networking trends and
innovations, as well as current product
updates. A magazine for technical, hands-on
Cisco users, it delivers valuable information
for enterprises, service providers, and
small and midsized businesses.

Packet is a quarterly publication. To
start your free subscription, click on the
URL and follow the prompts:
www.cisco.com/go/packet/subscribe

CISCO SYSTEMS

CISCO SYSTEMS/PACKET MAGAZINE
ATTN: C. Glover
170 West Tasman, Mailstop SJ8-2
San Jose, CA 95134-1706

Place
Stamp
Here

☐ **YES!** I'm requesting a **free** subscription to *Packet*™ magazine.

☐ No. I'm not interested at this time.

☐ Mr.
☐ Ms.

First Name (Please Print) _____ Last Name _____

Title/Position (Required) _____

Company (Required) _____

Address _____

City _____ State/Province _____

Zip/Postal Code _____ Country _____

Telephone (Include country and area codes) _____ Fax _____

E-mail _____

Signature (Required) _____ Date _____

☐ I would like to receive additional information on Cisco's services and products by e-mail.

1. Do you or your company:
- A ☐ Use Cisco products
- B ☐ Resell Cisco products
- C ☐ Both
- D ☐ Neither

2. Your organization's relationship to Cisco Systems:
- A ☐ Customer/End User
- B ☐ Prospective Customer
- C ☐ Cisco Reseller
- D ☐ Cisco Distributor
- E ☐ Integrator
- F ☐ Non-Authorized Reseller
- G ☐ Cisco Training Partner
- I ☐ Cisco OEM
- J ☐ Consultant
- K ☐ Other (specify):
  _____

3. How many people does your entire company employ?
- A ☐ More than 10,000
- B ☐ 5,000 to 9,999
- c ☐ 1,000 to 4,999
- D ☐ 500 to 999
- E ☐ 250 to 499
- f ☐ 100 to 249
- G ☐ Fewer than 100

4. Is your company a Service Provider?
- A ☐ Yes
- B ☐ No

5. Your involvement in network equipment purchases:
- A ☐ Recommend
- B ☐ Approve
- C ☐ Neither

6. Your personal involvement in networking:
- A ☐ Entire enterprise at all sites
- B ☐ Departments or network segments at more than one site
- C ☐ Single department or network segment
- F ☐ Public network
- D ☐ No involvement
- E ☐ Other (specify):
  _____

7. Your Industry:
- A ☐ Aerospace
- B ☐ Agriculture/Mining/Construction
- C ☐ Banking/Finance
- D ☐ Chemical/Pharmaceutical
- E ☐ Consultant
- F ☐ Computer/Systems/Electronics
- G ☐ Education (K–12)
- U ☐ Education (College/Univ.)
- H ☐ Government—Federal
- I ☐ Government—State
- J ☐ Government—Local
- K ☐ Health Care
- L ☐ Telecommunications
- M ☐ Utilities/Transportation
- N ☐ Other (specify):
  _____

CPRESS

PACKET™

Packet magazine serves as the premier publication linking customers to Cisco Systems, Inc. Delivering complete coverage of cutting-edge networking trends and innovations, *Packet* is a magazine for technical, hands-on users. It delivers industry-specific information for enterprise, service provider, and small and midsized business market segments. A toolchest for planners and decision makers, *Packet* contains a vast array of practical information, boasting sample configurations, real-life customer examples, and tips on getting the most from your Cisco Systems' investments. Simply put, *Packet* magazine is straight talk straight from the worldwide leader in networking for the Internet, Cisco Systems, Inc.

We hope you'll take advantage of this useful resource. I look forward to hearing from you!

Cecelia Glover
Packet Circulation Manager
packet@external.cisco.com
www.cisco.com/go/packet

PACKET™